Masters
of the
Stage

Masters of the Stage

BRITISH ACTING TEACHERS
TALK ABOUT THEIR CRAFT

Eva Mekler

 GROVE WEIDENFELD
NEW YORK

Copyright © 1989 by Eva Mekler

Published by Grove Weidenfeld
A division of Wheatland Corporation
841 Broadway
New York, NY 10003-4793

Published in Canada by General Publishing Company, Ltd.

Library of Congress Cataloging-in-Publication Data

Mekler, Eva.
    Masters of the stage: British acting teachers talk about their craft/by
Eva Mekler.—1st ed.
        p.   cm.
    ISBN 0-8021-1030-4 (alk. paper).—ISBN 0-8021-3190-5 (pbk.)
        1. Acting teachers—Great Britain—Interviews.   2. Acting—Study
and teaching—Great Britain.   I. Title.
PN2078.G7M45   1989
792'.028'092241—dc20
                                                                    89-7408
                                                                        CIP

Manufactured in the United States of America

This book is printed on acid-free paper

Designed by Irving Perkins Associates

First Edition

10   9   8   7   6   5   4   3   2   1

for Michael, again

Contents

Preface   ix

THE BRISTOL OLD VIC THEATRE
SCHOOL   1
Elwyn Johnson—Acting   3
Francis Thomas—Voice   15

THE CENTRAL SCHOOL OF SPEECH
AND DRAMA   31
Robert Fowler—Principal   33
George Hall—Acting   38
Anthony Falkingham—Acting   49
Julia Wilson-Dickson—Voice   58

THE DRAMA CENTRE, LONDON   69
Christopher Fettes—Principal   71
Reuven Adiv—Acting   79

THE DRAMA STUDIO   87
Patrick Tucker—Director of Studies   89
John Abulafia—Associate Director   110

THE GUILDFORD SCHOOL OF ACTING
AND DANCE   125
Michael Gaunt—Principal   127

CONTENTS

Ian Ricketts—Acting   142
Leah Thys—Movement   163

THE GUILDHALL SCHOOL
OF MUSIC AND DRAMA   177
Tony Church—Director of Drama   179
Virginia Snyders—Director of Studies   185
Patsy Rodenburg—Voice   194

THE LONDON ACADEMY OF MUSIC
AND DRAMATIC ART   213
Roger Croucher—Principal   215
Caroline Eves—Acting   226
Helena Kaut-Howson—Acting   241
John Waller—Stage Combat   249

THE ROYAL ACADEMY OF
DRAMATIC ART   259
Oliver Neville—Principal   261
Doreen Cannon—Acting   267
Andy Hinds—Acting   279

THE ROYAL SCOTTISH ACADEMY
OF MUSIC AND DRAMA   289
Edward Argent—Director of Drama   291
Peter McAllister—Acting   304

THE WEBBER DOUGLAS ACADEMY
OF DRAMATIC ART   315
Raphael Jago—Principal   317
Hilary Wood—Acting   329

Addresses   345

Preface

The last decade has seen a great influx of British plays and television programs to the United States. American actors are often awed by the quality of the acting they see in the Royal Shakespeare Company on tour or British T.V. productions that air so frequently in this country. How do they do it? What is it about their training that enables British actors to play Shakespeare and Sheridan as readily as Harold Pinter and Joe Orton? Because few students or teachers of acting are able to go to Great Britain to observe the training firsthand, a mystique has developed about the "British technique."

My purpose in writing this book was to find out specifically how the British train their actors: their procedures, the details of their curriculum, everything from the exercises they use with their first-year students to the direction they give their third-year students in productions. What I discovered was that there is no single "British technique"; that quite to the contrary, actor training is eclectic, heterogenous, and far from dogmatic.

American actor training has been dominated by a handful of individuals such as Lee Strasberg, Stella Adler, Sanford Meisner, and Uta Hagen—strong personalities who founded their own schools to teach and perpetuate their particular vision of the actor's craft. Often they were in open and acrimonious conflict with each other. Most young American actors flocked to one or another of these teachers and many got caught up in their debates, sometimes seeming to regard their teachers more as gurus than acting coaches. British training, on the other hand, has not been dominated by individual personalities. The schools there are enduring institutions that evolve as new teachers add their particular vision to the established methodology. Each school has distinguishing characteristics, but most are proud of their eclecticism and don't claim that they alone offer the one true method.

The teachers I interviewed, all of whom are from the major British drama schools, draw upon exercises from Stanislavsky and Michael Chekhov, as well as theater games, the Alexander Technique, and procedures that derive from Laban and the Expressionistic dance movement that was popular in Europe in the twenties and thirties. They also use various home-grown British techniques, such as the status improvisations devised by Keith Johnstone. These diverse approaches are combined with intensive training in voice and movement. Finally, students spend their last year of study performing in full-length productions from a wide range of theatrical styles: Shakespeare, Restoration and Jacobean plays, classical European drama such as Chekhov and Molière, as well as contemporary English, European, and American works. The training can be characterized as a combination of eclectic classroom work and practical experience in performance.

Unlike their American counterparts, who train in studio classes, the vast majority of British acting students study in drama schools. The training is comprehensive, full-time, and usually lasts three years. Classes are small, with only twenty-four to thirty students, and groups often split in half, allowing even greater teacher/student contact. The competition for entrance is keen. The schools typically audition over 1,500 applicants for approximately thirty places. What this means is that those students accepted for entrance are often quite talented to begin with.

Traditionally, British actors were able to perfect their craft through a kind of informal apprenticeship in the many repertory companies throughout Great Britain. Some of England's leading actors—Laurence Olivier, John Gielgud, Peggy Ashcroft, and Edith Evans—got their start and made their reputations in these regional theaters. In recent times the number of repertory companies has dwindled and only a few remain. The British schools understood how important it was for actors to perfect their craft by performing in front of an audience. Consequently, in the final year of training, most drama schools mount full-length productions directed by staff or outside directors, some of whom are prominent British actors or stage directors.

While Lee Strasberg may have been the most influential interpreter of Stanislavsky in America, most British schools have resisted Strasberg's emphasis on using personal events to interpret a character. They are wary of techniques like affective memory and emotional recall because they believe it leads to self-indulgent acting in which the actor's story is played out instead of the character's. Yet some drama teachers in Great Britain feel British actors are often not expressive enough, that their natural reserve and "stiff-upper-lip" upbringing is a barrier to fully expressing emotions and vulnerability on stage. As a result some of the schools have recently begun to experiment with American Method techniques borrowed from teachers like Strasberg, Uta Hagen, and Herbert Berghof, and have tried to incorporate them into their traditional approaches.

There was a time when drama training in Britain consisted mostly of studying voice and movement and being directed in classical plays. This was based on the belief that an actor learned his craft primarily by doing—that is, by rehearsing and performing. Now drama schools devote a great deal of time to teaching systematic techniques in the classroom. In the last decade almost all of the schools have established classes in improvisation and techniques that help students learn to relax, concentrate, create character, and become more spontaneous.

Since British acting, for the most part, takes place in drama academies, the interviews in this book are grouped by schools. These institutions have a long and respected tradition and most of Britain's major stage and screen actors are listed among their graduates. Each of the schools is represented by a principal or director of drama who may be solely an administrator or both a teacher and director as well. Their interviews usually provide a general statement of their school's history, philosophy of training, and curriculum. The interviews with acting, voice, and movement teachers give the reader a more detailed description of what actually happens in the classroom.

The British have a long and cherished tradition of theater, rich with models of excellence that inspire and challenge young actors. Laurence Olivier's Richard III, Peggy

Ashcroft's Juliet, and Edith Evans's Lady Bracknell are still discussed as standards of performance to strive toward. But students are also cautioned not to imitate their predecessors; on the contrary, they are encouraged to find their own unique Hamlet or Juliet. They are taught to honor their theatrical legacy as a source of creative inspiration, not as a set of models to copy, but as examples of actors and actresses who broke new ground and continually redefined the actor's craft.

The
Bristol Old Vic
Theatre School

The Bristol Old Vic Theatre School was opened by Laurence Olivier in 1946 soon after the foundation of the Bristol Old Vic Company itself. A close relationship still exists between the school and the company, which has, over the years, extended to the University of Bristol Department of Drama, the Bristol City Council, and the Avon Educational Authority. The school's association with these institutions enables students to perform in a wide variety of theaters: the Theatre Royal, the New Vic Studio, the Little Theatre, and the Bristol Hippodrome. The courses at Bristol Old Vic are essentially practical and the school does not adhere to any one philosophy of training. In outlook it is run as a professional theater, and staff regard a student's first day of training as the first day of his or her career.

The school offers a three-year Acting Course, and a two-year Acting Course more suited to the mature student. There are also one- and two-year courses in Stage Management, Design, and Wardrobe.

Elwyn Johnson

Elwyn Johnson is the Course Coordinator and Staff Director at the Bristol Old Vic Theatre School. A graduate of the Manchester Polytechnic School of Theatre, Mr. Johnson has appeared in many regional theater productions as well as worked for the BBC television and radio, HTV, and Channel Four. He spent three years in theatre administration and has directed at Salisbury Playhouse, the Strode Theatre, the New Vic, and the Redgrave Theatre, Bristol, among others. His productions have included Adian Chambers's The Dream Cage; *Shakespeare's* The Merry Wives of Windsor; Cider With Rosie, *adapted by Nick Darke from the book by Laurie Lee; R. B. Sheridan's* The School for Scandal; *and more recently, Dylan Thomas's* Under Milk Wood. *He has also directed Theatre in Education tours to Bristol schools and devised and directed two musicals for a tour of the southwest of England.*

Mr. Johnson recently appeared as Dr. John Watson in

The Crucifer of Blood *and* Tomfoolery, *both at the Pitlochry Festival Theatre.*

A long with being the Course Coordinator and Staff Director of the school, I also teach acting and text-study across all courses, work with our Stage Management and Design courses, direct final-year productions, and have taken Theatre in Education work into Bristol schools. Additionally, I have devised and directed Community Theatre tours with our students for their annual visit to venues in the southwest of England.

I suppose that the basis of my approach to acting rests on the belief that each student who leaves this school should be as fundamentally prepared as possible for any kind of work situation he or she might encounter. In a way, today's actor has to be all things to all people: he has to be able to play a turkey in a T.V. advertisement on one day and Hamlet the next. With the current trend in state funding for the arts, it's difficult to know how far to take them in one direction and how much to discourage them in another.

I have in front of me a section of Stanislavsky's *Building a Character.* Each time I come to evaluate where I stand on training, I try to find a relevant code to work from that gives a benchmark to the actor's craft. At the moment, I am working on Chekhov's *The Cherry Orchard* with one of our first-year groups. Stanislavsky is inextricably linked to Chekhov and there is no better person than Stanislavsky to put into words what I believe:

> The time has now come to speak of one more element contributing to a creative, dramatic state. It is produced by the atmosphere surrounding an actor on the stage and

by the atmosphere in the auditorium. We call it ethics, discipline, and also the sense of joint enterprise in our theater work. All these things taken together create an artistic animation, an attitude of readiness to work together. It is a state which is favorable to creativeness. . . . It is not the creative state itself, but it is one of the main factors contributing to it. It prepares and facilitates that state. I shall call it ethics in the theater because it plays an important part in preparing us in advance for our work. . . .

People are so stupid and spineless that they still prefer to introduce petty, humdrum bickering, spites, and intrigues into the place supposedly reserved for creative art. They do not seem to be able to clear their throats before they cross the threshold of the theater, they come inside and spit on the clean floor. It is incomprehensible why they do this! It is all the more reason why you should be the ones to discover the right, the high-minded significance of the theater and its art. From the very first step you take in its service, train yourself to come into the theater with clean feet.

How Do You Define "Clean Feet"?

I define clean feet as coming prepared to work. Acting is a very disciplined profession that allows you the license to be something you've never been. But if you come to a rehearsal without having "wiped clean" whatever just happened to you before you stepped into the room, you end up incorporating into that rehearsal what happened to you over breakfast or on the street. You are not ready, not prepared. It's a sad fact of life that an actor has to have a discipline above and beyond everybody else—and as a working actor myself, I speak from personal experience.

Even if his outside life is falling apart, he must remain intact, ready to take on the life he is about to portray. Clean feet means wiping out your personal story with its problems and worries when you walk into rehearsal at 9:30.

How Do You Help Students Achieve That?

When they come into this building they come with some preconceptions about the glory of the profession. I say, that's great, but first, through your work here, you have to find out both who you are and what parts of you can change. One of our greatest actors, Lord Olivier, is a chameleon with a magical capacity for change. He seems able to inhabit such a wide variety of people. His approach is a wonderful example to all of us. He's eighty years old now and has had a long, brilliant, and extraordinary career. Yet he still has a certain humility when it comes to his craft, and one tries to identify what that humility means. It is very easy for actors in exercises to stand alone and show off and say, I can do all that. What is more difficult is to put one's ability to the service of the play and to coordinate one's work with others. The atmosphere of any production relies on the ability of all the actors to feed into the whole. The beauty of Chekhov's work, for example, is that his characters represent everybody; they express what is in all of our lives. The character who has only three lines is as important as the one who has one hundred fifty-eight. And sometimes these characters don't move much, but are simply there. The actor must, therefore, know how to simply "be" on a stage.

6

How Do You Help Them Accomplish This?

For example, in the "being not doing" exercise I ask students to sit in a circle on the floor and I say, "With as little acting as possible, I would like you to respond to some key words." Then I ask them to become a group that is self-confident, arrogant, self-conscious, threatened, threatening, etc. I give them these emotional "buzz-words" that seem so simple to act, but as the exercise progresses, the students discover how difficult they are to portray and how easily one falls into playing clichés. The trick is not to play those clichés. They need to learn that they don't have to *do* anything. If they don't feel like moving about to express the spirit of the word, they have a perfect right not to do that. They can *be* not *do*. After I give them a word, they are to relate to each other in the manner of the word. They can either begin to interact with each other or move away, depending on how they feel. Some words may lead to silence and little movement, others to heated exchanges. It is important that the actors be true to their feelings and not force their responses. They usually start by overreacting, illustrating the words. It is the brave student who will simply sit and be. It's a difficult exercise.

There are also exercises that I use where I remove language. I split the class into two lines facing each other across a two-meter gap. Then I ask one couple at a time to come together and strike up an argument—not a fight—without using physical contact. They must communicate using only the letters of the alphabet—or numbers—in any order they wish. I also use this exercise for character work. I ask students to each think of a suitable alternative character to their own and I bring them together in different situations to strike up a relationship, but using numbers or letters instead of language. I point out to them the way their body-language increases or decreases when their language is restricted, when they cannot rely on text. In an extension of this exercise I ask them to spend about ten minutes putting together an improvisation around characters or situations of their own using only the words *yes, no,* and *oh* in any combination. When an improvisation is presented I ask the rest of the group to evaluate what they see. I will also use this technique after students have worked on scenes. I will ask them to replay their scenes using the alphabet or numbers as a way to underscore the physical interplay of their characters. This shows them how important it is for an actor to be physically conscious of how little or how much he communicates through his body and face. When students don't have the structure of the text to rely on they have to invent other forms of expression.

I also try to involve students in games to break down barriers and give them the freedom to make fools of themselves in public—which is what we are all about anyway. I start off by saying that I don't care how silly they feel, how foolish this is going to make them behave, because they have a right to fail here. Equally vital is mutual trust within a group; therefore we start with "trust" games. In one, a student will be passed around in a circle by classmates. The person being passed will have his eyes closed and let himself be guided by the others. He must let the circle take care of his body. The point is that the people in the circle have to catch the body as it is being passed in such a way that they don't hurt it. I give instructions that they take supreme and absolute care of the body. We play the game several times and as they get to know each other better the circle gets bigger so that there are wider gaps between the people guiding the body. In another trust game, an individual is asked to fall backward into someone's arms.

I use another trust game in which students are paired and one partner must close his eyes while the other takes him on a conducted tour of a space by giving verbal instructions on where to move. I first tell the guide where to take his partner and that he may not touch his partner. At crucial moments I change the route they are traveling by placing obstacles in the way of the walking couples in order to test their reactions and inject a degree of spontaneity. The couples then change roles so that each member gets a chance to learn to "trust" the other.

How Do You Begin Working on Text?

I ask students to look at the structure of the whole play and to answer the who, what, why, when, and where of their character's part. They learn how to read a text, how to look for clues to their character by what other people say about him as well as by what that character says about himself. They must then evaluate the two sources of information to arrive at a conception of the whole role. Then we lay down a rough blocking so that there is a framework within which to work. This can change, of course, as the script begins to come off the page and the interplay between the actors grows. We try to simulate a structure like the one they will find in the professional theater. Ideally, I have them establish the blocking and analyze the meaning all at the same time, rather than approaching them as separate processes.

In terms of emotional context, I think I would always prefer students to come to rehearsal with some awareness of what aspects of themselves are in their character. In that way they have a personal basis for their emotions, which they can then draw upon. I don't go through that with them in rehearsal nor do I use exercises or improvisations; I prefer to divorce the two. Using exercises in rehearsals can become an indulgence in which an actor finds what *he* has to say and then, inevitably, at a second stage has to reinterpret it in terms of what the character has to say. Time is the enemy, particularly working in repertory theater. I don't think it's the director's job to psychoanalyze the actor! In a well-written play the clues to character are all in the text. Throughout the training, students are asked to find different sides of their nature in improvisation classes. An additional way we help them discover these qualities is by casting them against type, leading them to find aspects of themselves they may not have suspected they have. If students are playing Lord and Lady Macbeth and the sexual tension between them is missing, then what does one do? I might, perhaps, by way of contrast, give them something in which the sexuality is easier to play, such as the scene between Lady Percy and Hotspur just before he leaves for the rebellion in *Henry IV, Part 1*. A drama school must be a place where actors can take risks and extend their range. Too soon—sadly for some, happily for others—actors become typecast.

ELWYN JOHNSON

How Do You Approach Character Development?

I frequently use status exercises as a way to open doors to
a character. One of these is a master/slave improvisation in
which the two students must find their character references by a liberal use of wit and invention; at all costs the
slave must avoid punishment by the master, who issues a
constant stream of orders. This derives from the early
commedia dell'arte, which gave birth to burlesque, music
hall, Chaplin, Keaton, and by direct descent, the unique
Dario Fo.

My own history in the repertory movement is based on
trying to play as many people as possible in as many
different ways as possible. As I say, one way we encourage
this is by casting against type: we take an eighteen-year-
old girl and cast her as Charlotta in *The Cherry Orchard*.
I might tell her, "You are not ready for this but you have to
find a way of playing it without caricaturing it, because
Charlotta is the embodiment of a real life. That lady
existed." Restoration-period theater is full of artificial
characters, though they weren't artificial for their time.
There was an artificiality of manners, of walking, of speaking, but you must still find the quintessential reality. The
easy option is to caricature, but what is the reality behind
that person? We must always look for the truth behind
the character, no matter how extravagant that character
may be.

Another character exercise involves asking the group to
choose a period in history and then each student must
come up with a character from that time. I then place
them in an unusual location where each character has to

form a relationship of some sort. Interesting and hilarious linkages can result. The "park bench" exercise also encourages basic character exploration. Two group members take up any character of their choosing and encounter each other at a park bench. That starts the situation. Then I send in the other members of the class, one at a time. As a student arrives at the bench, he must radically change the situation. As soon as the new situation starts, one of the previous couple must find a way to leave. There must be only two at the bench throughout the bulk of the improvisation. This can lead to humorous situations, but that is not the sole aim. For me, the value of this exercise is in the variety of people and types students create and the accuracy of their presentation, coupled with their development of a fast-response facility as situations change.

Lord Olivier, I believe, used to say that he worked from the outside in, and I suppose as an actor I do that too. I tend to start from how a character looks, using what it says about him in the play. I may not be at all like that person but I have to get as near as I can to him. There are also actors who work from the inside out. I suppose it's fair to say that one has to be aware of both processes. I prefer to give actors the freedom to do both.

Our technical training in voice and movement tries to hone the student's body into a flexible piece of equipment that can quickly adapt or respond to any section of the business, thus ensuring maximum employability in all areas. Too often students are tempted to say, "I'm very sorry, but I can only see myself as this one particular person who only does this one kind of part."

As we go through these first-term exercises I hold off

any criticism until the fifth or sixth session because, initially, students are learning how to become more self-aware. There are other parts of the course in which they receive sustained, constructive criticism. For instance, students have to audition every three weeks for the staff as a way to give them an awareness of what they will face in their final year and for the rest of their professional lives. We ask them to prepare one or two speeches and a song, or a radio or choreography audition. They come into the studio one at a time and do a five-minute audition. This is also a process of self-evaluation. They have to choose what they want to challenge themselves with. We try to give them an idea of what the big wide world is like; how, at the drop of a hat, they might have to charge across London to audition for Hamlet. That's why I am suspicious of too much improvisation work that can result in needing too much preparation time. One can't come to an audition and say, "I have to go to the side of the room and bang my head against the side of the wall before I am ready for this part!"

Although we spend a lot of time on classical theater, we also prepare them for Theatre in Education and Community Theatre, both of which are fighting hard to do the very best they can with a minimum amount of state funding. We take them on the road and put them in front of young audiences; and they quickly discover that children are the most honest critics there are. We put them into productions, often musicals, touring the West country and allow them to experience a wide variety of audiences so that they can get as much feedback as possible. This begins during the second year of our three-year course and continues into the final year. By that final year, students are in a strong position to judge where their weaknesses lie and what they must continue to work on in terms of voice, movement, and acting. Of paramount importance is that the learning process never stops, that it continues throughout an actor's career. At drama school we simply try to point the would-be professional in the right direction.

Francis Thomas

Francis Thomas teaches voice at the Bristol Old Vic Theatre School. Originally trained as an actor, he appeared in productions at the Nottingham Playhouse, the Royal Court, the Apollo Theatre, and the Pitlochry Festival Theatre before turning to teaching and directing.

Mr. Thomas taught a wide variety of subjects and directed student productions at several London schools before becoming Voice Tutor at Webber Douglas in 1976. He joined the staff of the Bristol Old Vic in 1979 and currently teaches voice for the drama department at Bristol University as well.

During the summer Mr. Thomas is Voice Coach for the Shaw Festival Company in Ontario, Canada.

What Is Your Background in Theater?

I trained at the Rose Bruford School as a teacher and actor. When I started my career in acting it was specifically to put into practice the technique that I had learned. After about five years acting, I was in a show that moved up to London, and London being the center for drama schools, I began to teach. I taught everything: acting, improvisation, basic movement; I directed students and I also taught voice and speech. Then I began to go more and more into the area of teaching. Because of my acting and directing experience I was able to approach the teaching of voice in terms of the needs of the practicing actor. As a result, I feel that I have been able to base my voice teaching on what I believe are the root needs of the performer. Obviously, I have been influenced by the important English voice teachers, such as Cicely Berry and Clifford Turner, but curiously enough the seminal book we used when I trained at Bruford was an American book, *Training the Speaking Voice,* by Virgil Anderson. I also began to see that certain yoga exercises were useful for breathing and getting a good sense of balance. My teaching is an amalgam of all these things, incorporating improvisations and acting exercises.

What I try to help students see right from our first session together is the purpose behind everything we do. While many of the exercises we do may not seem terribly exciting—for example, holding a particular sound for a count of fifteen or twenty—once students understand the purpose, however, they usually give the work their full concentration. We do some exercises that require great concentration, such as the one in which students have to feel that they are linking themselves through sound to a spot on the wall. In another exercise they have to bounce a sound just in front of them, and then bounce it farther and farther away as accurately as they might a ball. These exercises are very good for strengthening their concentration abilities in general, as well as, of course, for training their voice.

How Do You Begin Voice Instruction?

I begin by saying that voice production must take place without strain and that the mask of the face is the area where you can place the voice with ease. I then ask them to stand and imagine there is another person perhaps three feet away from them. All I want them to do is first direct a sound to that imaginary person in an audible whisper. Once they have got that as a feeling and are actually talking to this imaginary person, I then say, "That person is now moving away. Begin to follow them around the room, but all the time I want you to send your voice, still in a whisper, ahead of you so that you are following your voice rather than your voice following you." I ask them to imagine that the voice is like a beam of light shining from a lamp, the kind miners wear on their hats, and that it is pushing its way through the dark. I try to get them to feel that the sound they produce is always going out and going somewhere, rather than feeling, as people sometimes do when they get very quiet and relaxed, that the sound dribbles over their lips, almost like saliva. I keep suggesting that even in their most intimate feelings as an actor there is no place for the dribble. The voice always has to go out into the audience space, no matter what shape or size that space is.

As a next step I might ask them to imagine that they are linking themselves to a spot on the wall with a hum, and then to create a barrier with their hands between their eye-line and that spot on the wall so that they have to imagine the sound going through the barrier created by their hands in order to reach the wall. Again, this mental image helps them lift the sound out of themselves.

In another variation I tell them to hum on a particular note and to imagine that the vibrations of that hum are so strong that if we had the right sort of camera, we could get a picture of a series of vibration lines that would look like a little clothesline linking them to a spot on the wall.

I keep coming back to using images like this because, in a way, it's the only procedure to help them improve. Voice is unlike movement. If someone in movement class puts his foot in the wrong place, the teacher can actually grab the foot and push it into the right place. You can't do that with the voice. In all our exercises I caution them that whatever they are out to achieve, they must aim for maximum effect with the minimum amount of effort. Sending sound out doesn't mean straining. Many actors and students get so hooked on the need for effort that even breathing becomes a strain and you can see them pull breath into the body and push it down to the ribs and diaphragm. It is much better to use the image of a bellows, where air is easily drawn in as the bellows expand.

Breath is the basis for all my work. In his book, *The Life of Acting*, Bertie Scott suggests that almost everything the actor does is linked to breathing. That might be taking it a bit far, but certainly every sound that an actor makes, from the point of view of voice training, is being made by breath coming out. I try to make students realize that what they do with their breath is very important, and that in everyday life, it is taken care of automatically. Rarely does one get an idea and not have enough breath to express it. Yet when acting, many students find that they run out of breath in the middle of a phrase. So we do lots of breathing exercises, with some students using images as additional aids.

For example, I might suggest they breathe in and feel air centered down to the base of their lungs, like a reserve of untapped energy. Then I might ask them to use the breath to count aloud, first, making the count grow louder, and then to repeat the count while fading the sound and having it grow quieter—both under easy control of the breath. This type of exercise helps them acquire habits that will prevent them from speaking a phrase and letting it fizzle off at the end. They must never drift off at the end of phrases because not only will the audience become bored, but what is more important, they won't be able to hear what is being said.

Sometimes the teaching of voice can be a very gentle process. At other times it can be more athletic, such as when I ask students to do certain breathing and voice exercises while they swing the body or move parts of the body aggressively, as if they were executing a karate chop. I want them to think of the voice as a muscle that can be kept strong by being toned up. Even the quietest sounds require a sort of gentle muscularity. But I also stress relaxation, although never a total collapse.

I talk a lot about energy. Many students, when they talk softly and intimately, become totally devoid of energy. It seems to me that the one thing an actor can never lack is energy—even in what appears to be the most effortless conversation. Students need to discover for themselves the proper degree of energy that allows them to talk extremely softly and intimately, and really *to* someone and not *at* them, and yet still fill a theater with their voices.

How Does Your Instruction Progress?

In the first term students do a lot of work on relaxing, trying to feel that there are no obstacles to voice production. If you are trying to achieve the maximum effect with the minimum of effort, tension must not become a barrier. There are certain habits that are formed before people come here. Often students talk with a very tight jaw, so they have to learn to relax the jaw without making it flaccid. I also want them to learn how to get the maximum amount of breath while still drawing it in easily. When they take in their total capacity of breath, even though in normal breathing we don't do this, they should be able to hold it for a while. I want them to feel that at all times they can control their breathing without straining.

In every session during the first term there are exercises to relax the jaw, shoulders, and neck, and to learn how to increase breath capacity and control so that the breath never collapses.

During the first term we do exercises to try to strengthen the general tone, resonance, and placement of the voice. I especially try to help students who have acquired, through habit, a rather thin, high-pitched performing voice. It's curious that students who speak in a relaxed way at an acceptable pitch will, the moment they have to act, raise their voice an octave. I spend quite a bit of time during the first and second terms trying to encourage them to hear what their voice is doing without their becoming obsessed about it. It's a difficult thing for them to understand. I try to get them to listen to what they are doing. Once they begin to hear it, they can work on it. I want them to hear their voice in a technical, critical way. As actors they must be able to honestly evaluate their own voice and assess whether they have done as well as they should have done. And, of course, I want them to take what they learn into their everyday lives so it becomes a vocal habit. Eventually the performing voice ceases to be a phony thing that is switched on, and becomes a voice that is an extension of themselves.

Each term we add new elements to increase the students' range, flexibility, resonance, clarity, etc. Periodically, I will use a session to develop one particular area such as diction or resonance. For resonance, I might ask them to hum during every pause in our work so that there isn't a moment during class when they are silent. As I go from one exercise to another they must hum.

Another way we work on resonance is by going out on the downs near the school and, on a good day, spending almost the entire session developing a good, open, rich sound with a fair degree of power behind it. We are not actually shouting, but we are learning to make a sound which is so dense, rich, and resonant that it will fill the entire downs.

During This First Year, Do You Combine Text and Exercise Work?

It's mixed. In the voice classes most of our work is exercises, but at times we will take two or three lines of text, any text, and use that to increase the student's awareness of where the voice is placed. I may direct a student, for example, to use the consonants quite consciously in order to place the vowels in the front of the face. There are useful excerpts from the text in Clifford Turner's *Voice and Speech in the Theatre*. For range work I often use a speech from Milton's "Comus" and ask students to approach the first ten lines in a purely technical way, simply using the voice in its lower register—not just on one note, but exploring all the lower notes. They aren't to worry about the text making sense. Then we will explore the next ten lines using the middle range of notes; then ten more lines to explore the upper range. Then I will ask them to slide from one range to another. After that we will go back to the material, talk about the character, etc., and I will say, "Right, you are now Comus telling your followers that night has much more to offer than sleep. It is the time for nocturnal sport and orgy. Speak it using your full range of voice, but also convince your followers, whip them up into the right mood. They must believe you are right." In this way I use text for combining voice training and acting technique.

Do You Use Imagery to Foster a Student's Expressiveness or to Increase the Power of His Intention When Working on Text?

Yes. I might say, "You're talking to a crowd of people. Trap them into your belief, don't give them a chance to believe there is an alternative." Sometimes a student is not convincing because he hasn't convinced himself. It's got to feel wonderful to the student before he can sell the idea to others.

One afternoon a week during the first year of training I teach a class called Verse Speaking. We use lyrics and sonnets, and period prose, and narrative verse like *Beowulf*. Again, I try to persuade them to use their voices in a creative way. Yes, one does want good tone and breath support, but I also want to believe what they are telling me with that particular text. They may not get the chance to do this in every voice class, but they certainly get the opportunity to do it when they work on verse. It would be more accurate to rename the class Vocal Interpretation. At one class I ask them to read a prepared section from a novel where there is a narrator and at least two characters. They can only use vocal tone to create the different characters rather than different accents, moving quickly and accurately from one to another.

One Student Will Read All Three Characters?

Yes. And some find this very hard, but this kind of practice is invaluable for developing an accurate ear. I tend to be quite critical about their work, more so than I would be if I were watching them as professional actors in a performance. I prod them to keep discovering things about themselves and their voices. The whole process of training is more interesting when you keep trying to strengthen your weaknesses and extend your horizons.

Do You Work on Accents?

We do, usually toward the end of the first year. And at the same time I am always trying to help them develop an easy received pronunciation or Standard English. This is one of the trickiest areas. It's not that I am against regional accents. If I were teaching voice and speech to people who weren't going to be professional actors my main criteria would be: can I understand you? If I can, then I am really not interested in what sort of accent you have. But actors are expected to be able to speak in Standard English and to do so with great ease. If an actor is playing Professor Higgins or a character in an Oscar Wilde play, it can't seem as if he has a northern or London accent hiding beneath his received pronunciation. Therefore, actors need to practice that until they are absolutely at ease with it. Very often they can move into an Irish, South Wales, Cockney, or Lancashire accent with much greater ease than they can move into the standard sounds.

My wife, Lynette Erving, also teaches voice and we share the first-year classes. She tends to concentrate on the Standard English, although she still teaches breathing, tone, and articulation. She sets aside perhaps a quarter of an hour or so to look at a particular vowel sound or a particular sequence of vowel sounds needed to master received pronunciation. We try to use the standard sound as a model from which all the others deviate.

Do You Teach Students to Read Phonetically?

We do very simple phonetics. We have a few Canadian and American students, and reading sounds phonetically helps them with the subtleties of Standard English. It makes life easier to be able to link a particular sound to a phonetic symbol. They learn phonetics to the extent that if they are given nonsense words, they should be able to transcribe them.

As students progress, they are not asked to do radically different things, but rather to extend what they have been working on all along. As breathing becomes easier, they can spend a bit more time on resonance or placement or projection. In a way, we introduce the whole of voice training right at the beginning, then it just gets extended. All the elements of the voice have to be working well all the time. It's no use having wonderful breath control if you are totally monotonous, or getting wonderful variation if you don't have control over breath, or having wonderful variation, but no resonance. A student should feel that he has one voice that is capable of communicating anything that he can understand and feel.

In the final year students have fewer voice classes because most of their time is taken up with performances. So I try to give them a bit more time in individual tutorials. In the first year all the work is conducted in groups, except when they are doing vocal interpretation. Then I have an opportunity to make specific comments on their individual voices. I might also do this after seeing them present their audition speeches and scenes, which they work on themselves and then present to the basics teachers for comment. In the final year I'll see them in public performances and can work with them again in a few group classes, but mostly I meet with them on an individual basis for more specific guidance.

What Is Your Approach to Shakespeare? Do You Feel Scanning Is Important?

I am not sure that it actually helps students to know all the technical terms, like spondee, trochee, etc., so I don't teach them. I believe that students have, first of all, to get over their fear of speaking Shakespeare. Many students have great fear because it's almost a different language. Nowadays, students are less exposed to oral language at school. Reading aloud doesn't seem to happen very often now, whereas when I was a boy, one read aloud, teachers read aloud, and if you didn't speak clearly you were told about it. A lot of students come to drama school with very little sensitivity to language, so when they are faced with something like Shakespeare, there is utter panic. Either they feel that the language is totally outside them or they try to combat that fear by hamming it up. They seem unable to feel that Shakespeare's language is just a tremendously vivid expression of something that a human being has felt. In fact, they need to be able to feel the joy of his language and the excitement that went into his creation of new words and images. Then they have to work at the less glamorous task of discovering what it actually all means.

26

I remember a student doing a sonnet and the word *bark* came up. The line was, "It is the star to every wandering bark" (*Sonnet 116*). I asked him what the word meant, and he said it was the sound that dogs make. I asked him if he could make sense of the line with that meaning. He couldn't. So you must find out what the words really mean by testing them against the sense. That is most important—rather than worrying about what the meter is. And it seems to me that if one is talking sense, the scansion begins to take care of itself. Scansion can be disconcerting to students because they are so terrified about getting the meter wrong they can't speak with any commitment to the meaning. I tell them to be guided by their own sense of the music and the rhythm as it relates to the intention, rather than focusing on getting the meter right. I am much more interested in the language and the need to communicate the totality of the meaning. I prefer to let rhythm become a servant rather than some terrible master that puts students into fetters. We must never forget that Shakespeare was an actor, and when you focus only on the scansion, it can become a literary rather than a dramatic entity. We do look at iambic pentameter because sometimes you need to see how the sense of a line has changed it.

The way I work with Shakespeare is to ask students what they mean by a particular line. What is that line saying? They may be giving me just a general wash of noise rather than really saying something. I won't give them a line reading because if I do, they will hear what comes from me and be tempted to repeat it without motivation, and possibly even without conviction. I keep saying to them, "I'm not sure what that line means until you hit on a way of saying it so that it means something to me." In a training situation, I want them to do the work to discover what a line means.

Would You Ask Them Directly About Their Characters' Wants and Needs?

Oh, yes. I would ask what they are hoping to achieve by that line. Do they want to frighten the person, make them feel happy, etc.? If it was a poem, I would ask them what experience they are trying to stimulate in the minds and hearts of their listeners.

What Kinds of Voice Problems Do You Feel Are Particular to American Students?

One problem is the difference between some American and British vowel sounds. It's difficult to grasp the short English *o* as in *shot* and the short *u* as in *love,* and especially the difference between *ah* as in *cart* and *au* as in *caught.* Some Americans really get pretty good at Standard English. Some students have even auditioned for outside directors who weren't aware that they were American.

I have also come across a strident voice quality in many Americans, especially American women. Also, in certain parts of America there is a lack of range, a feeling that they want to stay in a very small area of the voice.

FRANCIS THOMAS

*There Are Certain British Actors, Like Richard Burton,
Who Have Special Voices. Is There Anything That Voice
Teachers Can Do to Help Students Find or Develop
Their Own Unique Voice?*

You must try to help the student discover *his* voice, not a
voice that is an imitation of some actor he admires. A lot
of it has to do with confidence and relaxation. Everybody
has a voice, but because of nervous tension and feelings
of insecurity not everybody uses his voice in its best
habitual pitch. If you can get a student to believe that
people want to hear what he has to say, then his voice
begins to find its own quality. It is a question of getting
rid of the obstacles to the true voice. But I think it probably takes longer than drama school for that real voice to
be discovered.

The voices that are unique, like Richard Burton's or
John Gielgud's, are a mixture of all their vocal properties,
the shape and size of resonators, etc., plus the feeling and
the thinking that they put into their work and the stamp
of their personalities. You can't divorce the voice from
what is going on inside them as actors. Burton was probably born with that basic equipment and all he had to do
was develop it. And I suppose that holds for the truly
great opera singers too. But I'm told that if you compare
the larynx of someone who is a wonderful opera singer
with someone who sings like a crow, you will find very
little difference. It's how they use the resonators and the
breath. There is very little difference between individuals
in the physical properties of the vocal cords from which
the initial sound is made.

Are There Any Areas of Voice Training You Feel Are Being Neglected?

I suppose if I have a hobby horse it is clarity. I get rather despairing when actors become sloppy and people can't hear what they are saying. Even in totally naturalistic drama it is the responsibility of the actor to be heard and understood. It gives me great delight to see an actor stand at the back of the stage and, effortlessly, speak the lines in such a way that you can almost hear them bounce off the back wall. That is a moment of joy to me.

The Central School of Speech and Drama

The Central School of Speech and Drama was founded in 1906 by Elsie Fogerty, who joined Sir Frank Benson at the Royal Albert Hall to devise a new form of training for young actors and other theater students. Their choice of name—the Central School—was intended to indicate an avoidance of extremism: the new form of training would have a definite yet flexible body of principles rather than a multiplicity of methods and theories. Gradually, training evolved into three separate but related areas: courses for actors and stage managers, speech therapists, and teachers.

In 1956 the school moved to the Embassy Theatre, Swiss Cottage, London, and in 1972 the school became grant-aided by the Inner London Education Authority.

Central offers a three-year Acting Course, a two-year course in Stage Management, a one-year Advanced Diploma in Voice Studies, and a course leading to a certificate in the use of Drama and Movement in Therapy.

Along with the courses for professional actors, Central collaborates with several academic institutions in granting degrees in Speech and Drama.

Robert Fowler

Robert Fowler is Principal of the Central School of Speech and Drama. Educated at Oxford, where he was a member of the Eglesfield Players, he went on to teach in Belfast, Northern Ireland, where he wrote and directed, lectured for the Queen's University, and toured England with classical plays. He became an acting member of Mary O'Malley's Lyric Theatre. After teaching in London's East End he became Warden of Bretton Hall, then head of English and Drama and Deputy Principal of Sittingbourne College. He was appointed by the Queen as one of Her Majesty's Inspectors in the Department of Education and Science, where he held national responsibility for Drama and Theatre Education and Training. He directed the department's course on the Teaching of Shakespeare at Stratford for several years and has been a member of the Arts Council of Great Britain Drama Panel, a member of the Royal Society of Arts Drama Committee, and the National Council of Drama Training.

Mr. Fowler has published many papers and articles on drama and education, and has been closely involved in many of the developments of the Arts in Schools and Higher Education.

For ten years before I became principal of Central I was Her Majesty's Inspector with national responsibility for drama and theater in all education institutions throughout England and Wales. So I came to Central with a broad-based experience of what went on everywhere else. You might call me a gamekeeper turned poacher— or the other way around. One of the things that I did as Inspector was conduct a course for teachers called The Teaching of Shakespeare, on how to teach Shakespeare as theater and drama. While there is a strong sense at Central that we are training people for a profession, that is, acting, we also try to give them an education that should be useful to them even if they never act professionally. Not many schools think in that context.

Over the past five years there has been great interest in drama and theater in all schools. There are now about 40,000 students studying theater arts and taking exams in this field. As a result, many teachers are needed, and Central offers a B.Ed. in drama teaching. So we have both an acting course and a B.A. degree course. We also offer a B.Sc. course in speech therapy, and a B.A. degree in drama and language. Because of this, Central is very different from other drama schools, and although these programs are now independent of each other, I would hope that as we develop they will move closer together and there will be greater sharing. For instance, I would like to see more voice teachers from the acting course also teaching the students in the B.Ed. Teacher Training course. There needs to be an eroding of the barriers between disciplines. For example, in our stage management program students actually stage manage the plays that the actors perform in. This is a good example of the value of a joint enterprise.

Do You Have a Particular Theory of Acting?

I personally am not committed to any one theory. The history of the word *Central*, as I understand it, is that it means central in terms of theories, that it is middle-of-the-way.

What Do You Think Is Special About British Training That Equips the British Actor to Play a Wide Repertoire of Theater?

I don't know the answer to that and can only speculate. It may be due, in part, to the British character, and also to what we called the "Dunkirk spirit" during the war; that is, a total commitment to a cause. There is a very strong work ethic in the acting profession, although some people outside the profession may not understand this. It has been one of my special areas of interest to combat the notion that acting is a sort of playing, and not hard work. In fact, I believe that if you train to be an actor, you acquire one of the best disciplines for any job that exists. As an actor you know that you have to be there on time;

35

you know that you are a member of a team of professionals with whom you have to cooperate or the whole thing doesn't work; you have to know your part; and you have to be sympathetic, responsive, and sensitive to other people. That special amalgam is something which English training inculcates. These are qualities that sustain people throughout their lives.

The English have a long tradition as well. We have Shakespeare, and he probably was an actor as well as a writer. All that helps. This doesn't mean there isn't a lot of room for development in drama training. I think we are moving toward a time when we will start giving actors more skill in directing so that they can learn more about acting by directing plays. That doesn't take place at the moment, partly because time is at a premium, but it's one of the things that I would like to see happen.

Another change I foresee in our curriculum is the opportunity for students to actually write plays. This kind of training currently takes place at The Other Place in Stratford, where you might get a writer working with a company and putting on plays written especially for that ensemble. I think that's an important learning experience for the actor.

Central Has a Long History of Graduating Some of England's Finest Actors. What Is Special About Central's Program?

I think Central is of very high caliber. One reason for that is our high application rate. We audition the majority of candidates who apply, so that in one year we could see as many as 1,600 students for thirty places; so by definition the raw material we get is of very high quality to begin with. We go to New York to audition and may see as many as sixty people for only one or two places. Again, we draw from very good material. There are some people who say that even if our students never trained, they would still be good actors. The English acting profession is an intriguing mixture: you can go to the Royal Shakespeare Company (RSC) and find very good actors who have never trained but went to higher education, joined their college or university drama society, and then went to the RSC or the National. You might not know whether or not they had been to drama school.

Apart from having very distinguished graduates, like Peggy Ashcroft and Laurence Olivier, who is the president of the school, we also graduated some of England's most distinguished teachers. Cicely Berry, one of our most respected and influential voice teachers, is a graduate of Central. Indeed, she still teaches here on a part-time basis. In addition to the program I talked about, we have a one-year course called the Advanced Diploma in Voice Studies, which is specifically for training voice teachers. So we have a lot of expertise in voice, which gives actors a special kind of confidence. And the voice is linked with movement, which is very important in actor training. The skill is to harmonize the totality of the physical elements along with the cerebral. For an actor to learn how to remain in control and be at ease within himself on stage is a great gift. For that you need excellent students and excellent teachers. Central is fortunate in having both.

George Hall

George Hall taught acting, movement, and music at the Central School of Speech and Drama, where he was Director of Acting from 1963 to 1987. He trained at the Old Vic Theatre School before appearing in various repertory productions and cabarets. He turned his talents to directing and worked on musicals as well as BBC Light Entertainment shows and the '69 Theatre Company in Manchester.

Mr. Hall is also a composer and has written music for the Royal Shakespeare Company, the Old Vic, BBC television, and the Royal Court Exchange, Manchester, among others.

He has been a vocal coach for West End musicals, including André Previn's Good Companions and The Black Mikado, and has worked with a great number of actors, notably Edith Evans and Laurence Olivier.

In 1985 he wrote the musical In the Picture with Ken

Hoare and is now working in cabaret as well as teaching music and acting.

One of the things I believe is that acting training is very much like homeopathic medicine, which states that there is no disease, there is only the patient. I think there isn't only one theoretical approach, one formula for good acting, there isn't really a method; there are only people in front of you who can act, up to a certain point, and who want to be better at it. If one is lucky enough to be able to help them to do it better, they are all going to arrive at that goal by different routes. One of the important aspects of English training is its lack of moralizing about one route being better than another. I would probably be accused of being result-oriented by one trained in the American method, but if I see a performance I love, I don't care how the actors got there.

I believe that the fundamental reason for running a theater school is a desire to improve the theater, not just to provide a service for a recognizable consumer group, that is, would-be actors. I also believe that one teaches well only out of a vision of the theater and a certain amount of rage about the waste of talented people one encounters who haven't found a way to realize their potential.

I trained at the Old Vic Theatre School. It was run by Glen Byam Shaw, Michel St. Denis, and George Devine, who were quite simply out to change the theater—that was the basic premise for their work.

How Did Michel St. Denis Propose to Do That?

My feeling is that he was very bored with the essentially naturalistic mainstream English theater of the thirties and early forties. He wanted to find a way to marry an actor's inner life with his outer skill. He always talked about the *Romeo and Juliet* that Olivier, Gielgud, Peggy Ashcroft, and Edith Evans did in the thirties. He felt that Gielgud had this wonderful ability to speak Romeo, but wasn't really in love; that Olivier had great passion, but couldn't speak the poetry at that point; and that in the middle was Evans, who perfectly combined inner and outer life. He wanted actors of great versatility and great range who could play what he called "big style"—Restoration, blank verse, Greek drama—without sacrificing inner reality; but also without what he called "the mud of naturalism." There was a lot of English acting in the thirties, forties, and fifties that was quite accomplished, but not very alive or authentic. That got a kick in the pants from the first signs of Marlon Brando that drifted across the Atlantic, and that was one of the factors that brought about a change in the English theater—that and George Devine's work in encouraging new writers, and Joan Littlewood's productions, which opened the theater up to a new kind of working-class actor. The theater always tries to steady itself between wanting to be real at the risk of losing clarity and definition, and being wonderfully shaped but superficial. Of course, the ideal of St. Denis was to get reality and form in absolute balance. That's what I was brought up with and it is at the heart of one's wanting to do the job.

The main difference between English and American training (and I am leaving out the schools like Juilliard and other more integrated programs) is that the studio system, which seems to be the primary way most actors in America train, means you take a movement class where someone tells you one thing about your spine, then you tear off across New York to your voice teacher who tells you something slightly different. You then tear off to your singing teacher who tells you something different again, as does your acting teacher! If the student is gifted and skilled enough he can perhaps make sense of these things, but not everyone can. Here at Central every performance is discussed by the entire faculty. Over the years teachers have developed a common vocabulary so that what is being asked of the student in voice class doesn't contradict what is being asked in movement class. In other words, an important aspect of drama training at Central is the desire to integrate skills and imagination and not have them at war with each other.

So the key to English drama training here is a vision of the theater and a desire to improve it, and a way of getting there that is based on the individual. I don't want to promote an acting mystique, but it is nevertheless a bit of a mystery how some people suddenly get better—or fail to.

Do You Teach Acting Technique?

I never used the word *technique*. To me that word implies that there is an existing answer—which I don't believe there is. I think what we do is endlessly pose the paradox

41

of acting: that is, saying to a student, "I believed what you were doing, but it was inaudible or boring or monotonous"; and saying to another, "It was bright, it was well-shaped, but it didn't have very much depth." Here is where the tension starts between a watchable result and a believable inner reality. I think we do that in increasingly complex ways over the course of training.

How Do You Begin Your Work with First-Year Students?

All of us here teach all three years. Acting study in the first term is about students being themselves, alone at home, using imagined objects. Then we ask them to re-create in the classroom what it's like when they are home. Most students can re-create that experience when no one is watching them, but the minute someone is observing, they tend to become apologetic (usually because they think they are boring), or else they go madly "show biz." We try to get students to critique each other in constructive ways, such as saying, "I believed what you did until the part when you did such and such when I thought you were out for a laugh or a consciously effective moment." That is the framework of the first term.

In the second term they move on to becoming somebody different from themselves. That takes two forms. Students go to the zoo every week and come back and try to become an animal of their choice, in an inner and outer way. I also do a series of classes that are like games where I ask students to try out different voices and walks. I am sure that it would outrage some acting teachers, but it's precisely what Alec Guinness did as a young man—he'd follow a person around London because he was fascinated by their walk. He thought that if he could reproduce that walk he would get inside that person.

I also remind people that there are more notes and rhythms in their voices and in their carriages than they normally use. From then on, exercises take any form that we think a particular group needs, including a certain amount of mask work. Apart from that, all the acting work is accomplished working on a play or scenes from a play.

Right from the first day students start to work on a whole play. A lot of people feel that you shouldn't do that until students know who they are. But I still don't know who I am so I would be waiting yet. We think that by collectively trying to serve an author and setting our sights on something bigger than ourselves we help students take their narcissistic eyes off themselves and refocus them away from constantly asking, "How am I doing?" We encourage a feeling of a collective ensemble that is trying to bring an author's vision to life so that it can affect an audience. This is fundamental.

How Do You Critique?

I believe a good acting teacher is someone who thinks of himself first as a member of the audience who has come primarily to have a good time, and only second as a specialist in acting or voice or movement. So the first thing a teacher should anticipate when he watches a play or scene is how exciting it is going to be. If it isn't exciting, then the teacher must ask himself why. It may be that an

actor lacked feeling or that his voice was extremely monotonous or that his jaw was tense; it may be that an
actress had a repetitive gesture that interfered with her
performance. The teacher needs to say, "I nearly had a
good time—what stopped me? Can I devise an exercise
that will help that person get released from where he is
caught?" For example, I might say to someone working
on a play by Oscar Wilde, "You are trying to have upper-
class nineteenth-century English, but why not do it in
your local accent just for today? You might discover something that will help you." There are a million things that
can be restricting someone, so like the homeopathic doctor, there isn't an illness, there is a patient who is strug-
gling and our job is to try and get onto the wavelength of
the difficulty.

What Is the First Thing You Ask Students to Do When They Begin Work on a Play?

The first thing one would get them to do is investigate the
background of the play and the author. For instance, a
year or two ago we were doing two plays; one was by
Arnold Wesker about the East End, and one was by Alan
Bennett about a Member of Parliament. Students in the
first play went to the East End and talked to people about
what it was like to live there in the thirties; those in the
second went to the House of Commons—only then did
they start rehearsing. I am a believer in not trying to do
everything in one rehearsal. One rehearsal might be
about asking students to read the text as if they were
saying the lines for the first time, and not about character
development. On other days one might say, "Let's begin

work on the character by focusing only on your Irish accent."

Do Students Work on Monologues?

They don't do any solo speeches until well into the second year. In a way, it would be wonderful never to do anything except a full play. I really believe in the experience of the whole play—but you can cover a much wider range by doing some scenes. So in the second-year Shakespeare course I might think a student needs work on a specific problem and give him a speech to work on that addresses that problem.

Do You Use Terms Like "Objective," "Obstacle," and "Intention"?

Teachers here work in their own way, and although we have a common aim, we have never stated it or written it down. A specific teacher may have an amazing ear for text and focus students on an author's choice of words. Someone else may work in a different way. Some may use these words, some may not.

Do You Have a Particular System for Analyzing Scenes?

A lot of theater training takes the instinct away from actors by tying them to particular formulas. Our approach, when we come across something a student can't do, is to sit down and look at it together. My feeling is, let's be thankful for things that work and not take them apart.

What Is Your Approach to Shakespeare and Verse Plays?

Shakespeare is very central to an English actor's experience. Like all language, it has its own inner music that is a reflection of intention, and when the verse comes apart in someone's hands it's usually because he doesn't know what he means or he doesn't know what his intention is.

What Do You Mean by the Verse "Coming Apart"?

If an actor is feeling the part but giving the audience no pleasure from his use of the language, it's usually because he lacks clarity of thought or is afraid of the style of the writing. Students work on a lot of verse and nondramatic text as a way to develop a feel for language apart from acting. They will read a piece from Dickens, for instance, to the class. The focus here is not on technique, but on how to keep alive this passage in Dickens. They become aware of vocal monotony, vocal interest, and of finding pleasure in the language. By the time they come to do Shakespeare they have acquired a lively reaction to language, and the desire to communicate is strong. So the most important thing is not to be afraid of Shakespeare. It seems to me that too many Americans are afraid of him and there is absolutely no reason for this. Doing Shakespeare is very much like doing the great numbers in a musical. Actors in such a show who understand that along with being real they have to give the audience the pleasure of the melody and the interesting rhymes—these actors can understand how to approach language in Shakespeare. Most of us are able to relish a stunning rhyme in Cole Porter. It's absurd not to relish a stunning turn of phrase in Shakespeare. We do a lot of work on musical theater and I feel that feeds Shakespeare very much.

Has American Acting Been an Influence Since the Fifties?

It initially had a huge influence. The tragedy was that the films Marlon Brando and similar actors chose didn't stretch them to a variety of styles. The only thing that stretched Brando in that respect was doing the film of *Julius Caesar*—which was wonderful. So what started as an exploration of reality became a style, and then a mannerism, and then had less and less potency. We had quite a few years where everyone happily mumbled Shakespeare, and then people got rather keen on hearing the words again.

The great thing that has shaped modern English acting is that a whole generation of actors have alternated between the movie studio, where they can be very small and naturalistic, and the big theater and blank verse. In film they have had the wonderful feeling of being absolutely true, so when they go back to the stage they want to maintain that—but they still want the audience to hear the text in all its glory. That tension between small scale

47

and large scale has permitted the lessons of the Method to be assimilated into the English theater without crippling it.

Do You See English Theater Moving in a Specific Direction?

If you look around you see a lot of trends, but they are contradictory. It seems as though the theater has changed, but then you notice that *The Mousetrap* has been running for over thirty years, so a lot of it does stay the same. People are darting off to do the kind of thing they wouldn't have dreamed of doing twenty years ago, but they are also darting off to do exactly the same dreadful old plays. This is necessary because there is not just one London audience but many with different tastes and different reasons for coming to the theater. Our training changes all the time to accommodate what is new in theater, but the foundation, for the most part, stays the same.

Anthony Falkingham

Anthony Falkingham teaches acting at the Central School of Speech and Drama. He has also taught at the Bristol Old Vic Theatre School and Bristol University.

Mr. Falkingham was trained at the Bristol Old Vic and has acted with the National Theatre Company, the New Shakespeare Company, the Ludlow Festival Theatre, and in many regional companies.

I am principally a director, but I am also responsible for basic actor training and overseeing students' progress during their first year at Central. My main interest outside of directing is in improvisation as an aid to training. The improvisational exercises that I do are geared toward expanding the actor's inner tools. I am also interested in *scene analysis* as distinct from *text analysis*, and I use improvisation as a technique in the early stages of rehearsal so that students can acquire a deeper understanding of the play and what each specific scene is about.

49

Can You Give Me an Example of an Improvisation That Is Designed to Deepen One's Understanding of a Play?

Take a play like *Uncle Vanya*, for example. We will work in small groups on a sequence of scenes from the play using the text, and the group will write out a list of intentions for each character. Then the students will improvise these scenes based on their character's intentions. After that we run all the scenes in sequence so that in the course of one afternoon's rehearsal, we go from having had only a cursory knowledge of the text to having an in-depth understanding of Act 1 of *Uncle Vanya*. Students will have seen the entire act run in sequence by different groups of students playing and improvising different characters. In that way, over a two- or three-week period, I will work through a whole play. The value of it is that students can look beyond what is in the text and on the page. Frequently, if one has a small amount of time allotted for rehearsals, there is an awful temptation for students to simply read the text and think they have encompassed the whole sense of the play as well as their character. Having to look very deeply into the text in order to draw out some sort of motivational list for those characters means that they have examined the text fully. Then they can see it transformed from what is a pencil-and-paper exercise into something living on stage that afternoon. It might not accurately reflect what will eventually happen, but at least it gives them a rough sketch or guide as to what the passage of the play is about.

I also use improvisations and exercises to create a sense

of ensemble. This is a developmental process and I use certain group exercises in the first term to develop their sense of group responsiveness and group identity and to enliven group scenes in the play.

In the second and third year, when students are performing publicly, I use group exercises to enlighten group scenes. For example, I am just about to start *Romeo and Juliet* and I will use group-improvisational exercises for the fight scene at the beginning of the play, for the deaths of Tybalt and Mercutio, and for the last scene of the play.

You Said You Use Improvisations and Exercises to Expand the Actor's Inner Tools. Can You Give Me an Example?

I use certain exercises to help an actor expand his self-awareness. In this category there are exercises that involve all the senses. These are designed to develop what I call "imaginative potential," so that students acquire a dramatic perspective and don't remain prosaic. For example, instead of doing typical sensory exercises in which I hand someone an empty cup and try to get them to imagine it filled with hot coffee, I will ask students to create the sensation of the bottom of a cup of coffee dropping out. That transforms the event from the mere prosaic into something which is dramatic and communicable. I do this in a group of ten. I let students work on it by themselves for five or ten minutes as I walk around examining what each one is doing. Then each will present his or her version to the rest of the class and we will critique it, looking to see if it worked for them, if it was

51

clearly communicated, if there was any hidden intention in what was happening—that is, if it became a performance as opposed to an experience for the student. In those early basic exercises it is important that whatever is happening to the actor be communicated. So an actor working on the sensory aspects of his experience will learn that he has to communicate those feelings to an audience.

Another exercise involves improvising any domestic activity, such as making beds, sweeping floors, getting dressed, and then adding an unexpected element to it, i.e., an accident occurring in the middle of the activity. To get this I might change the time needed to complete the activity, giving the students a specific reason for the change. So now the actor may find he is rushing because he is very late for an appointment, and suddenly an accident occurs. That always has dramatic force behind it.

From there we go on to look at the actor's relationship with people and objects. We would start to play two-handers, that is, an improvised scene between two people that focuses on three things: their relationship to each other, to objects, and to the environment.

When I start students working on the environment, what I initially direct then toward is the fantastic aspect of space. An empty room is unlimited in its potential, and these exercises are for stimulating the imagination. For example, I ask the group to sit in a circle and we do preliminary warm-up games. One of the games I use is for stimulating the imagination through the use of words. I ask them to throw each other a word, any word, and to respond with any word that comes to mind. Obviously a word like *chair* or *cupboard* quickly brings things to mind, but what's interesting and more difficult is to define for one's self what images the color purple conjures up or the word *hate*. Then we bring in surrealistic elements, like talking doors or arguing with posts. I don't mean that the actor enacts those objects, but that he winds up confronting them in an improvisation.

How Do You Incorporate the Image of a Talking Door in an Improvisation?

Say we are working on what I call an "inanimate/animate object lesson." A student might start by regarding a door as a door. If the door is locked and won't let him through, it might lead to an argument between the door and the student as to why it won't open or why the student can't pass through it. Now the student is subjectifying an inanimate object. I do the reverse exercise as well. I tell one student to treat another as if he were an inanimate object—a mailbox, for instance. The student/mailbox doesn't have to act like one, but the other student must respond to that student as if he were one. The fun begins when one student regards each of the other group members as an animated object and they in turn regard him as one. I ask students to integrate what others are doing and try to make sense of it in the specific world they have just created.

Do Students Know What the Other People Are?

No. They just have to make sense of the chaos around them. It's a type of jumble technique that I use in all sorts of ways. Once you disturb an individual's logical pattern, you can stimulate imaginative responses that are not a product of logical processes. This sometimes bucks the natural reserve that in England can be a form of self-censorship.

When students work together on improvisations in the first term, what I look for is the relationship between them as *people*, not as *characters.* During the initial training period everything is related to themselves. It is their own experience that they are trying to act out. But I always tell them that they are revealing themselves within a performance for us, rather than as any form of psychotherapy. In these exercises their relationship would, of course, be altered—in reality they are classmates, but in an improvisation they might be playing a brother and sister—but there would not be any fundamental character requirements.

Increasingly, during the first term, I add exercises to encourage an ensemble feeling in the group. I start with trust exercises and move on to exercises designed to stimulate a collective feeling among them.

Can You Give Me an Example of the Latter?

In one I send a student out of the room and the rest of the class decides to take on a uniform mood for a specific reason. For instance, they might decide that a cast list has just gone up and no one has done as well as they expected, so there is a mood of desolation. Then the student comes back into the room and through interacting with individuals he tries to pinpoint the mood and name it.

54

ANTHONY FALKINGHAM

Would He Question the Other Students?

He might feel it immediately, but if he doesn't he can talk
to them, although no one will directly tell him what has
happened. If the mood is directed at him, it is usually
easier for him to pick it up than if it is about something
that has happened to the whole group.

Another exercise I use involves movement. Everyone
stands together and starts to sway slightly from the right
foot to the left. Then, together, they have to decide to
take a first step—all at the same time. This develops into
a second step, and then develops into a walk, which gets
faster and faster until it reaches a peak, and then slows
down until they all stop. Students try to start together, go
through it together, and slow down together. The purpose
of this exercise is to learn how to adjust one's pace by
observing what is happening around one. I want to see if
students intuitively pick up what the whole group is doing. There might be one or two who actually try to work
against the group—which often happens in acting—and
that is then discussed.

I have another exercise called the "human machine," in
which I add a series of components one by one. Someone
starts with a rhythmic movement and a sound. The next
student adds a complementary movement and sound, and
so on, with an eye toward building the entire group into a
kind of movement and sound machine. They have to be
aware of what is happening to themselves and to others in
order to become part of this machine.

What Kinds of Exercises Do You Use to Stimulate Ensemble Feeling?

If I am directing a play with a lot of people on stage, I might assign students specific characters and divide them into small groups before I put the whole group together. When I directed *Camino Real* there were lots of people on stage all the time with distinct social divisions between them. In that particular production I extended Tennessee Williams's idea of famous literary people meeting up in the same marketplace by asking even those actors who were merely sitting around on stage without lines to choose to be a specific literary character. For instance, one young woman didn't have any lines in the script, but in one scene she had to order dinner on the terrace. She chose Lolita as her character and used it in her scene. I thought it important that each actor have a context within which to work. Making them famous characters gave them this context because they could refer to a book or a biography for information about their character. Though the audience might not know who they are, it does give the actor a specific personality and helps him find specific activities.

As another example, there was a moment in the play in which a student who had chosen to be Gertrude Stein walked through the market and met Alice B. Toklas on the terrace of the hotel. They had no lines, but out of their characters they created an activity, which was to discuss their Baedeker and what they had been doing in the town that morning. Then, in a later, highly dramatic scene— the arrival of the plane that is going to take them all away—these students didn't feel that they had to act generalized panic. They all had tasks to do that came out of the character they were playing. So it might be very important to Gertrude Stein to make sure Alice gets on the plane with her, and she might forget to take her valise—or whatever. Rather than choreographing a stage full of forty people, I created behavior this way. It's a good way to tap into the actor's creativity.

My philosophy, whether I am teaching an acting class or directing a production, centers on group responsibility. I think an individual actor works best by consensus. I know some directors feel that they need to trick the actor into becoming creative and sometimes become rather aggressive to accomplish this. I have never worked that way. I have always thought that part of my job as a teacher was to make the actor feel as secure as possible in his working environment because that's when he produces his best work—when he's happy.

Julia
Wilson-Dickson

Julia Wilson-Dickson is a graduate of the Central School of Speech and Drama, and has taught voice there. She has also taught at the London Academy of Music and Dramatic Art, Syracuse University in Britain, and the City Literary Institute. She is a dialect coach as well and has worked on West End productions of The Normal Heart, The Hired Man, *and* When I Was a Girl I Used to Scream and Shout, *among many others.*

Ms. Wilson-Dickson is a voice and dialect coach with the National Theatre Company and worked with Sir Peter Hall on Antony and Cleopatra. *She will continue her work with Hall at the National on productions of Sir Peter's* The Winter's Tale, Cymbeline, *and* The Tempest. *She also works with Peter Gill in the National Theatre Studio Company, and was voice coach for the season of plays that reopened the Cottesloe Theatre.*

My work is based on the belief that the voice is an instrument that cannot be treated as something that is separate from the emotions. Although in exercises we may need to look at the voice in isolation, it is essentially at one with the brain and the gut, so to speak. As an instrument it is situated within a moving, physically active being, and as a result, there can be many obstacles in the way of good voice production. There are also emotional and psychological obstacles that may need to be overcome.

How Do You Begin Your Training?

The first thing is to get people to understand their body in physical terms. Sometimes this can be repetitive and boring, but they do learn what is going on inside them when they make sounds. Having sorted that through, we then look at the breath. It's no use saying you will just *look for* the natural breath—it has to be *found.* One way you can do this is by repositioning the effect of gravity on the body and feeling how different positions affect the breath. The student usually discovers that the position that is best suited for producing a natural breath is different from the one he is normally in. I start by asking students to get down on all fours or lean forward, to realign the spine in relation to the floor. This primal position seems to give them a more open feeling in the back because the front of the chest drops and the sides expand. Steadily, I teach them how to use their muscles to work for extended sound when the body is upright. We go through floor, standing, and sitting work, connecting sound to the breath in each position.

Once I have established a vocabulary with students based on what is physically happening in their bodies, I can then give them a multiplicity of images to help them find their natural breath. It may be that ninety images will produce only one working image for one actor. For example, if an actor is trying to get powerful breath into the mid-body without tensing the neck (which needs to be kept open and free), he can imagine that his spine is like a piece of rope and that someone is guiding and tipping it forward. When he bends at the waist, he can imagine that his rib cage is hanging off the rope. Then, when it is tipped upright again, he may no longer feel the rib cage because it is balanced on the rope. Then I will ask him to imagine that the rope is being pulled gently upward and the rib cage outward so he can feel the rib cage expand while it is comfortably supported by the rope. I will often add variations, such as imagining that the rope (actually the spine) is being wiggled and I ask how that changes the feeling in the basket part of the ribs as it hangs off the rope. I constantly feed in images until it makes sense to everyone.

The other way to help students find their natural breath is through sense-fact. For example, I was working with first-year students on breathing right into the middle of the body. I asked them to imagine that their extended breath was a column of air that was heated from the middle. One young lady said, "I can't feel a thing in my back, it doesn't seem to want to open." So I ask her to bend at the waist while keeping her legs straight, and to stretch the upper part of her body so that it was at right angles with the base of her spine. When she stood up her back opened. It had felt closed to her because her spine had shortened and pressed down because she had been concentrating very hard. Imagery is important, but when it doesn't work there is usually a direct physical solution.

The balance between sound and breath changes as effort changes and the two need to work together. We also work on the lower girdle area and what it feels like if you cough or laugh—you can actually feel the area expanding. Students have to listen to all their responses and compare them until they have an accurate picture of how they respond physically when they try to produce sound.

Having tried to help the individual sort out his sense of his own body, i.e., his breathing patterns and how they work, I then look at sound directly. You cannot talk about sound without talking about the placing of the human voice. By that I mean that we have three resonators in the body and their balance is altered by the position of the tongue. Sound is determined by the relationship of the tongue to the soft palate and the larynx. These relationships produce the individual's voice quality.

Next we re-explore the production of breath. If you have support of the breath, then you can dare to actually open up the resonation areas. That's the next stage of work and one that is dependent on a very careful, trusting relationship between me and the person I am working with—together we try to get the balance right.

Are There Different Approaches to Voice Training?

There are approaches to voice training in some drama schools about which I am doubtful. One is when teachers separate voice from speech; that is, they see the essential vocal instrument as separate from what happens when it is divided up through articulation. I don't agree, because everything—breath, note, and word—is an integrated whole. Then there is the old-fashioned notion of "rib reserve" that is still being taught. Actors are taught to expand the rib cage and leave it out while they fill up with breath from the diaphragm. The belief is that you will never run out of breath because the ribs would contain a reserve of air. Can you imagine how people moved in this position? In the fifties there was an immense reaction against this approach and everything got thrown out, including the idea of approaching the voice physically. Then everyone said it's the diaphragm that we have to work on. As a result you will find a whole generation of actors who have overdeveloped diaphragms. Now we have come round, and rightly so, to teaching that breathing is a circle around the body, that you need to pull breath from the back, the sides, the front, the diaphragm, all of it. You will still find people who say that the rib reserve approach is relevant. I think it's relevant when it comes to supporting a singing voice, but it doesn't seem to work at all in terms of freeing the voice for the actor.

How Do You Combine Text and Voice Training?

Once a student at Central has a basic understanding of his own voice, he then proceeds to apply it to different kinds of text. First of all, he has to look at his pace. Perhaps he has developed a fast pace or, because of his dialect, a mode of speech that is nearly one-noted. Whatever it is, this has got to be discussed in response to text. Verse is a very good way of looking at this because verse, of necessity, requires emotional expression. Verse also allows you to hear when someone is not committing himself vocally—that is, when the link between the gut, the mind, and the voice isn't working or when one of those three is overbalanced. For instance, an actor may become overly emotional because he does not have an accurate understanding of the text. Verse can also highlight an individual's fears. An actor may be highly talented, but through verse, and sometimes through prose, I may be able to pinpoint his or her own particular fears about communicating text.

People sometimes ask me why by the third year of drama school all our actors' voices aren't of a very high standard, or why in the professional theater not all voices are what they should be. If I were to list all the things one is actually up against, one would wonder how most actors do as well as they do. It takes many years to overcome obstacles and get to a state of equilibrium. For example, one actress I know had to overcome a dialect problem. She is originally Scots but now has a complete English overlay. She is also an ex-sportswoman so that all her muscles are active in all the wrong places and her breath is not smooth and easy. Over the years I have watched her stand on stage in moments of acute discomfort and demand of her voice that it do what she wants it to without tension. But that can only happen when one is sufficiently sophisticated in voice control.

And there are psychological barriers to be overcome as well. I recently worked with an actress who has been told many times throughout her career that she has an attractive, if slightly broken voice. People say, you sound so

63

sexy, so vulnerable, I could take care of you for the rest of my life. But she knows that she has a voice that sometimes doesn't quite work, that limits her, and it distresses her on those occasions when her voice won't do what she wants it to do. But it's hard to resist misusing your voice when people find it attractive and you've gotten approval for it.

So when people say, why isn't the standard higher, I say I have been working on my voice for twenty years and I am just beginning to be able to tolerate it. It's very difficult to get the voice to do what you want it to do.

The accreditation committees that review all the drama schools complain, but if they listened to the raw material that we get in, I would hope they'd realize that, frankly, all of the drama schools are working miracles—and so are all the students who commit themselves to working on their voices. You must realize that many students come from families where monosyllables are sometimes the main form of communication, and that the art of conversation started declining about 160 years ago. It died a complete death between 1935 and 1980, when movies and television came in and we began to listen to people saying things—not conversing. We have developed a very strong visual sense, which has eclipsed the art of conversation.

What Are the Specific Vocal Demands of Playing Shakespeare?

Having looked at verse as an emotional tool, having looked at prose as a tool, we then come to Mr. Shakespeare. I believe Shakespeare was not only a writer of genius but a brilliant teacher as well. When you look at his work you find that even alliteration, assonance, and onomatopoeia aren't simply literary devices, but ways to unlock emotions. Take the line from *Macbeth*, "And take my milk for gall, you murdering ministers." There are four ems in that line and the pressure on those ems seems to release something in the human speaker. If an actor can get in touch with the feelings those sounds produce, he has a working basis for expression through sound—which goes right back to what I said about the need to find out what sound means to you in the first place.

Do You Believe That Those Four Ems, for Example, Will Release Something Consistent in All Actors?

Yes. Shakespeare uses language in a way that is totally expressive of what is going on emotionally in the text, and if you can find how those sounds unlock those feelings in you (or how those feelings unlock those sounds, either way), then I think you are on to something. Take, "If it were done when 'tis done, then 'twere well/It were done quickly" (*Macbeth*). As the line is composed of very short sounds, the speaker must be in a state of urgency. You can try to stretch out those sounds, but it ceases to seem effective. Emotionally, those sounds match up with what is happening. On the other hand, in the same speech you get, "and pity, like a naked newborn babe." Now, "like a naked newborn babe" is an expansive sound because Macbeth's grief, sense of loss, and inability to do anything about the situation he is in have increased. If you go through the whole of *Macbeth* you can prove this over and over again. And Shakespeare is not the only writer to do this. From Edward Bond in this country to Sam Shepard and David Mamet in your country, there are playwrights who are superb at capturing feeling through sound. The characters in Mamet's *Glengarry Glen Ross* are virtually monosyllabic, which so clearly captures how emotionally bleak they are. Every good writer picks up on how the rhythm and feel of language reflects the emotional state of his characters. And the actor has to be led into discovering that by examining language in a specific way.

There are also theoretical approaches to text based on an understanding of iambic pentameter that can help some actors in approaching the Shakespearean line. Oddly enough, iambic pentameter is a mode of speech that naturally lends itself to the English language. Think of the line, "Earth has not anything to share more fair." It doesn't sound like a line of blank verse, but it is. It is iambic pentameter and produces a rhythm that seems to appeal to the English ear, be it American, English, or Australian. "Let's have one other gaudy night." The feeling is embedded in the verse, and yet we are able to transcend the verse because it stimulates us emotionally.

If you look carefully at Shakespeare you will find that if you ignore all the punctuation except the full stop—the commas, semicolons, and colons in the middle of the line (which have been imposed by other people anyway)—if you don't breathe in the mid-line, but instead have a fractional pause to indicate the end of a line, you will find the emotional impact and meaning of the verse. "I left no ring with her what means this lady?/ Fortune forbid my outside have not charm'd her!/ She made good view of me indeed so much/ (no end stop, no punctuation at the end of the line) That methought her eyes had lost her tongue/

66

For she did speak in starts distractedly" (end line stop). You could say it in a modern, naturalistic way, but I think that you would lose what is actually going on in Viola. If I split the line "I left no ring with her . . ." and stopped as though it were a full stop (which some editions do) before I went on to say "what means this lady?", I would deny the importance of the second line. I think it should all be one thought: "I left no ring with her what means this lady?" Then if I run together "She made good view of me indeed so much that methought her eyes had lost her tongue for she did speak in starts distractedly," it sounds naturalistic, but I have ceased to be able—within the terms of iambic pentameter in which it was written—to be able to find out what is really important to me. I think it's more emotionally telling as: "She made good view of me—indeed so much, that methought her eyes had lost her tongue, for she did speak in starts distractedly."

It seems to me that if you don't look carefully at the iambic pentameter you are digging your own grave. Shakespeare had an instinctive ear. It sounds hypertechnical but I don't think it is. I think it is hyperemotional. There are some actors that I would recommend this to straight down the line because I think that's the way their brain works; and there are some actors I would push gently in that direction but not make too much of it because the seeming technicality can appear intimidating.

How Do You Combine Your Dialect Work with Text?

I first worked as a dialect coach so I cannot separate this area from voice. Dialect and voice quality are intermingled, particularly in this country. All the variations of tongue-placing and tone need experimenting with. There aren't that many teachers who do both. I am also interested in the voice in terms of acoustics and theater space. Along with teaching drama students at Central, I work at the National Theatre in the Olivier, and the Cottesloe for Sir Peter Hall, and I also give workshops there for actors. I attend play rehearsals especially to look after the younger actors and make sure they feel secure, and in case there are any problems to sort out generally.

Are There Many Voice Problems That Result From the Way a Play Is Staged or Interpreted?

Yes. Very frequently a director asks for a pitch change from an actor—off the top of one's head. The character of Stanley Kowalski in *A Streetcar Named Desire* often needs vocal weight using the chest resonators, or Caliban needs something similar, or Ariel needs to be pitched up a little. It takes some experimenting with the actor until one is sure it is a *real* and fully tried vocal transformation, not just done for effect out of context from full communication.

The Drama Centre, London

The Drama Centre, London, was founded in 1966 in order to make available to British students some of the major developments in European and American theater. It combines the achievements of the Method in the United States with the work of Rudolf Laban, a seminal figure in European dance and theater. It also reflects the English tradition, particularly that stemming from Joan Littlewood and Theatre Workshop. These various approaches are taught as modern developments within the great Western theatrical tradition that began with the Greeks.

The Drama Centre offers a three-year Acting Course and a two-year Professional Instructors Course.

Christopher Fettes

Christopher Fettes is Principal and one of the three founding directors of the Drama Centre, London. Virtually untrained except in modern dance, he worked with Joan Littlewood at Theatre Workshop and was one of the original members of the English Stage Company at the Royal Court Theatre. As a director his productions include the record-breaking Doctor Faustus *at Hammersmith and in the West End and* Bernice *and* Britannicus *at the Lyric, Hammersmith, both first productions on the English professional stage; Schnitzler's* The Lonely Road, *which brought Tony Hopkins back to Britain; and* Orlando *for Scottish Opera.*

The Drama Centre came into being twenty-five years ago. It quickly established itself and survived because it had the support of an extremely influential council, which included Peter Brook, Kenneth Tynan, George

71

Devine, who was the Artistic Director of the Royal Court Theatre, and Glen Byam Shaw, the former Director of the Shakespeare Memorial Theatre at Stratford-upon-Avon, who later took over the English National Opera. The reason was a simple one. The National Theatre had recently been formed, and the company that became the Royal Shakespeare Company had acquired a London base where they would develop a repertoire exclusive of Shakespeare. It was then discovered that our actors and actresses were, in the main, ill-equipped to deal with the requirements of these new and highly sophisticated repertoires. So the theaters had to embark on elaborate schemes for in-service training, which were difficult to arrange, tiring, and wasteful. All these very influential people, including by then Sir Peter Hall, gave the Drama Centre their full backing because the training represented something new and very complex, as far as English theater was concerned.

What Is the Drama Centre's Approach to Training?

Schools in this country have a very short history, and their approach to training has always been essentially pragmatic: training in voice and speech, a bit of movement, and lots of rehearsal with professional actors or directors who demonstrate what to do and how to do it. The British have always distrusted the realm of ideas, the intellectual, the high-brow approach. And they have always been insistent about maintaining an absolute separation between theater and politics. The Drama Centre, from the word *go*, rejected all of that. It was the heir, in many ways, of one of the most distinguished schools that Britain had ever had, the Old Vic School, which was run by Michel St. Denis, George Devine, and Glen Byam Shaw (though it was essentially St. Denis's school). St. Denis was in a sense the heir of the great French director of the twenties and thirties, Jacques Copeau. He was a European, and it was to Europe, not to England or the United States that the Drama Centre looked and still looks today. Now, because the political right had been thoroughly discredited all over the continent by the events of the 1939–45 war and the Holocaust, modern European theater has been to a large extent a reflection of the left, with Brecht the dominant figure. The only commanding influence from Britain that the Drama Centre reflected was that of Joan Littlewood and her wonderful company, Theatre Workshop. Joan, of course, fell foul of the Arts Council and was therefore ultimately destroyed because of her left-wing views.

There was also a strong American influence at work from the beginning, because unlike any other school in the country at that time, the Drama Centre had an acting class. The person who taught it was Doreen Cannon, who had formerly assisted Uta Hagen and Herbert Berghof in New York. After many years she was succeeded by Reuven Adiv, who had been an assistant to Lee Strasberg. So our training bears the stamp of these two very different approaches. Of course, things have changed and, we hope, developed since those early days. I think the acting training here is, in important ways, much closer to Stanislavsky than to his American disciples. We reject some aspects of the American approach and some similar approaches in this country because we have no use for the

73

notion of art for art's sake, and we do believe that theater is related, albeit in complex and subtle ways, to the real world. We believe that actors have to be sensitive to that world and responsible to it and for it. We are, therefore, very suspicious about too much psychology. We are suspicious about a lot of conventional theater, especially American theater and movie acting, because it evades its social responsibilities by taking refuge in "the inner life." And England is full to the brim of youngsters who want to do just that. It's a pernicious thing. So our emphasis is always upon what people do to one another in very specific places and at very specific times, which does not mean that motivation, psychological as well as sociological, is not very important. Of course it is, but the stage is not a place for self-indulgence.

The Drama Centre Is Considered the First Method Drama School in Britain. What Exactly Is Meant by That?

The Drama Centre became the first essentially "methodological" school in Great Britain and it was based on three distinct yet related approaches. First of all, there was the Method, but the more European, text-oriented form of Method as it exists at the HB Studio in New York. Secondly, the work of Michel St. Denis, which was taught here by the Joint Principal, John Blatchley, who had been Michel's assistant at Strasbourg. St. Denis's approach was very important because of its extremely strong emphasis on the body rather than the mind, and its view of actors as essentially rather mundane artisans, people with a craft, people who "make" things, like glassblowers and dress-makers and so forth. Again, this was a bit of a slap in the face for those in the mainstream of actor training because they were and still are desperately intent on the bour-geoisification—dreadful word—of the English theatrical profession. Also, St. Denis's approach was important be-cause of its typically French preoccupation with style, but style in the old-fashioned sense that derived from the interaction of the individual with the world in which he lives. Today, English theater is wholly devoid of style in that sense. Or, if you like, it consists *only* of style, but always the same style, whether you are talking about the National Theatre, the Royal Shakespeare Company, tele-vision, movies, or Shaftesbury Avenue—the same style, which bears only the most tenuous relation to what real people do in real life.

Of all the schools in Great Britain, the Drama Centre is the one that lays the greatest insistence on the classical repertoire. And not just the English classical repertoire, but the European as well. Oddly enough, our students have always reacted very favorably to this, and over the years far and away the most popular writers with students have not been Shakespeare or Sheridan or Arthur Miller or even Chekhov, but Calderón and Racine. Of course, one cannot train students to perform Brecht or Shake-speare or Molière. All one can do in a drama course is supply some firsthand experience of the nature of the stylistic problems involved in actually trying to play, say, *Fuenteovejuna*, in England in 1988; but that's worth do-ing, or so we believe.

Finally, the third and perhaps most important influence on our work was our ability to draw on the extraordinary knowledge and skill of another of our founder-members, Yat Malmgren, who is not entirely unknown in the U.S. as he used to teach at the American Conservatory Theater in San Francisco. Yat was one of the last of the great solo artists of European modern dance, which derived from the work of Mary Wigman and her close colleague, the choreographer and movement theorist, Rudolf Laban. Laban, together with Kurt Jooss, Hein Heckroth, and Michael Chekhov were refugees from Nazi Germany and settled at Dartington Hall in England. Laban went on to develop an astonishingly complex theory to account for the expressive quality of gesture. It is a system of move-ment notation that was widely used in the U.S.A. and became known in England as Modern Educational Dance. He himself, however, did not have a technique for training students. Yat, who has been a successful profes-sional dancer, a gold medalist at the Brussels Olympiad of Dance in 1938, and who subsequently trained with Ego-rova and Preobrajenska in Paris and became a soloist with the International Ballet Company, had precisely that—a technique for training. Certainly in England there has never been a teacher with so comprehensive a back-ground, so diverse a knowledge of the training methods peculiar to both classical and modern dance than he. But it was the Laban theory with its astonishing insights into the meaning of the expressive quality of movement that supplied the all-important foundation for the training. His theory implies that creative expression is not depen-dent on gaining control over an essentially alien medium, since the medium of expression is the body itself. Also, everybody is potentially a creative artist provided those qualities that serve an expressive purpose are first raised to consciousness and then systematically developed. This can be accomplished through a wide variety of exercises which, from day one, also involve the use of speech in order to develop an awareness of the relation of gesture to other things, such as the tone of the voice.

The remarkable thing about Laban's theory (perhaps this connection can be attributed to the presence of Michael Chekhov working in the same building as Laban and Jooss) is its close relationship to the Stanislavsky approach to character creation. In Stanislavsky's important but rather unsatisfactory chapter in *An Actor Prepares* called "Inner Motive Forces," he writes about character typology, which, though Pavlovian, oddly anticipates Jung's theory of character types. Jung's theory, in turn, exercised a very considerable influence upon Laban. I suppose we all remember the story of Olga Knipper's alarm when Stanislavsky stated that Astrov was deeply and sincerely in love with Yelena, because this meant that the character of Astrov was in no way to be distinguished from that of Vanya. Chekhov, however, had clearly conceived of Vanya as a "feeling" type and Astrov as a "sensing" type. With typical generosity and honesty, Stanislavsky came to acknowledge the scale of his error and in his subsequent work insists on the importance of diagnosing the character type at an early stage of rehearsal. When Laban was dying he entrusted all his unpublished work to Yat's keeping in the belief that it would have very little future in the context of dance in the U.K. He believed it could and should be developed by the man whom he indubitably came to see as his spiritual heir. No aspect of the training at the Drama Centre has had a more deeply and richly educative function than the work of Yat,

77

the most remarkable teacher of his generation in this country. His contribution is affirmed through his close association with the Royal Court, the National Theatre under Olivier, and his wide international influence.

So it is a very special kind of training here and we are special also in that we aim to supply not so much a training as an education in theater. Those of us who operate in this sphere know very well that training can become more and more refined, more and more diverse and complex and rich, without ever solving what is perhaps the most important question of all—which is not, How do you create good actors? but, How do you develop them into interesting human beings? Once the actor has sacrificed the fragile appeal of youth, that is where the emphasis must fall. The thought of going to a party to which most of the guests are actors or actresses is enough to stop the most intrepid person dead in their tracks, because the overwhelming majority of them bore one to sobs—off stage *and* on. The answer to the problem is anyone's guess, but if you run a school you really ought to have a go. Here we believe the development of the intelligence and a sense of responsibility, and the exercise of the nervous and muscular systems all play an essential part.

Reuven Adiv

Reuven Adiv is Head of Acting at the Drama Centre, London. Born and educated in Israel, he began his career with the Ohel and Chamber Repertory Theatre Companies in Tel Aviv. In 1954 he emigrated to the United States and studied acting and directing with Lee Strasberg in his private classes and at the Actors Studio. During his stay in America he appeared in off-Broadway productions, summer stock, and on television.

In 1970 Mr. Adiv returned to Israel. There he taught acting and was Principal of the Theatre Department of Hakibutzim Teachers College. He also appeared in productions at the Habimah National Theatre and in films. He has been with the Drama Centre, London, since 1983, and in 1986 became a permanent guest-acting teacher at the Swedish National Theatre School in Gothenberg, Sweden.

You Studied Extensively with Lee Strasberg in New York. Have You Changed or Adapted Strasberg's Approach?

Basically, I teach what I learned from Lee with the difference that I always keep students focused on why we do exercises. Lee did not stress this in detail. I believe that the exercises he developed will help actors contact and learn to use their own experiences. Maybe I was too young to understand, but I spent a great deal of time trying to decide what it all meant. I came to the conclusion that the Method exercises sharpen our awareness and help us reevaluate ourselves as individuals so we can come to know the things that affect us. They sharpen our alertness, our senses to the life around us. I want students to become aware of how the things they encounter affect them. Through his exercises I've learned how an actor can use himself to play a different individual under different circumstances.

Do You Start Students with Sensory Work?

Yes, very basic sensory work, such as creating a cup of coffee and drinking it, experiencing sunshine, cold, etc. But I add something to it. I tell students that if, for any reason, something comes into their mind which affects them, they mustn't interfere with it but allow themselves to be affected by it while they continue to work on the exercises. What is brought up will become part of the exercise. It may be that an individual has a certain association with drinking coffee. I want students to become aware of what enters into their thoughts, where it comes from, why it comes up. I want them to be in touch with what is happening at the moment.

Then students work on other exercises developed by Strasberg—on personal objects, private moments, song-and-dance, and affective memory exercises. Students can then begin to learn how to use those exercises in their acting if they need them.

For example, the song-and-dance exercise deals with being able to express in sound whatever inner reality the person is experiencing at the moment. In this exercise the actor is not working on a character but standing alone without a mask, so to speak, facing the audience. This is a confrontation between the actor and the audience and I try to make students aware of what is happening to them during this time, from when they get up from their chair, walk toward the middle of the room, and face the audience. In this exercise students start by picking a simple song. They sing it while looking at the audience, keeping to the melody but dividing the words into separate syllables, each held for a long time. They must keep their bodies relaxed while exploring the faces of individuals in the audience. Whatever feeling comes up in them must be expressed in the sound. In this way they are training themselves to reveal themselves constantly, to share their experiences with the audience. It teaches them to accept their feelings and express their momentary impulses, and in this way they are shared with the audience. That is what we do as actors—we share.

I also impress on students that when they work they have to pay attention to all the simple realities that are easy to ignore. For example, in a scene they may need to pay attention to the physical environment, to the cold or heat, to the fact that it's late at night. I want them to know where they are coming from or if they are tired. If their character is sixty years old, do they have any physical ailments. Young actors tend to miss these things. I want them to answer those questions each time they get up to rehearse. What if an actor does something special one night? How is he going to repeat it if he was not trained to investigate what brought this new element about? They must know the point of reference that brought this new nuance into their performance. So I teach them how to do that as well.

What Do You Mean by Point of Reference?

The point of reference refers to the character's point of view as well—how the world looks through the eyes of the character and the way in which the character's life has affected him. This has to do with the actor's imagination. If the character's point of view doesn't give the actor a sense that what he is going to do is very important, then the actor will start to indicate, force, and impose, because intellectually he knows behavior on stage must be important. Should the character's point of reference fail to work, then the actor's point of reference, his life experience, can come to his aid.

I then try to put the exercises into practice in rehearsals. Every term we take a play and use these exercises to see how they can help fulfill the objective demands of the play.

When Students Work on a Play, How Do You Help Them Become More Expressive?

I try to find the reasons why they are not being expressive. When I was a young actor, I wasn't sufficiently expressive when I felt self-conscious or when I was focused on what people thought of me while I was acting. So my mind was not where the character's mind was supposed to be. If these are the kinds of things that are blocking the actor, he must create the character's physical surroundings in more detail, pay more attention to these details, and create character thoughts. This will take his attention off himself. When I say to a student, "Stop thinking about what you are now thinking," it's as effective as saying, "Stop thinking about whether or not the audience likes what you are doing"—no matter what, he still can't help thinking about it. But if I tell him to think about the details of something else, like the character's needs and the means he will use to accomplish them, that will take his mind off of himself and on to the character's thoughts.

Do You Use Strasberg's Emotional Exercises?

We do not talk about emotions at all. Emotions are a by-product of, or response to, something that you want from the other characters in the play. Very often a student falls into the trap of working to express anger or frustration, rather than focusing on why, as the character, he has come into a specific situation, what problem he has to solve there, and what means his character will use to get what he wants and stick to his choices. If those elements bring up an emotion in him I tell the actor to allow its expression, not to judge it or inhibit it, and to stay with his action. Later on he can evaluate whether that character should express anger toward the other characters. Maybe the nature of their relationship is such that his character cannot express anger because it is contrary to his basic personality. Maybe his character feels insecure and wouldn't allow himself to show anger. If that is the case, the actor must find the means that the character can use to get what he wants when he cannot get it through anger. Perhaps his character would try to get the other person to feel sorry for him. There are many ways and means. This depends on the actor's analysis of the character's personality and the choices he has arrived at. I also put great emphasis on finding the character's physical life.

Do You Ask Students to Think in Terms of Objectives and Obstacles When Analyzing a Scene?

Yes. I use very simple examples from life. For instance, when we are hungry at night, what actions do we take to satisfy ourselves? What means do we use? It's simple. We get up, put on the light, open the fridge, take food, and eat it. We *do* something, and through the doing we achieve our objective. Students tend to forget these simple things. I remind them that every time they perform they must play the actions that take them in the direction of what their character wants.

Did You Have to Alter the Method Approach to Actor Training for British Students?

I don't think there is a big difference. Acting training deals with the human experience. It starts with trying to understand oneself and, later on, with being able to know the difference between oneself and the character one is playing. It's not difficult for any student, anywhere, to understand that. The difficulty lies in acquiring the freedom of expression that tends to be stifled in different countries for different reasons. Each society, each kind of upbringing, encourages and inhibits different aspects of expression. Acting training must remove the inhibitions. The actor must be able to explore a world that he doesn't know, that may be very different from the one he grew up in.

How Do You Work on Text?

I focus a lot on the meaning of every word. I would say to a student, "You are saying something, someone answers you, you answer back, what is that about? Why is it necessary to say exactly that and not something else? What causes the character to say that line and what is he trying to achieve with that line?" Those words and lines are based on the construction of the scene and the ideas of the play as conceived by its author. They reveal what it is about and how that specific scene contributes to that idea.

The Drama Centre, London

Therefore, I try to make them aware of the importance of every line and impress upon them the importance of reading the play very carefully and often. Research is also of vital importance and Christopher Fettes's analysis class is a model of how a play should be approached.

The Drama Studio

The Drama Studio was founded in 1966 by Peter Layton, and in 1980 an American branch of the school was opened in Berkeley, California. The school's purpose was to provide a new and more realistic approach to actor training—a training that takes account of the professional requirements and demands of the theater for which the student is being prepared.

The Drama Studio offers intensive one-year courses in Acting and Directing for postgraduates and other advanced students on both its campuses. In addition the Drama Studio has developed outreach programs, which include evening and part-time classes, a Young Actors' program, and workshops and seminars conducted by senior members of the teaching staff. An intensive summer program was added to the school's program in 1983.

Patrick Tucker

Patrick Tucker is Director of Studies and an Associate Director of the Drama Studio, London, and Berkeley. He has been teaching and directing at the Drama Studio since 1972.

After attending the Boston University Theater Arts program, Mr. Tucker returned to the United Kingdom to direct all forms of theater, from weekly repertory to the Royal Shakespeare Company, as well as productions for BBC Television. His most recent television production was twenty-eight episodes of Brookside *for Channel 4. His recent theater productions include* Love's Labour's Lost *for Southern Methodist University and* Another Country *for the Thorndike Theatre, Leatherhead.*

Although most of his directorial work is in Britain and the U.S., Mr. Tucker has also directed The Merchant of Venice *in Korean for the National Theatre of Korea, and* A Chorus of Disapproval *in Hebrew at Beersheba, Israel.*

89

How Do You Begin Training New Students?

One of the first exercises that I give new students is purposely designed to make them fail. I believe that we are more likely to remember through failure, and indeed, students always remember this one because they realize that they didn't do what I asked them to. They fell for an easy choice. If you succeed at something, you may never think about why. However, when you fail, you're concerned about why, and this is a better way to learn because you always *remember* it.

I tell two students that they are going to do an improvisation set in a launderette. I whisper a phrase in one student's ear and tell that person to somehow work it into the improvisation. The phrase is usually something unusual like, "I like to eat worms," or, "My sister married the Ayatollah Khomeini." Inevitably, after students do the improvisation, the rest of the class can guess which phrase I gave the student. I've done this exercise many times and no one has ever tried to play an Iranian in order to make sense of the line, "My sister married the Ayatollah Khomeini." Of course, the most logical thing to do is start the improvisation playing an Iranian, but no, students always wind up playing an Englishman or American who has to somehow twist these words to fit the situation, and they never manage to do that successfully. This is to show that acting should start from the text—not the situation. This exercise is also a way of demonstrating to students that their education, in the most general sense, has led them away from the path of instinctive acting and has taught them to be, first of all, concerned with being dutifully correct.

When I rehearse a play, I work with students in the same way that I work with professionals. When I work on a play with professional actors, I don't do read-throughs. Everyone hates them and just worries about pronouncing the words correctly and so forth, so why do them? I also ask the actors to learn their lines very soon after we begin rehearsing and I block the play on the first day of rehearsal. What that means is that instead of actors sitting around at a table during the first rehearsal, every scene is worked out within the correct context: a two-hander is seen to be a two-hander; a crowd scene is seen to be a crowd scene; in a read-through *all* scenes are read in the context of a crowd. If the actor rehearses with a script in his hand, he tends to follow the director's blocking without thought and he has not contributed to creating the pattern of the play because he wasn't there—his head was buried in the script. And because he was worrying about his lines, he couldn't experiment with them.

Too many people think that actors will be restricted if they learn the lines first. In fact, once they have learned the lines, they have total freedom to do anything they like with them. They can be said in a multitude of ways, and the different ways of saying them will lead to different thoughts, and different thoughts will lead to different blocking. I am a great believer that all patterns of movement are patterns of thought, and when you give an actor a different move it is usually going to engender a different thought. When actors are stuck in the script, however, a different move doesn't let them have a different thought. They haven't got the thoughts yet because they haven't got the lines inside their heads.

How Much Freedom Do You Give Your Actors to Change the Blocking if the Motivation Changes?

Very much or very little. By that I mean that I give them the impression that they have a lot, but they actually have very little. I give them hints about how to block themselves through the use of furniture—which is something that directors should do more often. Very simply put, if in a love scene I put you on the stage with a sofa stage center and I say, "Play the scene any way you like," the odds are you are going to sit on the sofa. If you do that, you will instinctively play the scene in a certain way without my giving you another note. However, if there are two chairs and I put them in an alcove and say, "This is a secretive love scene," you are going to sit in the alcove. Now, I've not told you how to play the scene, but I've set up how you are going to play it. So I have directed that scene quite explicitly without saying a word about blocking. You can change things radically just by changing the relationship between the actors and the furniture.

How Do You Instruct New Students to Approach a Scene?

I believe there are three important aspects to a performance: First, knowing what to do, that is, at what moment do you want the audience to know that you are jealous or secretly fond of another character, etc. Second, working out how to do it, which can be quite technical or obvious, for instance, by suddenly dropping a spoon when someone comes into the room or snapping a pencil when they turn toward you. I'm exaggerating, of course, but that's the *how*. And third, making all this look believable. For example, you cross to the bookcase, you take down the vase, he comes into the room, and you drop the vase. Of course, the actor has to motivate his move to the bookcase. Perhaps in the previous scene he has admired the vase, so that when he picks it up and then drops it, the audience doesn't perceive it as a device but as a naturalistic moment. But it's also a theatrical moment. It's the artist's job to make these "hows" appear so natural that the audience doesn't notice them. To me, that's what real technique means.

If you only travel the path of reality, it becomes a restriction. It reduces the play to yourself, to the middle class, to the twentieth century. It's possible to put Shakespeare in a contemporary setting, for instance, but in the process some directors also reduce the play. They say, let's put Hamlet in a bar. Is a man in a bar going to say, "To be or not to be . . ."? There is a lie between what this man is saying and how he is saying it. Contemporary people don't say, "Hark, who goes there?" They say, "Hello," or "Let's go, mate." They do not say, "Hie thee hither, that I may pour my spirits in thine ear." I care about the reality, which is what I got from my American training, but my focus is on creating the character who wants to say those lines, who wants to say, "Hie thee hither . . ." Then you've got true acting. So in a very approximate way, instead of the actor taking the text and fitting it to himself, I'm asking the actor to fit himself to the text. And that's important whether it's television, film, or theater.

Do You Instruct Students to Think About Objectives and Obstacles?

Yes. If the scene is not working I tell the students to work out their needs and wants. But I don't ask them to do it all the way through. I believe it's a tool for emergencies. I do use it, but I don't teach it to students until the need arises. You see, all actors want teachers to tell them what to do. I much prefer for them to find out for themselves. I believe that what actors actually feel is entirely irrelevant to what they do in front of an audience. There is no necessary connection between feeling good and being good. I know wonderful actors who feel nothing when they act.

Where Did You Study in America?

I was originally trained in physics in England, but was always interested in drama. So I applied to Boston University's graduate theater program, never dreaming that I would get in. But I did, and off I went to study in America. Now this was shocking since the English thought that it should be the other way around—that the Americans should come to us. The orientation at the school was Stanislavsky, of course. Some of the training I didn't find very useful later. For example, they taught directors to use certain kinds of improvisations to help the acting company work well together, and others to help actors feel they really live in the house or whatever environment the play takes place in. But I found that professional English actors already do this without the need for those kinds of improvisations.

94

What Is Your Approach to Teaching Shakespeare?

If you study Shakespeare you will find that there is a great paucity of information about how Elizabethan actors rehearsed. So I researched this and found out. Shakespeare's actors did a different play every day, six days a week, and then a new play every two weeks. They weren't given copies of the whole play, but sides or cue sheets the way some musical companies still do. So the actors only had their own lines and a cue line. In light of that and the fact that there were no directors, I assume that Shakespeare put his stage directions into the body of the play.

The first thing I do in my Shakespeare class is give out scenes so that the actors have only their own lines. I've typed out hundreds of sides from both the famous and little-known plays of Shakespeare. Then I tell the actors they have one week to learn their lines and work on the verse. They must *not* read the play, *not* find out who they are acting with, and *not* rehearse. All they must do is concentrate on their lines. The first time they know who they are acting with is when they meet that person on stage.

Then they present the scene. You get some of the most outrageous and funny performances, but they are also very exciting.

How Do You Critique Scenes Done in This Way?

I do it from the point of view of the language. I'll say, "Why did you do that? What does your line say? I don't care what it *means*. What does the structure dictate?" I

95

might say, "But look, your character has rhyming couplets here. Why do you shout this line when it is a straightforward line?" After I critique the scenes, the directing
students work them with the actors.

By the end of the semester every student has had two
attempts at presenting at least sixty lines of Shakespeare.
Then they work on a full play. The plays are presented to
the rest of the school and to invited guests. That's the
Shakespeare course.

How Do You Instruct Your Students to Analyze the Language?

In Shakespeare the end word in a line is always significant. The question is, why did Shakespeare write it that
way? He put that particular word at the end of a line in
order to give the actor extra information about what is
going on. It's the modern equivalent of underlining.

I learned text analysis from John Barton at the Royal
Shakespeare Company, but the difference between us is
that I fanatically put this into practice. He does it in his
verse classes and in his verse work with actors, but not
always in his productions. That's not necessarily a criticism of him. That's the way he works and he gets fabulous
results. All I am saying is that when I have applied this
principle 100 percent, it always works. I teach students to
examine the text as a series of explicit instructions from
the director/playwright Shakespeare to the actor.

For example, when Lady Macbeth goes off with the
daggers she says, "I'll gild the faces of the grooms withal;/
For it must seem their guilt." There is a pun on the words
gild and *guilt*. Now, however an actress plays her—

whether as a frightened child or a demonic woman—the fact remains that Lady Macbeth stops for a pun, and the question is why? What instruction is Shakespeare trying to give the actress about character? I insist that my actors note those clues and make choices based on them.

How Would You Interpret Lady Macbeth's Character Based on That Particular Clue?

I try not to give answers directly, but I let them find it for themselves. But basically, in that particular instance, I think there are several answers. Lady Macbeth may be afraid of going upstairs and she may need to crack a little joke to give herself courage. This indicates that she is not the strong character we think she is. Another reason may be that she thinks Macbeth is falling to pieces and she has to put on a brave face to give *him* courage by cracking a little joke. The third solution could be that she is so full of demonic fury and energy, and is so certain that this is the right thing to do, that she has no fear. That's an example of three wildly differing interpretations from the same clue, and I always tell my actors to do what they like based on the clue, but not to ignore it.

Another thing I do in my Shakespeare lectures and workshops is let the class know that I want them to learn from experiencing rather than by taking notes. I want them to feel what it was like to live in Elizabethan times. They can think about the information I give them, but not until they experience it can they really understand it.

So first I turn out all the lights and start my lecture by candlelight. Now I can't see them, but they can see me. Then I hand out more candles, which they light, and I ask them to introduce each other. Then I ask them to blow out their candles, gather together, and to tell me what they have concluded from this exercise. They notice, for instance, that they stood closer to each other by candlelight, and it seemed to them that everyone was more interesting. The reason for this is technically very simple: if I am talking to you by candlelight, the light level is so low that it makes your eyes sparkle, and mine as well. In modern times we are lit from above and the eyebrow ridge hides the eyes. With candlelight you can literally see better into the eyes. So the class discovered that their appreciation of each other was different. They also found that they had forgotten what people were wearing on their legs and feet, but they remembered what was worn around the neck, particularly anything sparkling. In Elizabethan times if you wanted to show people how rich you were, you put your best things around your face, like fancy collars and jewels.

Also, you can't rush about with a candle in your hand because it will go out, so you tend to walk differently. What I am saying is that the way people conversed and walked was altered by candlelight. If I told students this, they would simply write it down, but this way they have experienced it.

When Students Work with Shakespearean Text, or Any Text, for That Matter, Do You Ask Them to Think About Subtext or Prior Circumstances?

In Shakespeare the structure of the text tells the actor what is going on. By that I mean, is it prose or poetry, is it witty or simple? The subtext *is* the structure. If the actor responds to the structure, *that* is the subtext. If he works on it in other ways, he winds up reducing these wonderful characters. You don't need long rehearsals. Frankly, rehearsal can sometimes destroy actors as much as anything. Do you rehearse a symphony for six weeks? No. You have a couple of rehearsals and that's it. Actors *can* do the same. I'm not saying that they must or should, but I am saying that sometimes we get caught up in concepts that can work against good acting.

You Teach a Course Called Typecasting. Would You Describe It?

My research indicates that the bulk of acting from Dionysus to the present has been based on typecasting—that is, actors using their own personalities. The concept that an actor should be versatile is a relatively modern one. Now, I am talking about the bulk of actors, particularly the successful ones. Some years back when I would say this, people would point out that John Hurt or Laurence Olivier were stars and they were not typecast. Today everyone mentions Robert DeNiro or Meryl Streep. My point is that in every generation there are a few actors or actresses—very few—who are "allowed" to be versatile. When you see a Meryl Streep film you expect her to be different from the last one you saw her in, and you are disappointed if she is not. But when you go to see Paul Newman, secretly you know what to expect, and you get what you expected. And you are happy with that. That is not just true of modern acting. If you study theatrical history you will realize that actors like James O'Neill and Edmund Kean were successful because the audience knew what to expect and got it. It's a hard concept for us in the theater to accept because so many of us worry and care about differences. We say to our students, "I've seen that performance before," as if that were a bad thing. And yet, once an actor enters the profession, if people like his performance, they will want that performance over and over again.

Now as a concept of training it is absolutely vital and essential that actors learn to play different characters, but in preparing them for the "real world" I think it's a question of the actor finding the role that the world wants him or her to play. Marilyn Monroe had to search for her role, her look. Once she found it, she stayed with it and it was successful. Versatility didn't enter into it. Indeed, she was a good actress, but it was within the framework that the world demanded. The really great actors, like Humphrey Bogart, managed within a rather tight framework to find immense variety. Less great but successful actors, like the Sylvester Stallones of this world, have very little range.

So when you teach acting, you are faced with this conundrum: do you teach people this strange concept of acting, that they must all have ten, fifteen, twenty different parts at their fingertips (which, frankly, only the extraordinary actors are ever asked to do), or do you train them to do what you secretly know is going to be demanded of them? So, toward the end of their training, I think one should address what role students are going to be expected to play and teach them how to do that.

One of the things I do is teach students how to play their type, how to play what they are going to be expected to play based on how they look and naturally behave. I teach them two things: to play the way they look and to play the way they are.

Every actor in the Western world sends out an eight-by-ten-inch photograph. What does that mean? They are openly acknowledging that they are going to be chosen by the way they look. So I take their photographs, pin them to the board, and ask actors to "act" their photograph. I ask them to do a monologue, a speech, or a nursery rhyme, whatever they like, and we tape it with a video camera. I tell them to just do anything, and we, the class, coach them into doing it in the manner of the photograph. The class may say, "No, you need a louder voice, a higher voice." Or, "No, be stronger," or, "Be weaker," or, "Make it twenty years older." Every photograph is explicit in what it requires. In this way I get the actor to act his photograph—and the whole group is involved in the process. Then I say, "Right, now that's the photograph." If they say that's not me, I say, then change the photo.

Sometimes it's impossible to teach an actor how to act the way he looks because most photographs are not necessarily taken to get the actor work, but to make him look good. Most actors who are short like to look taller. The vast bulk of photographers will therefore photograph them with the camera lens slightly below the eye-line to make them look taller. That's useless. When I'm casting a play, I might look at a photo like that and say, "Hey, he could do for the bouncer." If, when the actor walks in I see that he's really very short, he's lost the job and wasted my time. So the moral here is, if I'm looking for "you" (whatever that means), I must be able to find you in the photograph. What I'm doing here is teaching actors how to cooperate with the photographer in taking the correct photo.

In the next step I ask the class, "What sort of part is this person going to play?" They might say, "impish," or "nymphlike." Then I'd tell the actor to go to the photographer and say, "I want the imp (or the nymph). Don't make me look glamorous." There was a girl in class recently whose photograph looked very glamorous, but it wasn't her. She herself was feisty and vivacious, but when we looked at her photo we all saw a boring, glamorous model. She couldn't even act it. If I had seen that photograph and sent for her, she would not have gotten the part of the glamorous woman. But if I was looking for an eccentric, zany person, I would never have sent for her judging her from her photograph.

There's a second part to this exercise. I set up a casting situation. The actor comes in for an interview, sits in a chair for five minutes, and then leaves the room. I, as the director, will usually write one sentence about him on a piece of paper, won't I? So, I say to each actor, "Now you write down what you think I am going to write down about you. And what the actor writes is often hilarious. One girl wrote "big nose." What big nose? No one had noticed. Or one boy put "tall, baby-faced, scar." None of us in the room had even noticed a scar, and we had been with him for a whole day. And it wasn't a baby-face, it was a boyish face. So the image we have of ourselves is sometimes not the correct one.

I sometimes teach this course to businessmen. I remember one man who kept trying to hide his paunch. I directed him to try to show us how big and chunky his paunch was. When he did it, of course, we didn't notice it. Sometimes when you actually try to flaunt what you are most self-conscious about, you can actually remove the barriers. Each of us has various barriers. The obvious example is the actress with a large bust size who must learn how to act without being self-conscious of her chest, the hiding of which becomes a barrier. Of course, some people will cast them for it, but then they have to learn to at least acknowledge it, not to hide it. I will ask certain students, tall girls for instance, to come to class for a week or two in high heels. Or I'll ask the girl with large breasts to wear tight sweaters for a period of time. You must get used to the experience of knowing you are tall or big-chested, because if you are cast, it will be in part *because* of that characteristic. We always try to camouflage our differences, to make ourselves like everyone else, and yet it's precisely these differences that will get us cast. I would say to the person with the big nose, "Enjoy people looking at your profile—or change it." It's the old adage: either use it or lose it.

*Drama Studio, London, Offers a Course in
Television Acting. What Kinds of Techniques Do You
Teach Specifically for This Medium?*

I try to get students to see television as it is, and not the way they think it is. It's more unreal than any other form of acting, far more unreal than even Restoration comedy.

What people do on television is technically untrue. For example, drinking a cup of coffee. If you want to see me drink a cup of coffee on television, it has to be two inches from my mouth. It looks silly in real life, but if you put a frame around it, it looks realistic. The same thing will apply to all sorts of gestures and behavior. On television you might see a husband and wife have a marital argument, but they don't argue face to face. They do it while the wife is washing the dishes and the husband is looking over her shoulder so she winds up talking with her back to him. The actors do it this way so that both their faces can be seen by the camera. The camera lies and lies.

If this were a television interview I could be sitting behind you and talking to your head, but on television with a frame around each of us, no one would notice. The unreality of television is very extreme. Because it is so intimate, people think it is the most real form of acting, and they don't watch and listen to what people really do and say.

Actors have to do visually more and vocally less on television. When I say "more," I don't necessarily mean popping the eyes. When we are thinking in real life, the face goes blank. That is because we are putting our energy inside ourselves and nothing shows on the face. A television audience interprets that as dead or boring. The secret is to put your thoughts onto your face.

Since your thoughts never stop, so your face must never stop. When we are thinking in real life or on the stage, our body continues to move although we are only listening. When you remove all those external messages, when you narrow the camera down to only the face, it has to stay alive the way the body naturally does.

But on television the actor has to do less vocally. I am working with an actress at the moment who said, "But I can't project less. If I do, I will lose my character." I said the trouble is you have to speak to the other person as if that person were two inches from you. Now if I were two inches from you I would be speaking very softly, very intimately. That's the secret. If I were angry and two inches from your nose, I would speak one way; if I were amorous and two inches from you, I would speak another way. So it's not as if I would say everything at the same volume. You are not supposed to whisper everything. It's the *degree* of intimacy that changes.

It's the same in the theater, but on a cruder scale. If it's a huge theater, the actors speak and act in a certain way to reach the back of the audience; if it's a fringe theater, the actors act and speak in a different way. You don't have to tell them that. It's the same on television, only the audience changes from being sixty feet away (in a long-shot), to being two inches away (in a close-up). The degree of intimacy varies more widely in television and that's another reason why it's so unreal.

I give my students this little lecture and then tell them that when they act for television they should not project to where their partner is, but to the microphone. That sounds simple. Then I say, "Let's do a little exercise. Everyone in class speak for thirty seconds to someone right of camera." Then I record them all. What I find is that most of them didn't hear me say *right of* camera and talked into the lens, and that ninety percent of them talked too loudly.

Another simple technique I teach for acting in front of the camera is to react first and then speak. If you are talking to me and I react before I answer you, the editor might, just as you are finishing your lines, cut to my face because he sees me decide to say something, and that's interesting. If I say my lines and react *afterward,* no matter how brilliant my reaction might be, the editor will probably leave it on the cutting-room floor because to leave it in will hold up the action. When an actor finishes speaking, the camera must cut to the next event, not

linger on what was going on. All these techniques go
against the actor's instincts and seem quite strange. But
when actors do this, their reactions come across as ordinary and natural. Even though they have worked their
heads off using these techniques, they end up looking
ordinary—which is a great triumph because without
these techniques they would all look bad. If you immerse
yourself in your role, you won't be able to fulfill the
technical requirements of television or film.

How Do the Technical Requirements of Television Conflict with Basic Acting Techniques?

If I were totally immersed in my performance, I'd be lost
when the director says, "Don't get within nine inches of
her because your nose will shadow her nose," or, "Don't
move off that mark," or, "Could you please cheat the eye-
line to the left because the camera is over there." If I
really "become" my character, I will not be able to fulfill
the technical demands in front of the camera. What many
performers do is subordinate these technical demands to
the emotional demands of the scene, with the result being that it might be beautiful, but the camera doesn't see
it because they aren't positioned right. That's why half
your brain has got to be aware of the technical requirements and the other half acting.

I recently saw *Rebel Without a Cause* on television and
suddenly realized the genius of the director. He did
amazingly long takes and I thought, that's how he got
James Dean's brilliant performance. I'm willing to bet
that it would be impossible to get that same performance
if the director had used lots of short takes and cut-a-ways.

Instead, he filmed the whole scene on one camera and used a couple of cut-ins of other actors. He was able to maintain the momentum of Dean's performance because it was filmed by one camera. If you have a great star, you can and should adjust your camera work to the requirements of the star. Some are better in big close-ups, some are better in long-shots. But when an actor is not a big star, he's got to fulfill the director's requirements and that's where technique comes in. That's why part of your brain has got to be in charge and able to fulfill the technical aspects, otherwise your best moments, however wonderful, will not be visible. Katharine Hepburn is brilliant at this. However intense she may be, if she is blocked by another actor she just eases over, which means that the take can continue. All of us in the television medium know that it's the technically perfect shot that gets chosen every time.

In England we use multicameras on our big series like "I, Claudius" and "Upstairs Downstairs." We film a complete scene at one time and you automatically get continuity of performance and emotion because it's in one take. The equivalent in the U.S. is filmed in little bits and pieces, and although the camera work and lighting are much better, you lose the continuity of the actor's performance.

You Teach a Class Called Entertainments. Could You Describe It?

Here, again, I emphasize the technical aspect of acting, not because I think everyone should immediately abandon everything they have learned, but because I want to do what Stanislavsky originally did, which was to teach his method to *trained* actors. His method was devised for actors who already knew how to communicate with the audience, even though they might be giving broad, bombastic performances. His goal was to make the communication appear motivated and real. Nowadays, Stanislavsky disciples still teach the Method to make acting appear motivated and real, but they don't teach actors how to communicate with the audience. I try very hard to be the other side of the coin—to teach actors to communicate.

For instance, if you are working on comedy and are supposed to smile at something, make sure you are frowning first. If you have to frown, make sure you are smiling first. Just before the other actor comes in with the funny line, find an itch on your wrist or something else to make you frown. Thus, when you smile, the contrast will make your reaction to the funny line clear. That goes back to my other first principle: What do I want to do? I want to laugh at a joke. How can I best do it? I can best do it by frowning first to make it clear. Now make that look believable. I will motivate the frown to look so believable that when I smile, the audience will not notice that what I was doing was a trick. The word *trick* upsets people.

I use another exercise to help students communicate better to the audience. I divide the class into groups and privately tell one group to improvise a scene in which one member has a dominant personality. I tell the next group to improvise a scene in which one of them is a real nuisance or pain in the neck. The next group chooses one member to be really timid, and the last group chooses one person to be a real hero. Then they do their improvisations for the class. Often the class can't quite guess what it was that was happening, or who was who, because the actors did not play their actions clearly.

Then I ask them to repeat the improvisation, but this time they must *literally* act the metaphor—that is, the person who is the nuisance must literally walk all over the other actors; the person who is the pain in the neck must literally inflict pain on someone's neck, etc. Now when they present it, it is magic. First of all, it's totally clear what is going on; and second, because they are skilled actors they do not appear unreal. Most actors think you can't do that, that it's too obvious—it's illustrating. And I say, but that's your job—to illustrate for the audience, but to do it so skillfully that they don't perceive it as illustration, but as perfectly natural.

Because there is so much unemployment in the U.S., too many actors spend too much time in acting class and teachers are always asking them what they are *thinking*. In a performance the audience either gets it or doesn't. And that's the bottom line. Maybe different rules apply for amateurs and college actors, but this is true for professional actors. When I teach, I want to train people how to be professionals, that is, how to better communicate with the audience. That's my job.

John Abulafia

John Abulafia is Associate Director of the Drama Studio, London, where he teaches acting. Founder of the Incubus Theatre and Theatremobile companies, he also ran the Pool Theatre, Edinburgh. A director as well as a teacher, his productions have appeared at the Oxford Playhouse, Leeds Playhouse, the Royal Court Theatre, the Open Space Theatre, and the Young Vic. He recently directed his own adaptation of Marlowe's Dr. Faustus at the CSC Repertory in New York.

Mr. Abulafia also directs opera at the Royal Academy of Music and the Royal Opera School. He recently produced The Marriage of Figaro *for the Mecklenburgh Festival Opera and directed the British premiere of* Sister Aimée *at the 1987 London International Opera Festival.*

Mr. Abulafia has written several stage plays, two books, and has just finished the script of a four-part television serial commissioned by Channel 4.

JOHN ABULAFIA

When I started to teach at the Drama Studio I was confronted with a group of people who had to learn all about acting in one year. The first thing you notice about new students is that they all act on one level. If they do a monologue, they will usually start on one level of extremely generalized emotion and go tearing right through it without much thought about the emotional changes within the speech. So the first thing I do is alert students to the fact that good acting is based on variety. To achieve this, there must be a part of the actor's personality that is standing back, controlling his or her body and voice as it communicates this variety. The actor, like any artist, must be subjective and objective at the same time. As one can't learn this all at once, I teach it in steps.

I teach two courses. One is built around improvisation and the other around text. I always try to relate one to the other.

What Techniques Do You Use to Teach Improvisation?

There are a lot of American techniques that I have incorporated into my own procedures, some of which are derived from Viola Spolin. Paradoxically, her work achieves its objective if the teacher makes it his own. Her ideas are marvelous and everyone can use them in a different way just because they are so fundamentally right.

My first port of call with the improvisation training is to introduce the idea of what it means to work together as actors. I do that with a game called "one-word stories." I choose two students and ask them to work together to make up and tell the class a story. One person says one word, the next says the second word, and so on. What usually happens at first is that the story dies on its feet. A student will often say, "I wanted the story to go this way or that way," and his partner was not doing what he wanted. I ask students to explain how they felt when the story didn't go the way they wanted it to. Usually, there is some admission that one felt angry when that happened. I can then point out what it feels like when one's imagination is being blocked by another actor. That block happens because one student actor is trying to control the story, and so control the other actor's thoughts. I remind them of the original instruction: working together to tell the story. I then ask them to see where the *story* wants to go instead of thinking about where they want it to go. When students understand this they can begin to create a story that takes on a life of its own. This happens when they no longer focus on themselves but on the task. Real creativity comes, I believe, from thinking about "it" not "I."

You often find that in the next phase these stories begin to get very wacky, which is nice because it means that students are letting their imaginations work. The energy flows freely between the actors. You can see different layers being peeled away in the types of stories that are created. Students' first stories are usually about fear—being chased by big monsters. The next are usually sexual and/or violent. Then, later, they get to sadder feelings as they let themselves be more vulnerable. Students have to go through these stages, so I let them.

This "one-word story" game becomes a model for working together: it is based on the principle of "accepting" instead of "blocking," which means an actor becomes more open to the possibilities offered both by the other actors and by the text. My work aims to bring actors back to basic principles, like "it," not "I." Even if they are acting the most complicated text, actors can always ask themselves what does the *playwright* want.

In the next phase of teaching I introduce the idea that theater is not just a verbal medium but a physical one as well. This is a theme that runs throughout my work. I am constantly helping them to use their bodies in a powerful and sophisticated way to communicate emotions.

There are several superb Spolin games that help here. One is called "calling out emotions." I cut out letters from newspaper advice columns and hand them out. I like to use these letters because they contain clear descriptions of what people are feeling. I ask students to improvise a scene for two people based on either the central emotional problem described in the letter or a scene that might have led up to that event. While they do this, I write out a list of emotions on the board: grief, anger, rage, lust, horror, etc. I also ask students to add these to their improvisations. (It has to be a feeling, not a word like *neurotic*. I would change that to *anxious*, for example.) I then ask them to improvise the scene. I usually find that they play it all on one emotional level. After we discuss the relationships in the scene, I ask them to repeat the improvisation. This time, however, the actors arc shadowed by two other students who stand behind them and read off emotions from the board. The actors have to continue improvising the scene, but now they have to add the emotion that was called out. The "shadow" actors keep calling out new emotions as the scene progresses. Suddenly, the scene begins to take off. You get enormous emotional variety and change because actors have to react instantaneously. This often makes the scene very funny. In this phase the actors may seem a bit like marionettes, but it's a good warm-up for them because their bodies become involved when the emotion is strong, and I encourage this. We begin to get information about their character from physical reactions, from changes in body language.

In the next phase of the game I tell them not to respond immediately, but to take time to incorporate the emotion being called out. Then we get real drama. You find that with emotional variety stage relationships acquire a past. It's astounding how two young actors will end up looking as if they had been married for twenty years.

This exercise introduces many useful ideas. First, the realization that it is emotional changes that make a scene interesting. Second, that the actor's energy naturally wants to be sent out, not remain inside. Third, that there is a direct relationship between energy and concentration: the higher the energy coming from the actor, the more concentration coming from the audience and the other actors; and equally, the more concentration coming from the other actors, the higher the energy. They discover that their energy will remain high without exhausting them because with each emotional transformation the energy is renewed. One thing I have learned is that energy doesn't stay in the same form for a long time. You cannot stay angry for two hours or be grief stricken for two hours. What happens when you change from anger to grief, for instance, is that it gives you a boost and your energy level goes up again.

A development of "calling out emotions" is a game

called "contact." After an actor has worked on the "calling out emotions" exercise, I give him a new scene with new instructions. This is to change his physical contact with his acting partner or the space around him every time the emotion changes. So now there is a specific physical change associated with each emotional change. This can be played with both improvised scenes and with a text. The results of "contact" are just as powerful, yet more subtle, than "calling out emotions." The great thing about these games is that students think they are just playing a technical game, but what comes up is often a very authentic portrayal of a character's feelings. The students begin to realize that they can only portray what they feel, through what their bodies are doing. And that's what I am after.

Another key idea I want to communicate to students comes from Keith Johnstone's work on status. Status has nothing to do with class. "High status" is created by taking up more space and more time. The bigger they are, the broader they are, the more measured they are, the more eye contact they make with another person— the higher their status. "Low status" is the opposite. The less space they take up, the less time they take up, the less eye contact they make—the lower their status. Status games are hugely enjoyable and very useful.

In the first "status" session I ask one student to stand and the other to sit. The sitting person is to read a recipe of his own choice to the standing student. I ask the sitter to read a recipe high status. He is to hold eye contact with the other actor for a long time and read the recipe slowly, with long pauses before each sentence. The only blocking I give is that when the recipe is finished the reader is to get up slowly and walk up to the other person and smile. There is a great deal of hilarity at this point because the meaning of the text changes. The recipe usually becomes a seduction and it's usually the person standing who is about to be eaten. It often acquires threatening sexual overtones, whether it's done by men or women. When the high-status reader gets up and walks toward the other actor, that actor will back off. It's because the high-status reader has taken up so much space that the other actor instinctively lowers his status and begins to reduce the amount of space he takes up.

Next, I ask the reader to be low status. He or she sits with knees together, toes pointed in, hunched up, making furtive eye contact, and usually takes a short pause *before* each sentence. Now you find that the other actor's status goes up. Often the sitter can't get up even though he has been instructed to do so. When I tell him to do so, he or she sort of apologetically limps toward the standing person. This simple exercise demonstrates that status is not static—it's always changing. Furthermore, we change status quite instinctively. Status is probably one of the most important techniques in an actor's armory because it means that he can play a variety of characters. In discussing status, I can talk to actors about the kinds of roles to which they would best be suited without necessarily typecasting them. There are some actors who naturally play high status, like Marlon Brando, and there are some who naturally play low, like Woody Allen. The goal of my work is to encourage my students to play a *variety* of statuses.

Status is not good or bad, strong or weak. Status is a way of getting what you want. I use another game that demonstrates this well. I ask an actor to sit in a chair and tell him to play high status. I tell another actor to find a low-status method of getting the high-status person out of his chair. Students find many ways to do that: they limp, collapse, have heart attacks, employing guilt or emotional blackmail as weapons to get what they want.

Status is very useful for learning to play comedy. Comedy is often based on the status difference between people (think of any comedy duo) and the ways in which the low-status person brings down the status of the high-status person.

In a more subtle version of the status exercise I get students to improvise the party they attended when they first arrived at Drama Studio. I ask them to play status based on a number that I give them (one is high and seven is low). The rest of the class watches and tries to guess the status of each person. At the end of the game the class arranges these seven in a row in terms of their status. Usually the class is dead right. You can then clearly see how status is a social phenomenon that we all use instinctively.

By the second term the students are ready to learn about "give and take," which, to me, is the basis of good ensemble acting. First I explain that a "take" is when an actor takes focus from the audience. I put three students on stage and tell them to do anything they like. The only rule is that if one of the three "takes" focus the other two have to "give" focus. That means they are actually to direct the audience's eye toward the actor who is the focus person. For instance, you may have a scene where one person is being dressed while two others are running around trying to get him ready for Ascot. The work in the scene is actually being done by the two actors giving focus. During this exercise sometimes two or even three people will take focus at the same time. When this happens I stop the exercise and ask the class if they know where to look. They usually don't. Then we go back to the rule: when one person takes, the other two give. The scene and its story become clear again because the audience knows where to look at any one time. The art of the game is to give strongly. Often, while one actor is taking focus, the other two will do nothing. The scene will be very boring. I make the distinction between giving passively, by keeping out of the way, and giving actively, which is to direct your energy to the actor taking focus. When students realize they can do an enormous amount on stage while directing focus toward another person, everything becomes more energized and fun. Americans, by the way, are *much* less shy about taking. They usually have trouble giving. The English resist taking.

How Do You Integrate These Games into Your Text Class?

Take Macbeth's dagger speech, for instance. If the actor playing Macbeth does it as a take, it's just an actor delivering a speech and the meaning is obscured. But if you instruct the actor to do it as a give, to give focus to the dagger, suddenly it becomes much more interesting and exciting because we see what Macbeth sees—the dagger to which his energy is directed.

I also find this technique helpful when I direct opera. The duet "la a dareim la mano" is the scene when Don

Giovanni is seducing the peasant girl, Zerlina. The singer playing Don Giovanni will usually do it as a take, directing focus to himself, and the girl will just stand there with nothing to do except look pretty. When I put the girl down-stage and Don Giovanni up-stage and ask him to do it as a give to her, the audience not only sees Don Giovanni, but Don Giovanni at work, seducing. I don't tell the actor to try to seduce her; I say, do it as a give to Zerlina. Invariably, the actor will do it as a seduction and Zerlina's reactions will become a key part of the scene. She *takes*. This fits with my philosophy of asking the composer or writer what he wants, not thinking of "I." I can work out how the story is unfolding, who or what is the focus, and then, as a group, we discuss it in terms of give and take.

I think it's important to make actors realize that they are never alone on stage. Actors must create the world outside themselves. As a result, I spend a lot of time using Viola Spolin's exercises to create an environment. These exercises involve sensorially responding to an environment. All this work must be done slowly and gently. We could work on the garden in Act 1 of *Uncle Vanya*, for instance, by creating the smells of the garden, how big it is, how hot it is, etc. I tell the students not to act, but to *react* to the environment. Again, to think of "it" not "I." Suddenly, lovely simple things begin to happen. Chekhov sets scenes in carefully chosen, specific locations. The actor has to find a way of creating the feeling of those places through the acting. When I ask students to think about the differences between the indoors and outdoors, they realize after a bit that you feel bigger outdoors because you can see farther, and there is so much more space above your head. It's a simple technical thing, but it's based on a very important principle: the actor is never there for himself, but to create outside himself.

What Is Your Approach to Text?

When I teach text I start by presenting students with a dreadful play in which the playwright has made everything obvious. I ask the students what they think of it. When they finally admit that it is boring, irritating, and undramatic, I ask them to tell me why. We arrive at the conclusion that it is undramatic because it has no subtext. Students begin to understand the nature of subtext and how to discover it. To explore this I hand round some scraps of real conversations that I have overheard in different places and have transcribed. For example, I have a wonderful conversation where four old ladies are talking about their bunions and arguing about whose are the worst. I have another one I overheard in a pub in which one man is telling another about a particular woman who wouldn't go to bed with him. In both cases what is important is contained in what is *not* said, or in lies, or in exaggeration, etc. We then stage these conversations.

After that I ask students to write their own scenes by listening to conversations and writing them down. We reconstruct the scene. In the next session we work on Bertolt Brecht's *The Fears and Miseries of the Third Reich* and Arthur Miller's *The Crucible*. We first look at the text and subtext of both plays, at which point I introduce the idea of beats. For me, there is a change of beat when there is a change of conflict. I begin by pointing out that the first thing to decide is not *what* the conflict is, but *where* it is. Let's use the "If it were done when 'tis done" speech from *Macbeth*. The conflict is within Macbeth. When Lady Macbeth enters, the conflict becomes between the two of them. What I try to do is get the students to trace where the conflicts change. We often go through a scene from Brecht or Miller and mark the play in terms of conflict changes. They see that in a play a story is not written directly but unfolds through the development of the conflict.

I also use the Cain and Abel story from the Bible. I write it out with the narration in red, the dialogue in black, and the rest scattered in between. We analyze the relationship between the storyteller and the audience. Usually, students say the narrator makes them feel like children. The narrator has all the information and they are passive listeners. I then put actors into the scene to play God, Cain, and Abel, but still keep the narrator. They usually say now they had two feelings: they felt involved with God, Cain, and Abel, but passive about the narrator. Then I eliminate the narrator and suddenly we have theater. The crucial thing is to ask where has the narrator gone. Students realize that the narrator has gone into the relationships between Cain, Abel, and God. It's that interplay that contains the narration and they begin to understand how a play's text works, how it's different from a poem or a novel. A good playwright tells a story through the characters' relationships or conflicts.

I am also very keen on actors learning how to do research. For instance, in Brecht's play *Betrayal* we have the line, "They've smashed the barrister's. He was al-

ready unconscious when they dragged him out of his flat."
Students often think "they" is the SS. But the play is
about the first round of terror after Hitler took power in
1933. "They" are the SA—a civilian militia, Hitler's popular army. The SS were a highly trained elite corps, but
the SA were little more than thugs, and all local people,
chosen area by area. So the SA were people very like the
neighbors of the characters in the play. Little points like
that are very important because it makes the action of the
play more specific. I also use Arthur Schnitzler's *La
Ronde* and try to feed in information about Vienna,
Freud, and Mahler. I ask students to listen to Mahler's
music and to note how he uses emotions in his music. It is
very close to the acting style the play demands—the
combination of tragedy and sentiment, a world both bit-
tersweet and funny.

In *The Crucible*, students have to understand what the
seventeenth-century witch trials were about. I ask them
to read Keith Thomas and Trever-Roper's work on the
period. They also need to find out what was happening to
Miller with the House Committee on Un-American Activities when he wrote this play, and who these characters
might represent. All this helps them understand the inner world of the characters and the environment in which
they lived. They also need to see why Miller was im-
pelled to write it and why it matters *now*.

To integrate the improvisation and text work I will tell
two students to take a scene from *The Crucible*, say,
divide it into beats, and learn the text and the beats.
Every time there is a change of beat I ask them to change
the emotion. We combine "beats" with "contact." I ask
them to change physically as well as emotionally on the

beat change. That means that they let their emotion move them around the stage. Suddenly, you find that the scene is beginning to block itself. Using this method any good text will actually block itself. As a director, I rehearse that way too; around the third week of rehearsal I might formalize the blocking, but my philosophy is that one finds blocking rather than decides it.

A final thought: I always tell students when they leave me that they are people *before* actors; I tell them never to use art as a substitute for life, and to keep all other interests alive, to read, listen to music, see films and paintings, travel, or just watch and listen to other people. I think actors can be the most boring people alive if all they think about is acting. In the end, it's just a job. I hope to teach them how to do their jobs well, that's all.

The Guildford School of Acting and Dance

The Guildford School of Acting and Dance grew out of the Grant Bellairs School of Dance and Drama, which was founded in London in 1935 by Bice Bellairs, who is now president of the school, and Pauline Grant, a famous British choreographer. The school later moved to Surrey, until Guildford became its permanent home in 1945. The staff at Guildford believes that today's "theater" includes television, radio, and film as well as stage, and the school is particularly concerned with training actors to be flexible enough to perform in all the performing arts.

Guildford offers a three-year Performance Course with an option in Acting or Musical Theater. The school also offers postgraduate courses in Acting and Stage Management, as well as an intensive summer course in Shakespeare or contemporary playwrights.

Michael Gau

Michael Gaunt is Principal and Head of Acting
Guildford School of Acting and Dance. His career
three areas of theater: acting, directing, and theater
agement.

After graduating from the Central School of Sp
and Drama he appeared in many regional productio
He has also appeared in some fifty television productio
for the BBC and ITV. In addition, he has performed i
fringe plays in London and appeared in commercial films.

Mr. Gaunt has directed many plays, among them
Mothers at the University of Surrey, All the Arts of Hurting at the Edinburgh Festival Fringe, and Entertaining
Mr. Sloane and Home at the Dundee Repertory Company. He has also directed the national touring production of The Revival of the Amorous Prawn, Private Lives,
and restaged A Matter of Choice for the Mickory Theatre
in Amsterdam.

In 1972 Mr. Gaunt received a scholarship from the Arts

127

ncil of Great Britain to study theater management
l later became assistant to Miss Hazel Vincent Wallace,
BE at the Thorndike Theatre, Leatherhead. He cur-
ntly represents the Guildford School of Acting and
ance at the Conference of Drama Schools and is chair-
an of the One-Year Course committee. He is a member
f the Accreditation Panel for the National Council of
Drama Training.

I think all the drama schools differ a bit from each other
and our difference is based on our roots. Guildford was
founded in 1935 as a dance school. In time the demand for
drama training increased and in 1964 we became a drama
school as well. But dance and movement are still very
important here. During their training our acting students
also study ballet, tap, Laban movement, period dance,
and movement, mime, and stage fighting.

We have what we call a Performance course, which is of
three years' duration. Within that, students can choose
the acting option or the musical theater option. At
Guildford we believe the actor also needs to be a good
singer and dancer as well. We also subscribe to the basic
principle that whatever an actor discovers about his character through study and preparation must be reflected in
his body and voice. Generally speaking, English actors
are pretty good with voice and not as good in movement.
So our emphasis is on three elements—acting, voice, and
movement.

Although a student may have opted for acting or musical theater, he or she is allowed to keep the option open
until the end of the first year. We may find that we have an

actor who ought to be developing his musical talent, or a singer who ought to be developing her acting more. Today, the marketplace demands a well-rounded performer. In drama training we are not just concerned with teaching students how to act, but with giving them the technical know-how an actor needs, a systematic way of thinking about the craft that can help them grow in all aspects of the profession.

On the one hand there is the actor and on the other hand there is the character. How is the character to live, to be? If we think of the actor in terms of mind, body, and sound, this is a convenient division of the whole. The actor uses his mind to study and absorb the text and to understand the character's place within the story—to be clear about the scenes and relationships. What is wanted by the characters and what are the obstacles that frustrate those wants? The actor becomes aware of how the character breathes and how the breathing changes as circumstances change. How does the character sound when expressing desires? How does the sound change when these are satisfied or denied? Breath, of course, influences the movement of the body when a want is expressed, satisfied, or frustrated. The actor should question the state of physical and mental health of a character. Is the body young and strong? Is it old and weak?

When I talked of the actor's mind just now I meant this to include the actor's spirit and power of imagination, because unless the actor gives of these as well as giving through the body and sound, feelings and senses, the work will not be organically based. The actor lends of himself to the character. Through the actor's sound the

129

character's voice is heard; through the actor's body the character's physical rhythms and movement are seen; through the actor's mind the character's thoughts and ideas are revealed. The audience sees the character before them—feeling, listening, thinking, and responding. Through the actor's craft and artistry the characterization is kept organic and fresh throughout the run of a play in the theater, or as long as is needed to get the take right in the studio. Today's actor needs the ability to be believed by the camera lens in close-up and by a theater audience seated at the rear of an auditorium. Now, let me return to the student commencing training at Guildford.

The first year is entirely nonperformance-oriented. Students are told that performance is the tip of the iceberg and although it may be beautiful, if it doesn't have a strong foundation supporting it underneath, it sinks very quickly. This foundation is technique. The study of voice, text, radio technique, improvisation, mask work, theater and television technique, mime, movement, dance, singing, and so on.

What Do You Teach?

As well as being principal I am also in charge of the acting course that I teach. The first thing I want students to do is to get away from the text, the word, and learning lines; instead they are asked to focus on their senses, their feelings, and how to communicate these through silence. Frequently, the great moments in acting are silent. My belief is that if an actor can create magic in an empty space, he can create it anywhere. Some teachers prefer to teach in groups, but I think that working all together gives students too much security at the beginning, and is not helpful in the long run. Acting is a business in which you are always alone to a greater or lesser extent, in which you feel insecure and frightened, and have to cope with your nerves. So right from the beginning I want them to become aware of either how easy or difficult it is for them to do this. If a student is concentrating, not on the word, not on the text, but on communicating a sense of place and feeling, then he has something to focus on—a basic intention.

I start by saying, "I want you to go into the center of the studio and, without words or overt gestures, to let us know where you are and how you feel. The way I want you to go about this is to stand in the room by yourself, find a silence, and from that silence begin to think about the place you have chosen and to visualize it. It can be fictional or one you know very well. When you have found it, think about how you feel." Later on, when students work in groups of two or three, I will say the same thing, but ask them to decide together where they are and what they are doing. If they were asked to play in a crowd scene, they would start by relating to the people near them and discussing how they feel about what is happening around them. Suddenly, that part of the crowd will begin to live.

After the actor has worked alone and before he tells us what he has experienced, I ask the rest of the class to describe what they saw the actor do. It's quite extraordinary how just by thinking, an individual can transmit thoughts and ideas, such as color or temperature. Once about eighty percent of the group had seen correctly that a student was sitting by the road and selling daffodils—and all without the use of words.

Then we work on the senses and sense memory. Students work one at a time and are asked what their strongest sensual memory is. I want to hear about any memory they can relate to one of their senses. Before we do that, I ask them which of their senses they value the most. Most students say sight. Then, as the memories are recalled, we find that sixty to seventy percent of them respond strongly to smells. Recalling and sharing sensual memories stimulates students' self-awareness, which is an important goal during this first year.

This kind of exercise also feeds into character work. When a student works on a character he should know which of that character's senses are defunct—either for physical or psychological reasons—and which are dominant. So we can talk about how certain personalities are influenced by particular senses while other characters have a limited sensual awareness. By then the students have come to understand this in themselves. When we play a character we need to know how he listens. It isn't necessary for an actor to cup his ear to indicate that he is listening; all he needs to do is listen! So right from the beginning the student must work on the connection between the senses and behavior, and how his character's sensory awareness affects his functioning in the environment. All these early sensual exercises are silent and only last between sixty to ninety seconds.

I also spend at least one session doing improvisations using only gibberish. I want students to make their character's intentions clear through vocal expression, but without using words. Again, we should know where the students are and how they feel. At this stage, I will often ask them to put subliminal ideas into their improvisations. I might say, "Don't tell the class, but would you both agree on a color to keep in your mind during the improvisation." Often, during the follow-up discussion, the other students will be aware of the color the actors selected.

What Other Kinds of Exercises Do You Do During the First Year of Training?

Some are influenced by Keith Johnstone's work on status. One of his exercises that I do is called "master-servant." I ask students to work out a specific environment and circumstance; for instance, one is a shop assistant and the other a customer. The assistant has a bad relationship with his wife and a headache today; the customer is a meek individual. I ask the students to play this out without words. Later, I will assign a simple dialogue. Then we might explore those statuses and lines through as many as twelve different kinds of improvisations in order to demonstrate how a text can mean whatever the actor wants it to, according to intention. It should be obvious in these improvisations who is high status and who is low status. At some point I ask the students to switch status. It is dramatically interesting when a dominant personality abruptly changes status because of the altered circumstances. Then the other students in class get to tell what they have seen.

During the early stages of this work it sometimes becomes apparent that a student has a preferred status when improvising or interpreting a character. He or she feels more secure playing high or low and has a reluctance to be flexible and explore new levels of status play. It is important for them to become aware of how limiting this approach is. Should the tendency to play the preferred status continue, in the middle of the improvisation I would then call for a status reversal. This usually works.

This work leads to devising an improvisational text in the second term. Students first improvise and work on characters and situations, and after about six weeks, put their own dialogue on paper and use it as a working text. So before they actually get to work with a playwright's words they use their own, which they have put into script form.

Throughout this improvisational work the class is asked if what they saw was believable, and if so, why did they believe it, and if not, why not. If an improvisation is believable, I ask the students to repeat it. It's very easy to get something right in rehearsal; it's very easy to get something right in an improvisation. The difficulty, as experienced actors know, comes in trying to repeat it. Often, when I ask students to repeat their improvisations they lose their initial spontaneity, and naturally the scene suffers. If that happens, I ask them to improvise around that initial improvisation. We also use these kinds of improvisations when working on scenes.

Can You Give Me an Example of How You Would Use Improvisations to Help Students Work on Their Scenes?

I ask them to improvise events in the lives of their characters, but that are not provided in the play's dialogue. For example, two students were working on a scene from Peter Nichols's *A Day in the Death of Joe Egg*. I asked them to improvise what happened to their characters before the events of the play took place, and also two years after the play ends. I asked them to use a minimal number of words and to use silence as often as they could.

In this play there is a complicated relationship between the husband and wife, and we wanted to know certain things about them. What were they like when they first met? How did they meet? I asked students to improvise that situation so we could find out who instigated the relationship. So they improvised the first date and the circumstances. Then they improvised the first time one invited the other back, and the first time they spent the night together. These improvisations were not based on arbitrary choices but grew out of what the students were feeling and the questions they were asking about their characters. We also improvised the announcement of the pregnancy—which occurred before the marriage. Who suggested marriage? How did the wife tell her husband that the doctors suspected there was something wrong with the baby? How did she feel about it? How did he take the news that the baby was brain-damaged? Then they improvised their meeting after the birth of the baby. We found that these kinds of exercises really strengthened and supported their characterizations. It shows that improvisation can become a concrete tool. I tell students that if they have a problem in rehearsal, stop talking about it and try to solve it. This kind of work, which takes place in the second term, prevents students from being general in their choices. We are always fighting the cliché and the generalization in performance.

In the last term of the first year, students are introduced to a text such as *Marat/Sade,* in which the emphasis is on ensemble acting, on movement, and singing. We never work with a set, but always with the audience on all sides, so that right from the beginning students get used to feeling exposed and learn how to use this experience. If a character has just gotten bad news, the audience should know of this, not only from the actor's face, but also from the way his whole body responds.

Another way I try to encourage spontaneity is to have students repeat an improvisation but change an event. For instance, what would happen if a particular character said yes instead of no? Then they improvise that. All of this work is without written text because I don't want them to be concerned at this point with the idea of presenting a performance. That comes in the third year. Whatever they do until then is either a project, an open rehearsal, or a work in progress.

At the end of the first year we have two directors work with twelve pairs of students on contemporary scenes. The scenes run approximately six minutes each and they have two weeks to prepare before they present the rehearsed work to the rest of the school. This is the first time the student body sees the third-term students working, although everything they have done will have been observed by all the senior members of staff and the various specialists who've worked with them.

In the eighth week of the first term we have an external examiner—someone who has been coming to the school for many years—come in to look at the projects. He is brutally frank. He interviews every student to find out what they think about the training and their progress. There are forty-eight students in this group and he gives me a full report on what he has seen and what the students have said. At the end of the third term we interview every student so they know how they are doing and what the next phase of work will be.

The second year is involved with classical acting. Students start with a Shakespeare rehearsal project, then go on to a Restoration project, and in the last term work on a nineteenth-century play. In the projects we don't do the whole play but work on meaty scenes so that everyone gets a chance to play the leading characters and everyone gets a chance to be cast against type. Personal research is of great importance. Students are asked to look at portraits of the historical period in which a play takes place; to read books, diaries, letters, and newspapers; and to go to museums to see the costumes and furniture. They are also taught period dance and movement, so that by the time they start rehearsing a play they have some understanding of that time—and, I hope, a point of view for their character.

These classical plays and their characters should have the same organic approach from the actor as is demanded by a modern play. Research and preparation enable the actor to empathize with past circumstances and conditions. From this base the actor's imagination can come into play. What did a man or woman living in Elizabethan England know that we no longer need to know? What skills did they learn that are no longer necessary? What did they believe that we do not now believe? What was it like to live in a world of unmade-up roads; a world without telephones, radios, and television sets; when men in one village regarded men in the next village with mistrust and suspicion? How easy it must have been to believe in a spirit world in those times, when the night was dark, the wind was high, the timber house creaked, and the candle flickered and went out! Living through a similar set of circumstances, our feelings, sensual responses, and beliefs would probably not be so different from those of our Elizabethan counterparts. The imaginative actor can breathe life into Shakespeare's characters and show us what they are—"only through their emotions is the effect made on yours," as Harley Granville-Barker put it.

The work in the third year is all rehearsal, production, and preparation to audition, and basic technical classes. I remind students of first lessons and that when they audition they should create the place and its silence, breathe as the character, get sensual as the character, and to begin only when they are ready. After all, what do we ask actors to do in performance? They must stand in either an empty space or one surrounded with canvas painted to look like anything from a castle to a living room, and in this space they have to create an illusion of reality. The actor has to make the audience believe what he is seeing. All third-year productions are fully mounted. The school has four acting areas licensed for public performance. Plays can be staged in the round, transversely, end-stage, or behind a proscenium. Generally, we present plays written after 1956 that contain present-day issues and concerns.

How Do You Help Students Become Emotionally Expressive?

I am presently directing the opening scene from David Hare's *Plenty*, in which the main character has to break down. How can a student arrive at an intense emotional state when she is only working on an isolated scene? First, the play must be well studied. To identify with the character she is playing, she has to borrow from her own experiences and substitute her own situation through her imagination for the one she is playing. This scene takes place during World War II in an open field in France. It is night. The girl is an English courier who is waiting for supplies to be parachuted down. If the actress was having trouble finding the character's emotional state, I would start by saying, "Imagine that it is very, very dark. Silence. Then the sound of a plane. You see the parachute with its supplies come down. You don't know if there are any German soldiers watching from the trees. Remember sounds that have made you frightened. Imagine how your senses magnify your fears at night. Imagine how you might become tense by the imminence of death. Any moment your body, which is so soft, can be ripped apart with bullets. Think of all of the physical aspects of your place and circumstance, and your fear. What is the state of your breathing?" This, however, may not be enough and the actress may need to find something else, some personal experience, like the death of a pet, to help her reach the desired emotional state. I don't suggest that students use the death of people from their own lives to trigger emotion, although an experienced actor might.

I am also interested in Michael Chekhov's notion of psychological gesture. This actress might find the key to her character in the way her body feels and reacts when she "lives" through the moment of being shot. I wouldn't necessarily suggest this, but I would bring it up if a specific student needed further help.

The final project in the third year is performed in a

West End theater and we invite about 130 agents and casting directors to look at 100 minutes of a nonstop show. For this performance we choose scenes from contemporary plays and look for a theme to link the various scenes. A few years ago we presented a show called "Younger Generations," in which every scene was about young men either going to war or coming back, or in some cases not coming back. There was a high emotional charge in the show that depended entirely on the students' understanding of past events through their research and imagination. In between scenes students presented relevant songs.

What Are the Various Courses of Study at Guildford?

Apart from our three-year acting and musical theater course, we also have a one-year postgraduate course designed to meet the needs of graduates or other qualified people who wish to continue their training. There is also a two-year stage management course. We also run a summer-school program with two options, either Shakespeare or contemporary plays. It's an intensive four-week course, in which the mornings are devoted to studying acting technique and the afternoons are for rehearsal. We rehearse scenes, not full plays. Many overseas students take this course to see if they want to train in England. About twenty percent then ask to audition for the full-time course. This year we have had applications from about fourteen nations. I like a mix of overseas students with our British students because it provides an added stimulation.

At Guildford we place a very heavy emphasis on career guidance in the third year. Cary Ellison, who was a casting consultant at *Spotlight* magazine, became our consultant when he retired. He comes to see all the third-year productions and assesses each student from a commercial point of view. He gives students a series of lectures on how to become a one-person business, how to write letters and prepare résumés and how to follow up on looking for work. He also arranges for students to be interviewed by an agent so they can learn how to present themselves. We also bring in Equity people to explain to the student body how the union works. We have different specialists from the Actor's Centre come in to explain how the center works. We have also successfully introduced a health and welfare team who lecture on diet, drugs, living alone for the first time, and so on, so that students who have come to us straight from home can make a smooth adjustment. Every week, one of the team is on hand for two hours to listen to and advise in confidence on any problems a student may have. We try to look at students in a complete way and provide them with the tools they need to enter the theatrical profession. Caring for the 200 students who study in our four courses is a rewarding challenge for the Guildford faculty.

Ian Ricketts

Ian Ricketts teaches acting at the Guildford School of Acting and Dance. He also teaches theater studies at the University of Surrey, has been a Visiting Fellow at the University of Reading, and has contributed to the London programs of Ithaca College and Highline Community College in Washington, D.C.

Originally trained as an actor, Mr. Ricketts appeared with the Royal Shakespeare Company; the Open Air Theatre, Regent's Park; the Hampstead Theatre Club; and in the West End; as well as being a member of many regional companies. He has also taken part in numerous documentaries and plays on radio and television.

Mr. Ricketts also writes. He has published papers and articles on a variety of subjects, ranging from Shakespeare and acting technique to examining and education.

Almost everything that I understand about human beings and relationships returns to the fact that man is a sensory animal. Everything that he thinks and feels is a result of something that at some time has come to him through his senses. Directly or indirectly, his thoughts will arise from his sense of smell, hearing, sight, and kinesthetic appreciation of the world. That's why when I teach students how to build characters I try to begin by helping them find a connection with their sensory sources. Whether you come from Cambridge or Los Angeles you still smell, see, hear, touch, and taste. Everything that you do is contingent upon the body and your consciousness within it. Inspiration itself derives from breath.

I suppose you might say that what I do is try to get students to perceive the truth beneath appearances and to rediscover the things that are simplest. I use examples as often as possible from men who are indisputably wise and have shown us how they came back to the things that are essential, men like Aristotle, for example, who observed that "the things that we must do when we have learned to do them we learn to do by doing them." It's not until one begins practicing the thing one cannot do that one discovers the part of one's self that can do it.

The sensory world matters to me a great deal. When I was a young man I knew a friend of Jung's who had come to England just before World War II. She was a profound influence because she helped me to learn to trust those parts of the mind that are not open to rational proof but that determine one's tastes and aspirations, and one's deepest caring about people.

I suppose another important strand in my development

as a teacher would be the fact that I was old enough during the war to learn about the economy with which physical tasks can be performed. In all action there is the ingredient of *submitting* as well as that of *doing*. You can only lift something if you receive from it information about its weight and texture and form, just as you can only relate to a person by receiving whatever it is that he or she brings to you. This feeds directly into the listening part of acting.

How Do You Begin Your Course in Character Building?

I always work in a circle because in this way everyone can see everyone else and receive from them and learn by observing others. Also, of course, the circle is equal and continuous and the idea is central. Often young people think they are sitting neutrally and not giving anything away. Then I ask all the students to freeze in the position in which they are sitting and tell them to look around the room and take notice of how each one of those fifteen or twenty people is in an entirely different and distinctive posture, and how this reflects each one's state of mind, his or her mood and form and nature.

Soon after that I take the class out into the air, irrespective of the weather, and we agree that we will all go separately and only rest our attention on smells and sounds and touch and tastes. We can use sight too, but principally we employ those senses that are less often used. I tell students that every time a thought comes into their mind that takes them off on a tangent, they should let that go and come back to the moment and the place they are in. If students find a whole train of thoughts going through their minds, I ask them to just stand still and notice things close to them—the feel of their clothes or the ground they are on or the sounds within their body, such as their pulse or breath—and then to allow their attention to move further away. We are fortunate in Guildford because the castle grounds are there and we can wander by the river and find quiet places. Students almost always respond to that because they notice the delicacy and richness of the sensations. What is equally important is that they notice how their thoughts move. One's mind is forever leaping onto things and going off into dreams because one's senses are a catalyst to the memory. If they become aware of the paths their thoughts take and know they can come back to the place where they started, then they will be free to take up a character's train of thought and follow it without fear.

The following week I sit them in pairs in a circle and one student describes to his partner a few minutes of an experience in terms of one sense other than sight. The partner can ask any question he wishes. The event might be the first five minutes after getting out of bed in the morning and a student might choose touch. Usually students say they can't remember the first thing they touched that morning. Eventually, they remember something, however, even though they did not attend to it consciously at the time: the texture of a tap and a finger slipping on it that brought on a rush of water, or the pressure of the tap in their palm. They will recall exquisitely precise details, and they discover how listening to and asking questions of each other enables them to re-

145

member something they had not deliberately learned. They had taken it in because their senses were open and had received the information.

This Sounds Very Much Like the Classical Sensory Work That We Do in America, but You Seem to Focus Students on Relating It to Another Person Rather Than Experiencing It Privately.

What you can remember depends on the person with whom you are sharing it. I might know exactly what I wanted to say to you in this interview, but if I had memorized it and said exactly *that*, you would know that what I was saying was not being said to *you*. You would know in your heart and stomach that what I was saying was a preconceived offering that didn't really belong to you at all. If what I said was for you, you would know it with that part of the mind that is independent of reasoning. This is what I am moving the students toward. They often have a rich intuition that will feed upon any material that is brought to them, but they don't see how much their behavior depends upon what they receive from other people, upon the quality of attention in another, upon that other's listening in their presence.

After we have worked on the senses I then move to working with objects themselves. I try to work with objects that people have not seen before. I have a box full of extraordinary things: some are very simple, like old tools, sheep shears, an otter's skull, a Civil War brass buckle, an Elizabethan schoolhouse key; all of them are things that the students have not seen before. We sit in the circle and

I pair off people and ask them to close their eyes. I open the box and put one of these objects into the hands of one member of each pair. The one who has the object describes it to his partner. They can name it if they choose, but they don't have to. The one without the object can ask any question about it, such as its weight or smell, or ask for details if they know what it is. Suppose it were an apple and suppose I knew nothing about apples. I would experience the object in my hand as being smooth-skinned, cool, and just filling my palm. That's it. I wouldn't be able to go further with my description. But supposing you, my partner, had been brought up on an orchard and your father had 106 species of apple trees that you knew. Your questions about the apple would direct me to a sensory perception of it that I would not have thought possible. You could direct me to the stalk and the area around the stalk, and ask me to compare that to the rest of the skin. Was there a lump at any point on the top? As a doctor can diagnose a patient, with your eyes closed you could ask the questions that would enable you to create a picture in your mind of that object without touching it and, of course, would enable me to exercise my sense with regard to this object in a way that I couldn't before. So it doesn't matter who has the knowledge, the one who questions always determines in part what is experienced.

Then I ask the students to pass the object to their partner with their eyes still closed, and then the partner explores the same object. If I didn't know about apples and you did, as you explore it all kinds of things will appear to you which did not appear to me. My notion of weight or texture might be unlike yours. Even through my use of words your experience of it might have been quite different from mine. Then students open their eyes and see the thing for the first time. I remind students of Gloucester's lines in *King Lear* when, after he loses his sight, he first begins to "see": "I see it feelingly," he says. Students acknowledge how much more comes to them when they allow an experience to go beyond the visual. Of course we all practice seeing, but we often see through or beyond; we rarely see in. And seeing in depends upon our being able to receive things for their own sake rather than with some motive for their use.

We then move from objects that are comparatively large to ones that are small, and the partners switch roles. I have a tiny eighteenth-century whistle that a lady wore round her neck to call her servants, a little nutmeg grater, an apothecary's balance—things of that kind. Now their perceptions have to become much finer. I use all sorts of strategies to defy their expectations. For instance, if I thought you were a girl who disliked everything to do with animals, I might well give you the badger pelt so that it could actually reach you through touch before you could reject it by sight. By the time you realized what it was, it is at least possible that its texture, smell, and feel would have won your curiosity, if not your liking. I try to help people beyond their likes and dislikes to seeing things as they are. I try to free them from being driven by their existing tastes.

I also have some objects that reveal things to the touch that might not be evident to the eye. There is an eighteenth-century opera stick with a dagger in it. It looks like an elegant cane with a silver ring, but once you feel it, you find that the ring turns and a ruthless weapon emerges.

Then there are carved cherubs from a sixteenth-century Flemish church, items like that which are charged with history.

My next task is to show how our values influence our judgment. Among the items in the box I have a folded piece of paper with Maunday money in it—silver that a reigning monarch used to distribute to the poor the day before Good Friday. Sealed in another piece of paper I have a bit of earth from the tomb of Sir John Moore, a figure in English history who is now vastly admired but was harshly criticized by the government in his day. I then compare these two pieces of paper: one containing an object that is of extrinsic value—silver—and the other, which has no worth at all unless by association. Which does one choose? Once students have heard John Moore's life described there is no question as to which of these two properties is of greater worth. So I introduce the difference between extrinsic and intrinsic value, and point out how something is prized only to the extent that one understands what it represents. The actor rarely has real silver or actual earth on stage, but through his imagining they can become real for him. The truth of the idea matters more than the thing itself.

Now we move from the temporal to the abstract world, to the conflict between the dark and the light, and the feelings of good and bad. I ask everyone to make a list in private of those qualities that might be ascribed to them by their severest critic. They must try to be truthful. After that they draw a line across the page and for an equal time they have to set down those qualities that might be ascribed to them by their deepest appreciator. These may be qualities that no one else has noticed. They then look at the two and I invite people to comment on anything that might appear on the lists. Almost everyone finds that some of the qualities that appear on the first might, under different circumstances, also appear on the second. The "obstinacy" on the first can become the "determination" and "courage" on the second. Students begin to appreciate that their characteristics are not objectively determined by either the seemingly good or bad, but are open for selection.

At this point I tap the unconscious world by asking one person to begin to tell a story. The moment he comes to a pause the person sitting on his left must take it up. Students do not decide in advance where they are going with the story, but they must not end it nor attempt to be entertaining. It should continue until I stop it. These stories vary much in their quality.

What Is the Purpose of This Exercise?

Almost invariably when they tell the story students discover that there are certain themes and patterns that repeat themselves: a child or a dispossessed person who has special powers or perceptions; there is usually a river in the story that someone has to cross in order to be safe in a forest or cave on the other side; an animal is almost always present in some way beneficent rather than as a threat; there is usually some unnameable dark force at the center of the story, and it's often circular, repeating itself. That's the point at which I usually stop it.

This exercise is an example of how something can emerge that is always coherent and sometimes brilliant and is a result of no one having decided in advance what it should be or what pattern it should take. The story depends entirely upon the particular people there. Its shape is equally a part of everyone's contribution. It isn't one person's story, but it belongs to the group.

In the summer I take students into the woods and along the river at night. It is very quiet and I tell them there will be no conversation. We meet toads, deer, insects. Nobody talks. We experience things like cow's breath being carried down the river and the extraordinary sounds of the woodland at night. Eventually, I take them down a steep hill that is so thick with trees that nothing is visible, even by moonlight. I tell them to hold each other's hands because there are all sorts of hazards (all of which can be safely negotiated if one is aware). They become finely alert to each other, to sounds and smells, and in this situation there is nothing that their intellect can do to bail them out. They have to hear, feel, smell their environment. Afterwards they come into my home and we have flapjacks and tea and such, and then they go home. This seems to be a rather important thing to do and it always seems to work—though in very different ways for different people.

How Do You Hope This Experience Will Be Translated onto a Stage?

I think it gives students a trust in stillness. Every time they perform an exercise of this kind they have to confront the great commonplaces again, but with the support and the discipline of a group. All movement begins out of nothingness and goes back into it. Action of the body begins with the action of the mind. If one's mind is preoccupied with other things, then these will intrude into one's voice and body and give the lie to one's performance. But if one is absolutely still, just receiving, then one is safe and that which is appropriate will come. If one brings this stillness into a character, then one's mind is free to imagine truly as the character. So acting is taken out of the realm of display. It is based on trusting one's behavior without trying to shape it to entertain. By the time they begin to work on nonverbal relationships and how to define a character's circumstances in their second year, students have learned not to get obsessed with illustrating, but to allow themselves simply to live out the problem in the scene. It can be wonderfully simple and moving when they do.

How Do You Introduce Text into Your Course?

I start by reading a biography to the students of someone who has died. They don't know it, but it is actually an amalgam of a number of people that I have known. In this biography I have thoroughly described a life, and I ask each student to invent for himself, without telling anyone else, how they knew this person: where they met him, under what circumstances, etc. The students don't discuss it with each other. The deceased in the biography has decided that all those who have known him should be brought together, if they choose, at his funeral, and wherever they are in the world, their expenses would be paid. So regardless of their financial circumstances they can come to the funeral. When they arrive they are put up in a Victorian hotel in the west of England. I describe the hotel in detail to them. They are given dinner and then they go into the lounge and each student is to write a letter to anyone in their world. It doesn't have to pertain to this occasion at all. That is their first active part in this improvisation. They become a character who has known the deceased and they take on that character's mannerisms and ideas.

When they write their letter they try to write it in the handwriting of that character. I then make a circuit of the room and each student in turn reads his letter as the character, within the stage convention of a letter read aloud. Then each character is interviewed by the deceased's executors and solicitors who are going to distribute his estate and give each of them mementos. This gives students the experience of role playing and it also allows them to deepen the character they have established, to take up a character they have imaginatively created rather than someone they actually know.

Do Students Continue to Work on Improvisations in Their Second Year of Training?

Yes. In one improvisation I do with second-year students I tell two students that they have been very close friends. They create the history and the circumstances of their friendship in detail. But something has come between them. Perhaps one committed an indiscretion or there was an absence of understanding, but something happened to separate them, and they don't see one another again. Now they are grown up. Each student decides for himself what's happened during the time they were separated. It may be that they haven't thought of the other person for years. Each decides separately what has happened to his life. Then I ask them to agree upon where it is that they will meet again. It should be a place in which they are unable to avoid each other, like a railway carriage or a theater foyer. It may be five years or forty since they last met. This is the exercise. For people who are able to give themselves fully to this, it can be poignant and exquisite to watch. One can see so many strands of pain, resentment, hope, and concealment. Nothing much may happen in the conversation that ensues and there may be no visible action. Yet for those who watch, what happens can be instinct with life. Some of the finest work I have seen students do has arisen out of devices of this kind. I encourage them to consider events from their own experiences so that they can accept how the deepest shadows of their personal lives can be useful to them when they take up another life as a character. In the exercise I have just described, the characters make no reference at all to the event that parted them, but an observer can see that the conversation taking place has nothing to do with what is really being exchanged. A text carries within it that possibility, that subtext. All of Shakespeare's plays contain the substance of a life that is not openly declared but transmitted indirectly. In Chekhov, particularly, there are characters who find it impossible to say what they truly think or act upon what they know—and the talk continues forever. All the work that I am describing is geared toward encouraging people to believe in their own powers of perceiving and feeling on behalf of another and as another in such a way that when they come to seek out a character intuitively they are not seeking for ways of demonstrating, but are inquiring *into* that person.

What Kinds of Exercises Do You Give Advanced Students?

We try and help people with the problem of audition pieces because they are a horrid but necessary part of an actor's life. I work on this by asking students to think of a time from their own past when they first stood alone. They can interpret that any way they like. It might mean having been physically left alone, being separated from a parent in a large department store, for example. It might be something that happened to them as adults, perhaps their first sense of independence. I ask them to describe that incident to the class. I use this exercise to remind them that they don't have to relate something gallant or exceptional to hold the attention of an audience.

After all the students have described their own moment of being alone—which is usually entertaining and commands a certain respect—they can see how little they need to do, how utterly simple a truth can be and still engage an audience. I then ask that the following week they should choose a simple skill and instruct the rest of us in such a way that we might be able to perform it. It can be anything, like the correct way to make tea or boil an egg, how to shine shoes or mend a bicycle puncture. Everyone comes in with something and they get to describe it for five to ten minutes. This usually holds an audience's attention because it's something that matters to the one who transmits it. There is nothing dramatic about such a skill, but it is wholly real. I tell them clearly that no single speech in any text will ask them to hold an audience for longer than that.

For the following week I ask students to consider an issue about which they have passionate views, like feminism or AIDS, and to come to speak to their fellows about this subject. Their classmates can interrupt them with questions, so they have to control their audience with their argument. Those who watch and/or participate see what happens to people when their emotions begin to sway their judgment. From this example they can understand how a text with an argument can be passionately felt and expressed and also, how an audience can be encountered directly.

I do very little work with text in character building. It's almost always based on experiences I set up. I describe the exercise in detail in advance and they discuss it with their partner. Then they act it out and they learn by what happens to them in the event itself.

Do You Critique Students?

Yes, but very little as a rule. I found being criticized the most difficult part of being a student, and I try to make criticism of the kind that enables people to see more of what they need rather than pulling them to bits about what was not evident to me. I always want to acknowledge those elements of what they do that have worked and of which they might not be aware. I am sharply critical when people introduce devices or solutions or ways out because the circumstances I set up are designed to preclude this; the structure is there to enable students to enter a problem, not avoid it. I detest trickery because however clever it may seem, it trivializes and as such it tells a lie.

What Other Exercises Do You Give Advanced Students?

I ask students to work on animals. We go to the zoo, but before we do I ask them to observe an animal in the wild, such as a rook, a woodlouse or a hare, or some domestic animal like a chicken or a cow. I ask them to observe the animal without preconceptions, to take up its space and world view, to inhabit it during an ordinary day in a routine activity. I try to encourage them to consider tiny creatures, not just the large ones, and to look at indigenous animals, not simply those that are found behind bars.

I discuss the ways in which animals are stereotyped or maligned; the hawk is not cruel and can even be magnanimous; the wolf is a hunter, but to its family, gentle; pigs needn't be dirty and badgers are often more civilized than men. Then they must devise a sequence of circumstances that are both human and animal, that is, in which the animal moves imperceptibly into the human and back into the animal. For example, a student could be a toad eyeing a fly and the human counterpart might be a director salaciously observing his secretary, and then a toad again preying on the fly and preparing to pounce on it. A group of girls could be peacocks in forage and displaying, and become girls in party dresses searching beneath tables for a lost pin or ring, and then peacocks lighting upon grain. A student can be a man lying on a beach on a towel who sees a woman walking by and raises himself in order to see if she is worth the effort or, if not, sinks back onto his towel. Once we had three men doing this in total unison, and they looked like lizards. On another occasion I saw some donkeys leaning up against barbed wire in the frost at night and they were like people in the Gulag. For one moment they looked just like imprisoned men. We discuss examples where human beings behave in animal-like ways, and students devise the circumstances to be developed so that the human gradually becomes more animal-like—perhaps a situation connected with food or quarreling. Then they can take the exercise right back into the animal world, becoming totally animal again but retaining as far as possible the dignity of that animal. There is that delicious moment when you are not sure whether this is a person who is animal-like or an animal who is person-like and the edges become blurred. The circumstances need not be charged with great action, but they must be true to the animal.

We will also look at the human walk. We take up walks from the group without saying whose it is and we find walks that are curiously related, men and women who seem to walk in almost identical ways. I ask them to walk as themselves first while observing each other. Then during the week they are each to observe another student and when they come back to class they get up and walk around the room in the guise of the other, but not declaring who their subject is or caricaturing. The class has to guess who it is. Sometimes several people have chosen the same person and you get as many as six different aspects of the same character revealed through their walk. This activates the students' interest in observing things that are seemingly of no consequence but infinitely complex in possibilities.

We also study an old man or old woman. We discuss how old people are stereotyped—that one can be old and very active and fit, or young and in physical decay. Age can touch the body and mind. This is something that the students may not have thought about. Then I pair up the students and ask them, as old people, to do very simple things: put on a coat, help one another take off the coat, go for a walk together, wash up, take tea together. I sometimes take that into an improvisation where two elderly people have known each other for a long time and one comes to stay with the other who is unwell and has been advised by the doctor to stay in bed. The patient does not want to do this and the other person has to find ways to keep him or her in bed. These exercises focus on everyday events that involve lost independence. I will also give two students an improvisation in which they are two elderly people who go to a children's party and I ask them to play with a balloon after the children have gone to bed. This sort of activity is immensely rewarding as it calls simultaneously upon restraint and suggestion.

In another improvisation I describe circumstances in which a boy has fallen in love with a girl but his closest friend disapproves of her because she is so unlikely a partner. She is the kind of girl who can be described as a siren with a mind, the sort who makes macho men go wobbly at the knees. In other words, she can think for herself, but she also has the gifts of nature. She unaccountably falls in love with this rather serious young man who has nothing of what she would normally regard as vital equipment. But she may have other reasons. I ask a student, as this young man, to write a letter to his friend telling him of his engagement, knowing the sort of reaction his friend is going to have. While the boy is writing to his friend, he must consider all the internal conflicts that bear upon what he is trying to set down on paper. So we have a young man writing a letter while all the unspoken parts of him are considering what he should say to convince his friend. One student plays the private and another the public self.

Following this, I then ask another student, as the friend, to reply to the young man. He, in turn, wants to spare his friend's feelings, to be true without being brutal, and yet to prevent his engagement. Again the private and public selves are shared between two people. Now I ask a student, as the girl, to write a letter to her mother—who has no illusions about her daughter's behavior, and as before, there are two persons for each character. In the next improvisation the young man and his fiancée make a visit to the boy's aunt. She is the kind of aunt who in England tends to wear well-cut tweeds and rule country houses with a rod of iron. So now the four parts of the young couple go to tea with the two selves of the aunt, herself attended by a maid with public and private worlds, and it takes some handling. But it's often an exciting exercise where pain and hilarity mix. It shows that what we see and think is less concealed than we imagine and how convention supports disguise for the comfort of all.

I take a number of situations where one is overwhelmed by his or her emotions and in the power of another. They are always fictitious. For instance, a young man is trying to write a novel and he has gotten to the third chapter, in which he is writing about a girl. But he has set himself a task he cannot perform because he has never really known a girl, the way she might think or feel. He is in a bookshop one rainy afternoon and he can't believe it but there, before him, is the girl in his novel— exactly as he described her. He knows that somehow he must engage her in conversation, not because he has designs upon her at all, but for the sake of English literature, for his novel. The girl can choose to be any number of characters with specific imagined circumstances. I usually give this improvisation to a student who is accustomed to playing authoritarian, self-possessed, dynamic people. Here he has to be determined, yet discreet, because of the limits of his situation. In all the exercises I assign students I carefully construct the boundaries of what will take place so that the character's inner world will be engaged, not merely the outer.

How Would You Help a Student Become More Expressive?

I never ask students to work on an emotion directly because an emotion is a conceptual experience and it is a complex of many strands of thought and feeling. To label it is to suggest that a particular emotion is the end of one's work when, in fact, one's end in working is to discover how many parts make up the form, how many colors give the impression of green or gray and how, finally, it can be felt when only just suggested. If individuals have a problem with emotion I will speak to them according to what I know about them and may suggest an emotional correlative from their own lives.

Acting often seems a fearful thing—no privacy, no certainty, no posterity—but in fact it points to a skill of lasting consequence, that is, the freedom to choose our attitude toward a given set of circumstances. In some measure this characterizes every artist: he leaves himself for the sake of another and there finds another part of himself. The survival of the race depends on the practice of this craft. It entails no prejudice, no dogma, because what the actor looks at and experiences is all of humanity.

Leah Thys

Leah Thys teaches movement at the Guildford School of Acting and Dance. She was trained as an actress and drama teacher at the Royal Conservatory in Belgium and there was introduced to the movement work of Rudolf Laban and Kurt Jooss.

Ms. Thys worked in repertory theater throughout Belgium and appeared in numerous productions with the Royal Flemish Theatre and the National Theatre, Ghent. She also made frequent appearances on Belgian television before coming to London in 1983. Since then she has appeared in many productions with Studio '68, including Noël Coward's Family Album, *August Strindberg's* The Stronger, *Edna Ferber's* Stage Door, *and Israel Horovitz's* Line, *among others.*

Ms. Thys is also a director. Her most recent productions were Cymbeline *for the William Poel festival at the National Theatre and Peter Shaffer's* Black Comedy *at the Webber Douglas Academy.*

I trained in drama in Belgium at the Royal Conservatory. It was a three-year course in drama. And I have always acted, even during the years I've been teaching, because I couldn't teach if I couldn't direct or act as well. They have to go together for me.

I teach movement to first- and second-year students at Guildford. My approach is based on a combination of Rudolf Laban's "space knowledge" and Kurt Jooss's "eukinetics," that is, dynamics that express emotions. Laban's work emerged out of dance and is especially good for dancers. Since I train actors my point of view is its use in acting. Both these men taught and performed in Germany in the twenties and thirties. Jooss had a performance group called Expression Dance. He became world-famous for his choreography of *The Green Table*.

My teacher, Lea Daan, was trained in these two traditions and then adapted them for the Flemish. I do the same thing now: I base my teaching on what I learned from her, but I have adapted it for the British. As different people live by different codes, there will be a different way of approaching the course. I believe this course of study is useful for all nationalities and cultures because it deals with universal emotions. What one has to do is adjust it to address the emotional forms and inhibitions that are specific to different groups of people, in order to help them get to the truth of an emotion. There is as much psychology as technique in this approach. For instance, at the end of the first year I ask my students at Guildford to write down what they have gained from the course or how it has influenced them. Most of them feel that it has changed them as people, that it has influenced the way they look at things, the way they live. That's where the influence on their acting comes from. Once you have done these exercises, you can no longer be an actor who only acts with his head. What I work toward is a clear link between head, mind, body, and word.

Would You Describe This Course of Study?

The first part of the course focuses on getting to know your instrument, that is, how your body works. We investigate the movement of the joints and look at ourselves as skeletons. I usually start with what looks like a warm-up, but I want students to concentrate on the skeleton while they are doing it. This is followed by exercises for the muscles before we concentrate on the nerves. At this point everything they do is geared toward the idea that as human beings we can only move in six directions. If you look at your skeleton, how does it move according to these six directions? Which parts permit large movements and which small?

What Are the Six Directions?

Forward, backward, left, right, high, and deep. These make up the three dimensions in space. I insist on calling the last two high and deep, and not up and down. This is important because the words *high* and *deep* imply limitless space.

After loosening up the body, students try to come to grips with space that is limitless. They learn how to just stand and get their body well centered and sensitive to these directions. For now I don't want them to express any emotion because when one is well centered one is not expressing anything. It's where you start from. Being centered is more than just a neutral position because actors have to conquer enormous spaces and be aware that they can do it. They have to start concentrating on the concept of space as limitless.

What Instruction Do You Give Them?

I always refer to nature. That's where it all starts. Unless we understand ourselves as being part of the universe, part of nature, we can never come to an understanding about our own rhythm—which is the rhythm of nature. Once we learn and understand the rhythm of nature, we can then express ourselves in "tensions." This is based on how we breathe. The study of these tensions is very important. There is a constant flow of dynamic and static tension in nature. If the tensions are right, the communication of emotion will be honest. What I do is feed students' imagination to get them to go forward and backward, to get them sensitive to what that means. The notion of moving forward can bring to mind the image of a lane, for instance, but one that goes on forever. The notion of high is more than just standing on a mountain. It's being able to imagine going up endlessly. Twenty years ago, before we were on the moon, space was more limited in our imagination than it is now. When we work on the concept of left and right, I ask them to think of a flat land, like Holland, that is flat and unbroken for as far as they can see or feel or imagine. Space doesn't stop at your fingertips when you stretch out your arms to the left or to the right. It goes on and on. This helps students become sensitive to their bodies in space and teaches them how to use their bodies so that they can make me or an audience *feel* the space around them.

Once they can center themselves, that is, just stand in a space and be free of tension, then they start to explore the six directions in space. Let's take forward: how can you move forward? What can your body do in forward, and are there limitations on the body? What are the combinations in forward? You can have forward/high, forward/deep, forward/left, forward/right, and directly forward. Some students come up with very theatrical movements, and some with very simple ones. I don't care which, as long as I see a truthful movement, one in which the whole body is sensitive to its direction.

When You See That a Student Is Not Truthfully
Moving Forward, What Do You Do?

If someone cannot move forward, I ask them to stand and walk forward while imagining that they are going to walk through a wall that is ten or twenty feet in front of them. They have to create the feeling with their mind that they are about to walk much farther than they actually do.

Some people think that the direction deep stops at the floor. I might help a student get the feeling of going deep by using the image of diving into water. Later on, when they are asked to express the emotion that belongs to the spatial area deep, the deeper they can go, the more pro-

found their pain can be. The greater their spatial knowledge, the better they can express the emotion that is
triggered by that direction.

This Sounds Like Sensory Work.

I do that all the time. I ask students to sit without moving
and I feed their imaginations. I take them through a
landscape and cultivate their sense memory, which is very
important during this first year of movement work.

After we work on the six directions in space separately,
the next step is combining these directions, still without
expressing anything, but with a great sensitivity toward
the spatial direction in combination with the right tensions. Students often feel that a particular movement
stimulates an emotion, and at this stage I don't want that.
I keep the emotion and the movement separate at the
beginning.

When we start to work on emotions, I say, "There can
be no truthful communication unless the emotion has its
rightful place in space." Any uplifting feeling belongs to
the spatial area high. You can sit on the floor and still
develop this sensitivity in the direction high. This stems
from Kurt Jooss's work. So we work on the six directions.
The first is high: the character of the movement is light;
its emotions range from longing to joy. The next is deep:
the character of the movement is heavy; the emotions
range from boredom to anger. Left or right: the character
of the movement is narrow or broad; the emotions range
from shyness or caution to power. Now, power can be
positive or negative. When you combine it with deep or
heavy it is dangerous; if you combine it with high and

light it is friendly. Then we work on the direction backward: the character of the movement is quick; the emotion is fear. If you go backward slowly, it's a deliberate action. When I talk about emotions, I mean the inner conflicts that provoke the emotion. I only want to see the emotion. The actor has the freedom to use whatever he likes to get to that emotion. I don't want to see what it is that makes them happy or afraid, just the happiness or fear. The last phase covers the direction forward: the character of the movement is slow: the emotion is peace or relaxation.

We work on these separately at first and then combine them. I call these emotions the primary feelings because they are straightforward.

During the first year we cover the body, space, directions in space, and then emotions. It's a lot of work because each student has to be worked with individually. In the second year we start to work on the notions of central and peripheral feelings, which are more complex and a more accurate reflection of human nature.

What Kinds of Exercises Do You Ask Students to Do Using the Primary Emotions?

Students have to prepare an exercise in the direction high, for example. The character of the movement must be light and emotions can range from longing to joy. I want to see how they physically express all these emotions in a choreographed piece that they create on their own. Sometimes I will let them use one word, like yes or no, but it must start from an inner conflict that they have created, and they have to make these feelings visible.

Is This an Improvisation?

Yes and no. I ask them to create a movement pattern, which is like a little speech. It expresses the direction, but without words. The movement replaces the verbal expression. Then, when I direct them in plays I only have to say, I want you to make something more broad or narrow, and they will know what the emotion is and how it affects their body.

What Kind of Prompting or Imagery Do You Give Them to Help Them Get in Touch with Their Emotions?

For example, a student was sitting on the floor, legs crossed, and working on the direction high. There was a lightness in his body and a smile on his face. I could see that in his imagination he saw a butterfly, and it made him very happy. But I didn't want to know that he was seeing a butterfly; I only wanted to see what the butterfly evoked in him and I wanted him to express that. I didn't want him to follow the butterfly with his eyes, but instead to focus on the feeling rather than the image, and to take that feeling and put it into a movement that is light. The purpose of this work is to teach students how to translate the inner experience of a character into movement.

Students are then asked to create an exercise that incorporates all six directions, the character of each movement, and the underlying emotions. For instance, a person can start deep and heavy and end up light. I ask them what has to happen *psychologically* for that to take place, for a person to become light, for example. When people are very angry (direction deep), they often become frightened of their own anger (direction backward, and narrow). How does someone get out of narrow into broad? At the end of the first year, each student presents a piece that incorporates all the directions.

In the second year we begin to work on the four central and the four peripheral feelings. When we have explored the central and peripheral feelings, we can combine those with the straightforward primary feelings, and we have the whole scale of human emotions.

What Do You Mean by Central and Peripheral Feelings?

Central refers to the core feelings of human nature, the forces of nature within us. We have to learn to use these natural forces. For instance, a volcano: the strength of a volcano is in us. I have students delve into themselves and try to get the feeling of a volcano erupting, a feeling that is like a total release. Then they have to find the movements that express that release.

The first central feeling I start with is gliding. You can describe it in a technical way, but when I talk about it I ask them what kind of person would we describe as a glider in life? It's a person who starts something and never finishes, one who doesn't stand still, who is always moving but without clarity of direction. When people are gliding, they no longer have a purpose in life: they are aimless. How do you truthfully get that sense of aimlessness into the body, and later on, into the text? Surprisingly, the image of a volcano exploding leads them to gliding. They start with the explosion and inevitably end with gliding because the flowing lava glides. They also discover that in gliding there is great sensuality.

Then we work on thrusting. That's the moment when a volcano erupts, when you are carried away. Thrusting is more than just a strong movement. The emotion behind it is destructive. It's the feeling of wanting to destroy, to break. You cannot talk about how to play Othello if you do not understand that force.

I would describe gliding by saying it is central, the rhythm is slow, and the character of the movement weak. Thrusting, however, is central, quick, and strong.

The next central feeling is pressing, which is strong but slow. As an example, I tell each student to put one hand on another student's forearm and to imagine that the hand on their arm, with its slight pressure, will not leave for the next twenty years. Now they begin to understand what pressure is. We try to find examples from real life that reflect that kind of pressure. Then we discuss what kind of pressure a character might be experiencing that would lead him to murder another person.

The fourth feeling I call flopping. It is central and quick, but weak. An example would be a character that has disintegrated, someone who has given up the struggle and is resigned.

Do You Translate These Feelings into Character Work?

Yes, but we never do just one thing. We do one and go into something else. You can glide for quite a while. Take Irena in *The Three Sisters*—you might ask, why doesn't she go to Moscow? Because she glides.

Next we work on the four peripheral emotions. A peripheral emotion is something that is imposed from the outside, such as society or education. It is not natural or from nature. If in central we talk about gliding, then in peripheral we talk about floating; it's lighter than light. For example, Juliet in *Romeo and Juliet* is so in love that she moves away from reality. Her feelings no longer come directly from nature. Floating is a very young feeling. I always tell my students, you may be forty years old and have to float in order to play Juliet. Floating is peripheral, slow, weak; I would use the image of a seagull that starts by gliding and then floats.

In the central emotions we have thrusting; its peripheral counterpart is slapping. It's quick and strong, for instance, telling a joke that hurts another person. In central it would kill, but in peripheral it becomes a more sophisticated way of hurting.

In the central emotions we have pressing; its peripheral counterpart is pulling. This is the most adult feeling; the ability to say no when everyone else says yes. If you put that in a dramatic conflict, you've got Antigone: someone who can say no when it would be so easy to say yes. Nora, in *A Doll's House*, is another example.

The last peripheral emotion is flicking or fluttering. It's quick and weak, a kind of trembling movement, a sort of ecstasy of feeling. Joan of Arc on the stake, for example, has to believe very strongly in what she is doing or she couldn't go through it. Nina in the last scene of *The Seagull* is another example of where an actress would use fluttering.

This is one way of understanding the actor's process, of understanding how to express the truth. It's basically similar to Stanislavsky's circles of concentration. I prefer this approach because, if the space knowledge is correct and these emotions are expressed truthfully, they will grab the audience. There is a greatly theatrical aspect to this work. It is beyond reality in a way, and yet it is real.

We do exercises that isolate and clarify each of these central and peripheral feelings. Then we combine them.

What Form Do the Exercises Take?

At the end of the second year, students present a movement exercise based on a character. For instance, if a student has chosen Lady Macbeth she will, with or without the lines, physicalize all the emotions that Lady Macbeth experiences. Then she will present the exercise without words, using only the thoughts of her character. She must decide how her movement grows out of all the central and peripheral emotions.

How Would You Use This Approach When Students Are Working on a Play?

When I direct them, I tell my actors to forget all about it. They will have the course in their body, and their body will remember. It's their secret.

For example, I was directing *Waiting for Godot*. The actor playing Pozzo could not get a sense of the inner strength that Pozzo has to have. So I asked the actor to go through exercises for the left/right/broad/power experience—the primary feelings combined with central pressing—and just by doing that, he got the sense of inner strength in his body. He couldn't have conveyed it through his voice alone. His body had to embody that strength.

Toward the end of this play Gogo is asleep and Didi sits next to him, tired and depressed. Didi is very narrow. He would like to share his feelings with Gogo but he cannot. Using the left/right spatial knowledge helped the actor achieve a feeling in his body that expressed this need.

This approach to revealing emotions goes against a lot of what is in the English personality. The English do not express emotions readily—they take a gin and tonic. A production of García Lorca's *Yerma* I saw recently did not work. Why? Because the people around the main actors were not right. They didn't have the physicality of the Spanish; they needed more body awareness. In young people all the emotions are there. You just have to unlock them. I see the need for this kind of work. It's learning how to physicalize an emotional experience.

The Guildhall School of Music and Drama

The Guildhall School of Music and Drama is a conservatory that prepares students for all branches of the music and drama professions. The school was founded in 1880 and was situated in Blackfriars until 1977, when it moved into new premises in the Barbican Centre—Western Europe's largest complex of arts facilities.

The two Royal Shakespeare Company (RSC) theaters in the Barbican Centre are physically connected to the school, and the RSC company and Guildhall work closely together. Directors and actors from the company work with students in the acting department, both in the classroom and on productions.

Guildhall offers a three-year course in Acting, a two-year course in Stage Management, and a one-year course in Scene Painting.

Tony Church

Tony Church has been the Director of Drama at the Guildhall School of Music and Drama since 1982. He is a renowned Shakespearean actor and continues to work with the Royal Shakespeare Company (RSC) and other theater groups, including many in the United States.

Mr. Church was a founding member of the RSC in 1960 and later Associate Artist of the company. He appeared in major roles in Stratford and London, including Quince in A Midsummer Night's Dream, *Polonius in* Hamlet, *Lockit in* The Beggar's Opera, *and Cornwall in Peter Brook's production of* King Lear. *In 1967 he was appointed first Director of the Northcott Theatre, Exeter, and, apart from performing in productions, he directed* Hamlet, Twelfth Night, *and* The Boyfriend.

Mr. Church's appearances in feature films include Darling, Tess, *and* Krull. *He has recorded twenty-six roles in Argo's Complete Shakespeare and written articles for The International Shakespeare Association and Cambridge University Press.*

His teaching career has included visiting professorships at several American universities, such as UCLA, SUNY Brockport, and Brooklyn College. He was chairman of the Arts Council Drama Panel from 1982 to 1985 and is currently a member of the British Council Drama Panel.

A cting, I believe, should be theatrical and authentic at the same time. These are the same goals that Michel St. Denis sought when he joined the RSC in 1963 as a director at Stratford. I have always been in favor of having a drama school that had a connection with a national company, but although technicians and actors from the RSC come in as specialists to work with our students, we do not have a strong link with the company; that is, we don't get any special advantages in terms of the RSC hiring our actors. You will find recent graduates of Guildhall scattered all over the country, and they compete for acting jobs just like everyone else.

In What Way Do You Feel Guildhall Differs from Other Drama Schools?

We are peculiar in that we receive a mixture of private and public funds. Because of this we have more freedom in the way we allocate our funds, and as a result, we have a very high proportion of teachers to students, more than other public institutions would allow. This is necessary in drama because when one teacher works with more than twelve students at a time, the training, in my opinion, must be superficial.

In our classes we normally have one teacher to twelve students. In the second-year project we will have a music director, a choreographer, and a director for every twelve students. For half an hour every week every student has a solo singing lesson. In our combat class we have one teacher to six students. We have three singing teachers who work with students. That is a very high standard and we devote a lot of time here to developing voices with secure foundations. We feel that students should build a strong foundation before they perform in musical shows and they are not permitted to sing in productions until the end of the second year of training. Similarly, Patsy Rodenburg, our voice teacher, won't allow them to work on Shakespeare until halfway through the second year because students need to acquire an enormous stretch of breath before they can learn proper support and placement. At the beginning of the second year, students take a production on a school tour. They rehearse a play twelve hours a week for six weeks and then they tour different schools and present the play.

In our final year the students are formed into a professional company that presents nine plays, three each term. Each student is in two productions a term, and gets at least three good roles to perform per year. Last year's final project was *Love's Labour's Lost* and *Romeo and Juliet*, and students took the plays on tour to Greece. We also have a television project in which short scenes from these plays are filmed so that students can see themselves and learn the differences between acting for the stage and acting for the camera. We are now trying to create an option in the third year where students could choose to work on a play for a community theater as a final project.

In the final year we also have what we call the Professional Kit Bag courses. Four or five regional theater directors come to Guildhall and hold a dummy audition session, in which all of the students are critiqued. Students also meet an income-tax specialist and a representative of Equity, and at least one agent or casting director.

The BBC presents between 800 and 900 plays on radio each year, so we have a class in radio acting. Students receive training in narration and voice-overs. Years ago English actors could extend their training by performing in regional theaters, but since this practice has diminished, we believe we have to provide the students with a great deal of performance training in the final year.

Since we are training people for a profession, we have to look at what is happening in that profession. That doesn't mean that we don't set standards for performance, but we do have to prepare people for careers as they actually exist. One large area of employment in this country is Theatre in Education (TIE) and Community Theatre, that is to say, companies that specialize in these two activities. TIE involves actors in preparing shows, with teachers, to take into the schools for all age groups. Sometimes they are text-based shows, but they are often based on devised documentary material. These shows often require audience participation. Community theater is equally varied but aimed at the older age groups, youth organizations, the handicapped, etc. Companies are small, poorly paid, travel incessantly, and play about ten short shows a week. The work requires—and gets—very dedicated performers. We can only provide an introduction to it, but we feel we must give both these areas more time in our training schedule in the future.

How Is the First Year of Training Structured?

The first acting classes focus on improvisations, character work, and narrative work—all without text. We then gradually introduce scripts. We usually start with the beginnings of British theater, the Mystery plays. This is very simple, almost cartoonlike theater. We then increase rehearsal time for scripted drama—such as projects focusing on Ibsen, Brecht, and Chekhov—and in turn, the time devoted to craft classes tends to decrease. The training is broadly based but with a constant emphasis on the imaginative approach to language. The English theater scene is multifarious and requires actors who can perform in a range of theater styles.

What Do You Mean by an Imaginative Approach to Language?

None of us want to produce students whose voices are inexpressive and unimaginative. English drama schools were very famous for producing "voices," and the voices were always the same and had very little to do with content. If an actor is imaginatively in touch with what he is saying, his voice will be colored by that and become expressive. It's very important to make clear that we are not in the business of doing voice production with actors.

But on the other hand, we also realize the importance of this and work toward enabling the actor to freely express his emotions. We want to encourage students to be responsive to language, which they have not been trained to do. Few nineteen-year-olds have a natural response to language these days, and often find that their speech lacks vigor or expressiveness when they first come to us. The response to language has been on the decline for twenty years and is worse now than it has ever been. In the fifties and sixties we had a revival of interest in regional accents and dialects. Now, television has put such a bland smudge over language altogether that even people who come from the North speak with weak, falling off, poorly articulated accents. Today there is a lack of enthusiasm for the natural taste and value of words. An actor cannot perform the body of classical theater unless words become like food, palpable things that he can smell, eat, and touch. That's what we try to instill.

Virginia Snyders

Virginia Snyders is Director of Studies at the Guildhall School of Music and Drama. Originally trained at the Old Vic School under Michel St. Denis, George Devine, and Glen Byam Shaw, Ms. Snyders went on to appear in productions in various repertory companies, toured in productions for the Arts Council, and performed with the Old Vic. She has appeared on television as well.

Ms. Snyders taught at the Central School of Speech and Drama, the Rose Bruford School, and the British Drama League before taking up her post at Guildhall. She has lectured and taught at the Circle in the Square and New York University in New York City. Her freelance work includes advising Thames Television on a series of Restoration comedies and coaching for feature films.

One of the things we feel strongly about is equipping students to work in a wide variety of acting and theater styles. It is of no use for actors to be able to work well in only one way because the first director they meet may work in a totally different way. So they have to have great flexibility in their technique. I think that is the reason we don't talk a lot about theory at Guildhall. What we do is give students an enormous amount of practical experience in acting and, like many of the modern drama schools, the essence of our training is Stanislavsky. But that doesn't mean that we slavishly adhere to his exercises. We use many of them in all sorts of ways, but we also use other kinds of exercises as well.

Many people have a misconception about the British technique. They frequently think that our technique consists of a kind of vocal finish or an ability to move in certain ways. They don't realize that all technique must be centrally related to the actor's inner motivation. If that inner life isn't there, no amount of decoration around the edges will produce a good performance. For us all voice and movement work must be a means of expression, a way to illuminate the character and the text.

How Do You Begin the Training?

In the initial stages of our training we do an enormous amount of improvisational work, and not very much rehearsal of plays. Gradually, as the training continues, the balance switches and we spend more time on rehearsal and less on technical classes.

When I say rehearsal, that includes what Americans would call scene study. This goes on as a developing process through two years of training. The third-year course is actually run like a repertory company, in which students do nine productions during the year. They spend one day a week in classes, but we hope that by that time they have learned how to use improvisation as a rehearsal tool, whether it be with a director or simply as part of their own homework. We expect them to know by then about limbering their body and their voices and to have incorporated this work into their preparation as a result of what they have learned during their first two years of training. In the first term they spend about seven hours a week on scene study. The rest of the time they study improvisation, voice, and various kinds of movement including period and country dance, acrobatics, and stage combat. Later, they study tap and jazz-dance. They do a lot of voice work. Many young people nowadays may write a bit, but they don't read much. So we spend a lot of time reading text so they can get a feeling for different kinds of language. They have lectures on the history of theater, but we combine that with the study of period plays, and incorporate both into workshops so they can translate that information into practical acting experience. We start with Greek plays and work through to modern text focusing on one play a week. This is separate from their scene study. Students also work on poetry, starting with medieval poems, and work their way through to modern verse.

In scene study we frequently begin with medieval plays because they are marvelously humane and the story line is very clear. These plays require a lot of research, but although the text is difficult, they are not hard to speak.

The words may be obscure, but unlike Shakespeare, the verse line is not very long and doesn't require great breath technique.

Obviously, one of the very important aspects of the early stages of training is relaxation. For us, learning to be relaxed and simple, learning not to be afraid to stand still and do nothing but think, is an important area of work. This takes place in all the classes: voice, movement, acting, improvisation, etc. Actors should never confuse tension with effort.

Because actors are going to have to work in varied circumstances they have to learn that different people will have different opinions of their work and, in the end, they will have to be their own judge. We don't have a very clear-cut method nor do we insist that all staff teach in the same patterns. Granted, we want like-minded people to work together, but at the same time, we don't expect all the teachers to use the same vocabulary or approach to acting training. It is important that the actors themselves learn to sort out differences of opinion. After students work on exercises the staff as a group will talk to them briefly, and then each student goes to each member of the staff for a discussion of that piece of work. Quite often they find that the staff do not agree about their work and that is something they have to deal with. If they want they can always go back to a staff member for clarification. Also, we don't expect the students to progress in the same direction at the same pace. Sometimes a criticism may not be useful at the moment but begins to make sense in a few months' time. We expect students to realize that ultimately the only person who will go with them on every job interview is themselves. They cannot be dependent on other people's judgment.

In the beginning the improvisational work is geared toward students' learning how to be themselves and how to be honest in what they do. By improvisation I mean sensory work as well. We tend to label things in a deliberately general way in this school because we don't want students to think that they only use improvisations in their improvisation class. There is an enormous amount of overlap in the teaching and I think that is very helpful. For instance, our voice staff attends rehearsals to watch the students work and talks with the directors about whether the actors are using their voices adequately. Movement staff will also watch rehearsals and offer comments on what they observe. The students know that if they need special help there are people they can go to for such things as accents or period movement.

After the initial improvisation exercises, in which the actor learns to play himself, we gradually introduce exercises that enable the actor to adopt different physical and vocal rhythms. One of the early exercises we do for this is to study animals in the zoo and create improvisations based on them. We try to help students get in touch with more instinctive drives and rhythms of moving and breathing that are not their own. In the animal exercise the primary focus is still internal. In a later exercise students work on circus acts, in which the primary focus is on relating to other actors and an audience

Could You Describe the Circus Exercise?

It's used in a number of different ways. A class will work for several weeks developing a circus act. They have to find a timing and a rhythm that makes the act work. The students start by looking at professional circus acts: watching clowns, animal trainers, jugglers, tightrope walkers, and reading books on circuses. Some of the students will elect to try to develop a skill, such as juggling. Others will choose to mime their act in a kind of structured improvisation. They must find how to shape an act so it communicates directly with the audience. This particular exercise always involves relating to the audience of fellow students and teachers.

Actors need to find a way to be outgoing and include the audience while keeping their inside work alive. Otherwise, it's easy for an actor to become self-obsessed to the point where he is acting for his own pleasure and not for anyone else's. That becomes self-indulgent.

What Other Kinds of Exercises Do Students Work On?

There are many kinds of "trust" exercises that students work on at the beginning, from the kind where a student falls and someone catches him to learning how to flow with someone else's work. For example, one student will start an improvisation with a certain set of circumstances and the next person will walk into it with a totally different set of circumstances. The first student must not stop what he is doing, but contribute to the new circumstance while maintaining his own. Neither of the students should kill the possibilities of the new influence. Then a third student will join them with something else. He may come in and say, "There is a fire down the road." Everyone has to incorporate this new information into what they are doing. They have to be flexible enough not to block their imaginative possibilities.

What Kinds of Exercises Do You Give Students to Help Them Create Different Kinds of Characters?

Students start as themselves and work toward developing other characters. They begin by trying to create someone they have observed at great length, someone in their own family, or someone they know very well. After working on that person for several days, they will be paired in an improvisation with another student. By then they should know enough about the new person they have become to be able to live as that person in an improvised world with unexpected events.

Do You Use Stanislavsky's Exercises?

Not directly. His work crops up in all sorts of improvisational classes and in much of the scene work. It is a gradual process that comes from teachers in a variety of ways. Because our teachers may not say specifically that they are doing Stanislavsky exercises, our students are quite surprised (if they haven't yet read Stanislavsky) at how many of his exercises they have actually done in varying forms. Though it is not compulsory, most students do read *An Actor Prepares* and *Building a Character*, which are the two most useful of his books when in training.

What Is It About British Training That Enables the Actor to Play the Wide Range of Theatrical Styles?

I suppose this is partly because we see our training as a commercial training for the theater and not as a university course. This is not true in many American academic institutions, where students can choose the courses they want to take. We don't give our actors that choice. We say that everything we provide is useful and don't argue about it. They may not see its need now, but they will in five years time. Obviously, this can be hard to take because it assumes a "we know best" attitude. But we have to assume that we do. One of the things that actors have got to learn if they are going to have successful careers is to risk trying many things they may not be very keen on doing, including learning to work on period material that they may not be interested in. Also, we have a lot of teachers and that prevents us from becoming dogmatic in our approach.

We use an enormous variety of text material throughout the training and feel that the order in which the work is presented to students is important. We usually start with early, medieval plays because of their directness, simple staging, and short verse line; we introduce Chekhov a little later in their first year when they are ready to understand the idea of subtext. They then apply this understanding to different kinds of material. If they are introduced to subtext at the right point in their training, it can inform everything else they do afterward. In the same way it is no use working on Shakespeare in the early stages of training before students have adequate breath support. All that will do is create a lot of neck and shoulder tension in the actors as they endeavour to get round the text. It's important, then, that Shakespeare comes in their second year when they have acquired some of the machinery they need to do it with comparative ease. Otherwise, Shakespeare becomes a barrier. In the same way it is important that students have been through the early research, exercises, and self-awareness exercises so they can find both the similarities and differences when working on Shakespeare and the Jacobeans, realities that are appropriate to the lives of those times. I think introducing these texts at the right moment helps students to play a wide repertoire of theatrical styles.

Where Would You Place Pinter in This Progression?

He requires a strong sense of poetic imagery. I don't think he is first-year material because you need a lot of understanding about how to fill silence and pauses with intention. And his plays have a very condensed poetic language. So, yes, it's second-year material, or even later.

I must add that in talking about a three-year course where students are working a very full five-day week, one is going to give a misleading impression by discussing just a small part of their work. It is difficult not to overemphasize some aspects at the expense of others in response to these questions, and we should regard this as a brief conversation about some aspects of our training that, by its nature, must be an evolving and developing process.

Patsy Rodenburg

Patsy Rodenburg is Head of Voice at the Guildhall School of Music and Drama. She is also a principal voice coach for the Royal Shakespeare Company and the English Shakespeare Company. From 1984 to 1985 she headed the voice department at the Festival Theatre in Stratford, Ontario, Canada.

Ms. Rodenburg has worked as a voice coach for many of the major theater companies throughout Britain, including the National Theatre, Shared Experience, Cheek-by-Jowl, and Clean Break. She continues her freelance work in theater, television, and films, and teaches throughout Europe, the United States, Canada, India, as well as Great Britain.

I divide my time equally between working with professional actors and with students. In general, professionals are much easier to teach because they know what they need and they know whether you are knowledgeable enough to help them. I think one of the big differences between Britain and America is that some actors here continually work on their voices, that is, they continue to come for classes even if they do not have a voice problem. Once I have established a working relationship with an actor, he will come back whenever he starts a new project. So there is an ongoing belief in the voice as an integral part of the actor's craft.

Speaking is a physical activity and unless an actor technically and physically works every part of the voice, it will not respond organically when he needs it. But I do not want an actor to stand on stage and think about his rib cage or how his voice sounds. I want him to be organically reactive and emotionally responsive to the moment with a voice that is totally free. In order to get to that point, I think you have to spend hours standing and working every muscle, just as a ballet dancer will spend hours exercising muscles at a barre in order to be able to leap without thinking about it. After having spent a bit of time in film or television, an actor might come back to me because he has lost strength in certain areas and wants to rework them. Or an actor may come to work on a specific text, or because he has vocally blocked himself in some way.

What Kinds of Text Might an Actor Bring to a Voice Teacher?

Different plays make different demands on the voice. What is so remarkable about Shakespeare is that he totally marries the emotional with the intellectual, so an actor not only has to be able to extend vocally in an emotional sense, but must also convey intelligence and ideas in the words. Restoration text is more intellectual and requires tremendous skill in articulation. Specific texts have specific demands.

How Do You Begin Working with New Students?

I don't separate voice training from acting training, and I definitely don't separate it from text. Text work has to be part of the voice class, but not immediately, not in the first year of training. That year is a technical year, which has to do with students learning how to unlock bad vocal habits. I think that one of the misconceptions in voice work—and there are many—is that the natural voice is confused with the habitual voice. One of the big battles is to make someone realize that a free, open voice is not necessarily his habitual voice. It takes about a year to find that voice and to be able to support it muscularly with sufficient breath, and to develop range, resonance, and clarity of speech. During that year students don't touch text while they work with me. What they do work on are their own language skills.

I will give students exercises in a variety of areas, such as storytelling, speaking to someone of a higher status, and using jargon so that language codes are explored. In this way they begin to understand how they use language and, therefore, they learn to adapt these methods when they encounter a text that is not in their language code. I send them off to listen to people who use words they would not use, their aunts or mothers, for example, and then I ask them to think about how they themselves use words that another generation or class would not.

Could You Describe the Storytelling Exercise?

I ask them to tell a story about something that has actually happened to them, a time when they were frightened, for example, and I give them certain rules to follow, for instance, that the story has to be told in the first person.

One of the things I feel strongly about is that there is not one way to teach voice for all students. There are certain exercises that one finds work for some people but not for others. The exciting thing about being a voice teacher is that you don't know what is going to work or what voice problem will emerge. So the specific things I do change from student to student, from year to year. What I can say is that until students develop a physically free voice they can't begin to fulfill a text, because a physically free voice is connected to a free intellect and imagination. You can't think clearly if you are tense or if your voice is tense. So all these first-year exercises are technical and freeing.

Some of the language exercise work that I do are not unlike the improvisational work that is done in America; that is, the student finds someone to observe and tells a story to the class as that person. But I focus on the way the character speaks and the words he or she uses rather than on complete character work.

Could You Describe the Technical Work on Voice?

I work a great deal on centering the body which is derived from the Alexander technique and focuses on freeing the neck, the shoulders, and the jaw. Students spend hours breathing and expanding their capacity—learning to breath with only the right sort of tension, which means none in the shoulders, upper parts of chest, neck, or jaw. They then spend a lot of time strengthening the muscles of breath and extending this capacity so that in the end they can quite easily attack four or five lines of Shakespearean verse on one breath. At these times I use text for the purposes of the exercise without analyzing it for meaning. Students spend a lot of time learning to free the voice and place sound forward in the mouth. They then spend time extending their range to about three octaves. They work on opening up different resonators, on articulation, and learning Standard English. This is what they have to achieve in the first year.

In the second year all the voice work that I do, apart from several voice workouts a week, is through text— Shakespearean text primarily. At the same time students work on projects using other texts and I sit in on these projects to help them, just as I do when I work with the Royal Shakespeare Company, for example. I sit in on rehearsals and assist the director with vocal problems.

Could You Give Me an Example of the Kind of Vocal Problem You Might Encounter in a Rehearsal?

I might notice that an actor is reaching an emotional part of the text, and instead of freeing his voice, he might begin to sit on it, not using the language to explain what he is experiencing. He might be pushing or ranting. I would then try to free that tension and connect his breath to the text and the word. This will enable the audience to hear the words and, at the same time, permit the actor to experience and express his emotions without them becoming muddy with tension.

How Would You Do That? If Something Emotional Were Interfering with Voice Production, How Would You Try to Correct It?

If there is something interfering with the voice, it takes the form of tension that blocks voice production. This tension appears all over the body. It appears in the shoulders or the neck or the jaw, or the position of the head or the collapse of the spine. I not only listen to actors but I look. There have been times when an actor has tried to reach a particular emotional level and winds up catching and hurting his voice. When I work on this I might do something simple, like adjust his head or jaw a half inch at that moment in order to keep the voice free. Or it might be much more complex than that. If I have a dialogue with an actor, if they know the way in which I work and I theirs, I can probably find a solution in half an hour. Students get to know how I work over time and by their third year, when they are involved in their final productions, I watch rehearsals and work with them outside rehearsals as well to help them free their voices and use them to make the most of their texts.

I do have to say that I have to have a good relationship with a director in order to tell him, for example, that he can or can't ask an actor to shout in a certain spot. I will only work with directors who are concerned about the actors' voices. I suppose those who aren't wouldn't have a voice coach in the room to begin with.

When and How Do You Introduce Text?

Students start with Shakespearean sonnets in the second year and spend a whole term in small groups speaking sonnets. The sonnet form presents all sorts of problems for the speaking voice because it is a powerful form and the actor only has fourteen lines in which to express enormous emotions. Working on them is a way of learning how language can free our voices intellectually and emotionally. We do a lot of work on how the language affects the voice. If Shakespeare chooses particular vowel sounds it is because emotionally those vowel sounds are the right ones for the emotion contained in the text.

Can You Give Me an Example of How Vowel Sounds Reflect Specific Emotions?

Take, "When I do count the clock that tells the time." If you speak those lines correctly you will hear a tick-tock sound. So Shakespeare is on the side of the actor vocally. He writes for the actor and he uses all his skill to give us the right word, the right sound. If you trust that, he does fifty percent of the work for you. Another example is, "No longer mourn for me when I am dead." This is full of open vowels that slow you down and give, if spoken fully, a sense of mourning. Or, "The expense of spirit in a waste of shame is lust in action." This one is about the chaos and madness caused by lust. The verse is shattered and lines tumble into each other giving the feeling of madness, if you follow the structure.

In general, I think that vowel sounds in language represent the feelings and consonants the intellect. That's quite general, but true, I believe. The emotion and the intellect must marry, otherwise we just end up making sounds. Whenever we speak words, even in the throes of an emotion, there is an intellectual process going on. If Shakespeare doesn't have a word for something, he puts in an *O* or an *Ah*. These are most important moments in Shakespeare. He has run out of words.

Do You Teach Scanning?

Yes, in the first year. We do a text class using poetry and I take students from Anglo-Saxon poetry through to modern-day poetry. They discover that in each period a new form is introduced. For instance, the Anglo-Saxon poets relied on repetition and onomatopoeic qualities in language. Working on these poets helps students discover how powerful an onomatopoeic word is, or how powerful repetition is. Then, as we move through other periods, they get a history of the development of language and the development of style.

When I work on scanning, basically what I work on is the imaginative response to language. I don't want the meter to be dead; I also want to know exactly why someone is saying something, why that person needs to speak. I don't only want to hear the form. My argument is that good writers use form to help actors discover the intellectual as well as the emotional intention, the meaning as well as the feeling. If the actress lets herself go through the thoughts contained in Juliet's "Gallop apace . . ." speech, the rhythm will make sure that by the last words she is out of breath—which is what should happen. Juliet is out of breath because she is so excited.

Interestingly, Shakespeare helps the most when he breaks his rules. If I were in a relaxed Elizabethan mood, I would be able to speak very free, regular, iambic pentameter. If something chaotic started happening to me, I couldn't continue to speak in that way. Shakespeare will break his own forms to reflect these emotional disruptions. But in all voice work you have to know the rules before you can break them.

The iambic pentameter is the rhythm of a heartbeat driving on with dramatic force, which makes it a very potent form. I always try to relate these technical aspects to a dramatic core rather than an academic one. Yes, I can teach students the academic notes in the back of the text, but I always look for the dramatic ones. Shakespeare chooses to write in this form because of its dramatic effect, and when the meter is broken it becomes a clue that there is an emotional change taking place. Often, the more complicated the thought, the more complicated the emotion. Sometimes I look at some of the sonnets and think, what is he going on about? Then I suddenly realize that he is discussing something very complicated; for instance, someone has been unfaithful to him, he wants to forgive, but he is furious. The sonnet structure will then reflect his very contorted thinking. Then I realize, of course, he is in such an emotional turmoil that the form of his thinking becomes complicated and contorted. These are the kinds of things I hope inform the actor rather than inhibit him.

After studying sonnets students move on to soliloquies or monologues, and finally to a scene. We spend a whole term on a scene, which they first perform for me and later present to the rest of the staff. Then they work on several major Shakespeare productions.

As the training progresses students have more and more individual contact with me, which often has to take place informally. So, initially, there are formal classes usually for eight hours a week, and by the third year they generally come to me individually. In the second year they also start dialect work, phonetics, and learn how to transcribe phonetically. They can learn dialects through listening or through phonetic transcribing.

Do You Teach Them European Dialects as Well as the Various British Dialects?

Yes. Some we only get to teach if students need them for a part. My belief is that if they learn how to listen they'll be able to pick up a dialect. Listening is a part of voice training and we do many listening exercises in the first year. They listen for the placement of the voice and the vowel shift and learn how to transcribe the sounds they hear into phonetic symbols. So although they develop a large collective library of dialects and accents, in the end they should be able to transcribe any new dialect they need on their own. Obviously, we emphasize the dialects that are the most important for work in this country.

The other important thing that happens in the voice

department at Guildhall is that throughout their training students receive an individual half-hour singing lesson each week with a classical singing teacher. This links very strongly to the voice work, although there are times when the singing teacher has to stop teaching a certain technique if it's in opposition to a technique that the voice staff use.

In the first term, students don't perform very often. I don't like them to expose themselves too quickly as they will fall back on old tensions. But twice a term we have informal shows. When the class works on poetry they present an evening of poetry. For instance, we will have one evening of early poems up to Chaucer, another on the Elizabethan poets, and another on the Metaphysical poets. We will also have an evening of poems from the Age of Reason and one on the Romantic poets. Students will then present evenings on the Victorian and on twentieth-century poets.

What Are the Different Vocal Demands of Different Period Plays?

My starting point is this: you are true to the text and the text comes first. You can only be true to the text once you can realize that text accurately through your voice.

When you look at a Restoration text the first thing you notice is that the thoughts expressed are much longer than those found in twentieth-century text. You cannot apply your eighties rhythms of thinking to it. Every word spoken in it is important. Today, most of us ramble on, while in a Restoration text every word is purposeful. If you cut a few words you can change the whole meaning. It's very structured writing. The voice must reflect this intensity and clarity of thought. As one starts to get very clear about what one is thinking, the voice naturally lifts and sounds higher.

Another thing students might notice when they look at Restoration plays is that the characters have a real need to be heard and to speak. In fact, in that society people were only allowed into certain rooms if they could be witty and tell stories. That is something that a young person today has trouble grasping. Once they have done their first year's work they know that they have to want to speak— and not to grunt. In Restoration texts words are actions, tools, levers, seducers, which today we have replaced much of with body language. So to trust and use language is one of the greatest skills an actor can acquire. That doesn't mean that actors can't interpret; it means that they have to find what is embedded in the text through language, the choice of sound, the choice of thoughts, and the construction of each thought.

How Does Shakespeare Differ from Other Texts?

His language is structured too, but it's of a more poetic nature. It's more emotional and has more imagery From their work on sonnets students will have learned that everything has to be reasoned. You cannot put across an argument with a hole in it. So the first thing they discover when they work on Shakespeare is that they need a lot more breath for him than they would, say, for Pinter. Since they have to sustain their thinking for a much longer time, they need more breath. Breath is directly linked to thought. You take in enough breath for the thought that you want to convey. Today we live with very short thought processes, so we don't normally experience our full breath capacity.

The human voice is a remarkable instrument. If you put someone across a field and called across, the voice would carry naturally, but if you stand someone on stage and his ego and fears get in the way then those natural processes get blocked. A lot of my work focuses on unblocking the tensions that the environment, society, and emotions put on the voice.

Also, a lot of my work aims at helping the actor discover the *need* to speak and the *need* to use language imaginatively. If children are not encouraged to speak and use language, how can they think clearly or understand the world? The reason we want to go to the theater to hear wonderful text is because it illuminates our experience for us. It is the actor's duty to excite people through the imaginative use of his voice. My job is to give actors choices. If they can't get their mouth round the text then they have no choice but to say it in a certain habitual, unimaginative way. If the actor's imagination is taking him somewhere that his voice won't follow, his efforts to express will be strangled with tension.

Does Chekhov Have Specific Voice Demands?

I think if you can get through a Shakespearean text, or Restoration, which I think is harder to speak, I don't think you will find other texts difficult. Wilde is an exception because he is living off the *crème de la crème* of a certain society—a group of people who went about with their brains ticking a hundred times faster than ours do. Most people fail when they work on Wilde because they make it seem effortful, and wit has to be effortless. I've talked about being physically strong, but if you are going to speak Wilde or Shaw, you have to be intellectually strong as well. People find Shaw difficult to speak because few of us get excited by a clear argument, but that's what Shaw's characters do.

What About Molière?

Molière in English translation has the problem of rhyming couplets, which can be a nightmare. If the actor pursues the thought and lets the couplet take care of itself, something nice will happen to the ear. We should hear the sense before the form, but the form should be there as a support.

How Do You Help an Actor Find His or Her Unique Voice Quality?

Every voice is different. Voices are more accurate than fingerprints. I want to help actors develop free, flexible voices that can embrace any role. I try to center their voices, which means position each voice with the minimum tension possible. That takes about a year to do.

I don't like to sound mystical, but often the voice will not be centered because of an emotional block that gets translated into a physical tension. Sometimes there are areas that I can't go into. I can only free a voice up to the point that the student allows. Sometimes three years later an actor may be able to go further. I don't think a voice is ever fully trained. It changes with the experiences we have in life. The year of centering is spent in unblocking the tensions that block the voice, but often they are actually rooted in something a bit deeper. So, although I can say that I center a voice in a year, it's only if that person is ready for it. I don't do exercises to push them further if I don't feel they are ready.

Once the voice is centered, it can move in all sorts of directions. I try to get students to start speaking a new text in a neutrally centered position so they start without tension that might ultimately inhibit their understanding of the text. In rehearsals, as one's understanding of the text develops, the voice must be free to change, to reflect those discoveries.

What Are the Kinds of Obstacles to Voice Production That an Actor Might Encounter in a Professional Production?

I've had actors who were asked to do specific things in plays that were dangerous, such as screaming, shouting, or having to speak over music. There are some things that directors or designers will require of an actor that are physically impossible. If you put certain costumes on certain people their voices will become bound and therefore very vulnerable to abuse. The actor may not be confident enough to stand up to the director, so I often have to stay sandwiched between them. The human voice can be very frail. With the wrong tension in the voice you can easily abuse it, which is frightening for actors because they live through their voices.

Another problem I might be called upon to solve is the actor who has been doing a lot of television work and gets into a play in a large theater and can't be heard.

Do You Teach Your Students Standard English?

Because we have a tradition of voice training in Britain we have bound ourselves to a convention that is not freeing: Standard English. We have told young actors that they cannot use their natural dialect. I think that cuts off an actor from his roots. That doesn't happen so much in America.

Students should be able to speak in their own dialects as well as Standard English. While Standard English is a very free, open position for the voice, most dialects are very held in, for complicated physical reasons. But I don't think that they should have to speak it all the time—in their private lives as well. I don't see why actors have to begin to work on a text in Standard English. The rigidity in English training has to be addressed. There is a political point contained in this. For many years we were told that the great texts of our culture could only be spoken in a middle-class sound, that is, standard received pronunciation. I find that very worrying.

I also hope that we can get away from wanting to hear beautiful sound without any meaning behind it. I would be horrified if an actor I had worked with was referred to as having a "beautiful voice." It's the voice serving the text that's important.

Do You Feel English Actors Need to Be More Expressive?

In some way all the great plays are about passion, and we often wind up with actors who have very clear voices but have become a bit suburban and passionless. I think a lot of English actors find passionate text difficult.

Being emotionally expressive has a lot to do with breath. That's where a voice teacher can help an actor release emotionally. If you watch someone hold back emotion it's usually because of some block in their breath. You can often see that and devise an exercise to get it released. For instance, if you can get their breath very low and very free, then they can experience more. That's something I often do in rehearsal. The block often has to do with sexuality or addressing one's own aggression. Without talking about the specifics I will give them an exercise that gives them a breath memory of the experience they are blocking.

One way of doing that, of helping them to let go of their breath and stop controlling it, is to have them run around. When they suddenly have to breathe for a real purpose, and speak text at the same time, they often lose control and become emotionally released. The memory of this experience can inform their work next time. If they haven't breathed in a particular place in a long time, when they do take a breath there, they will start to feel things they might not have felt before. This is based on my experience with many actors. In private sessions, where the work is very intensive, when I get them on very deep, low, free, open breaths, a lot of people start to cry. That happens first. Then they often start talking about the moment they lost that freedom in their voice. Over the last ten years I have come across more than thirty people who, when they get on to that breath, will talk about childhood sexual abuse.

I think my students would say that after their initial year of voice training I teach acting, and they will come to me with an acting problem. They don't separate the voice from acting. Thanks to Cicely Berry, one of the great voice teachers, voice specialists have acquired their own dignity, so that directors will invite us to rehearsals and talk to us and work with us. They are not afraid to ask for help. Until directors in America allow that to happen, the actor is going to undervalue voice work.

The London Academy of Music and Dramatic Art

Founded in 1861, The London Academy of Music and Dramatic Art (LAMDA) has sought to remain progressive and innovative under its recent principals: Michael MacOwan, Norman Ayrton, Michael Barry, and Roger Croucher. In 1978 Roger Croucher was appointed Director of the Acting School and in 1980 he became Principal. As a former theater director in London his stewardship at LAMDA continues their tradition of appointing a principal from the professional theater. His goal has been to prepare actors to play a wide variety of theatrical styles. To that end he has revised the curriculum so that students receive training in both naturalistic and French expressionistic techniques.

In 1963 LAMDA's experimental theater, the Mac-Owan Theatre, was opened by the Academy's patron, H.R.H. Princess Alexandra. It is a highly flexible playing space that enables directors and students to present productions in any form—proscenium, in the round, open stage, or arena staging.

The London Academy of Music and Dramatic Art

LAMDA offers a three-year Acting Course, a one-year Acting Course for overseas students, a two-year Stage Management Technical Theatre Course, and a Summer Workshop for students who wish to work on an intensive Shakespearean program with the LAMDA faculty.

Roger Croucher

Roger Croucher has been Principal of the London Academy of Music and Dramatic Art (LAMDA) since 1980. After leaving Oxford, where he studied under Professor Nevill Coghill, he trained as an actor at the Central School of Speech and Drama. He joined the Royal Shakespeare Company (RSC) to play under the direction of Sir Peter Hall, among others. He appeared in many RSC productions, including Troilus and Cressida *and* The Devils. *He has also appeared in many television productions for the BBC and ITV, and in films.*

In 1970 Mr. Croucher joined the Royal Court Theatre as a director. He presented such new plays as Boesman and Lena, *and directed* Entertaining Mr. Sloane *and* Beckett 3 (Come and Go, Cascando, Play). *He served on the British Council's Drama and Dance Advisory Committee and has lectured extensively on theater and drama training in New Zealand, Brazil, Turkey, and India, as well as Europe and the U.S. Most recently he has been a judge of the 1988 Olivier Awards.*

O ne of the things that is important here is the tradition of having a principal who is from the theater. It's not just an administrative post. I trained at the Central School of Speech and Drama and I worked as an actor for twelve years in various companies including the RSC. Then I turned my career over to directing and worked at the Royal Court Theatre for five years where I helped to found the Theatre Upstairs. The Theatre Upstairs was famous for brilliant new writing in the seventies, and introduced Athol Fugard and Caryl Churchill. Many actors and directors cut their teeth there. So I am an actor and director by profession. When I was offered the opportunity to become the principal at LAMDA I was very pleased because I had directed there and really loved it. I had some ideas that I thought would be helpful to actors and wanted to introduce them.

When I became principal I made a number of changes in the curriculum because I think that the actor should be trained in a double tradition: he should learn Stanislavsky and the naturalistic school, but also the French expressionist tradition of Copeau and LeCoq. I am strongly committed to combining both. So side by side with our basic actor training we have introduced movement classes that derive from LeCoq and other expressionist traditions. These classes begin in the first year with actors studying animals. The student observes an animal at the zoo, works toward creating it, and then enlarges it in various ways by bringing the animal into improvisations and text work.

216

The animal exercise is a prelude to other work, including movement improvisation, mask work, *commedia dell'arte*, and clown work. These classes form the core of the first two years of training at LAMDA. The third year is primarily devoted to performance. Side by side with workshops and classes students take expressionistic movement work, which is very freeing and builds a lot of confidence. It helps produce an actor who is willing to take risks and is not simply stuck in the Royal Court naturalistic tradition.

What Do You Mean by the Royal Court Naturalistic Tradition?

The foundation of the British actor is naturalistic—what you see in the well-acted traditional West End play. George Devine, Michel St. Denis, and Glen Byam Shaw at the Old Vic School were responsible for promoting that style in Britain, and Michael MacOwan brought it to LAMDA during the fifties. He was a believer in the ideas of the Old Vic school and so am I. But I don't think young actors need stop there. Of course, they have to be able to be realistic and natural, but they are going to have much more asked of them nowadays. They should be able to survive whatever a director throws at them. That is my philosophy of acting and it is different from the naturalistic tradition I myself was trained in. When we were asked to do something unconventional we found it very difficult. When a director like Peter Brook or William Gaskill decided to tear up the script, many actors were at a loss as to how to work. They no longer are. I believe that the actor should be confident enough to feel there is no style of theater that he cannot tackle.

In What Ways Have You Adopted Lecoq's Ideas?

LeCoq's is a movement tradition that can be joined to text. For example, students study a specific animal, and then they work on text through their animal. In movement improvisation students are given the assignment to observe people, to discover how specific people move and how an individual's body is affected by various factors, like the work they do, for example. One exercise students are given is to observe the people in the café opposite the Earl's Court Underground station and create a scenario based on their observations. They present this to the class. We use this particular café because it has many unusual types of people in it. It's an interesting place for an actor to be—it increases the actor's awareness and sharpens his eye. This exercise stimulates the imagination, and it also helps an actor to release tension by getting into someone else's life and manner. Students first present their character without speech, but in order to successfully accomplish a silent character, students have to create the character's inner life and become this person. They do this for up to an hour in class. That's a wonderful way to learn that acting isn't about demonstrating, but about creating a living character who can exist without language. It's a particularly helpful preparation for playing Chekhov, where what the characters don't say is often more important than what they do say.

We then expand this into group work, and five or six

students will work together on an improvisation. Each student is his or her specific character and must stay true to that character in the improvisation.

How Do You Evaluate the Success or Failure of This Exercise?

You can see immediately whether students have moved from their own self into someone else. You can also see when they haven't because their bodies don't function normally. You can see whether their body is beginning to change into something different from their own; you can see their weight being transferred, hear if their voice has changed, and above all, you can see it in their eyes. Now that I have seen this exercise a number of times I notice the same characters from Earl's Court Café coming up year after year. And students are never told who to study. It's up to them.

One of my favorite exercises is called "matters." This is the study of the four elements: earth, air, fire, and water. The actor is asked to explore the world around him, and this can be anything from fluff to chewing gum to hard metal. I shall never forget a class I observed, taught by the director Jane Gibson. Students were exploring the properties of metal springs and then three of them were transformed into a family comprised of different types of metal springs. Dad was a kind of heavy industrial spring that doesn't move; Mum was one of those large floating kinds of springs; the son of the house was a floppy spring like the kind you find in a ball point pen. The students found the movement and personality for their characters through exploring their movement as springs, and then they improvised the family breakfast as these springs. It was one of the most hilarious things I've ever seen and it is a marvelous exercise.

Do You Teach the Stanislavsky Approach at LAMDA?

Yes, and we are not alone in this. The Stanislavsky approach is the basis for most European training today and we work from the exercises that Stanislavsky described in his books, especially *An Actor Prepares*. It's a very down-to-earth training method and it does not involve pushing emotions to their limit, but rather teaching an actor to live truthfully in his environment. We don't teach Lee Strasberg's version of Stanislavsky, with its great emphasis on affective memory. Most good teachers will be wary of a student becoming indulgent with his emotions, and that is why you will find teachers concerned about this exercise. It often leads students into emotional areas of indulgence and extravagance. This is not what I feel Stanislavsky was about at all.

Some of the Teachers I Have Interviewed Feel That the Emotional Range of British Actors Could Be Expanded. Do You Agree?

I think this was a widely held view twenty to thirty years ago, however I don't think that English acting would be so admired today if it wasn't expressive. When one looks at the performers who are best known and most widely admired, I think they are very expressive emotionally and have the ability to involve an audience in their inner life. For instance, anyone who saw *Nicholas Nickelby* saw what most people thought was very passionate acting. This may have surprised those who thought the English were laid back and only good at naturalistic work. Leading English performers are no longer the polished beast of yesterday. Whether it's Jonathan Pryce's Macbeth or Judi Dench's Cleopatra, you are talking about an actor who has an instrument that is capable of expressing great passion, not one who is just technically skilled.

English actor training has changed a great deal in the last thirty years in order to meet the needs of the many different kinds of companies we now have in England. I have been at LAMDA for ten years and hope that some of what we do now will continue to encourage actors to commit themselves to being emotionally expressive. That's what the good actor has to be.

What Aspect of the Training at LAMDA Focuses on Helping the Student Become More Expressive?

Although that is an interesting and fair question, in fact we don't do specific exercises that focus on that. I have seen certain exercises in other schools where students were doing what I would consider to be self-indulgent work. We focus on emotion when it is appropriate for the specific text. If an actor is working on Macbeth, say, then clearly he is going to come across a certain number of raw emotions that he would want to express—or that the

221

director will want him to express. And that will be different from the range he might want for Hamlet—which would still demand great feeling and emotion. I think it is dangerous to use exercises that separate the emotions from the text. If an actor is studying an animal, that will produce a set of sounds, and emotions will be released. Similarly, emotions will come up if an actor is working on a clown. Improvisations will produce raw emotional responses, and if they don't the student will be critiqued for that. I prefer to throw the challenge out to the actor, but within a structure, not through freewheeling exercises for emotional release. We don't do, and I am not in favor of doing, what I would call general, primal exercises. For one thing, when emotions are worked on in a general, nonspecific context, actors find it difficult to recreate them.

You Mentioned Clown Work. How Is That Incorporated into the Acting Training?

Clown work is from the French tradition and, of course, has roots even further back. During the second year of training each actor is asked to find his own clown—he has to discover what it is about himself that is ludicrous or even timorous or fearful, and has to create his own clown character based on that, just as he has to find his own animal. All sorts of exercises have been developed to help students develop the clown into a living entity, something the actor could go out on the street with, if necessary. In class we might grill the clown, that is, put him in the middle of the ring and ask him questions about his life. So the clown learns the perimeters of his existence.

You Seem to Distinguish Between Class Work and Workshops. How Are They Different?

Basic actor training, that is, exercises like the ones I described, take place in classes. Scene work is separate; it starts gently during the first year and then leads up to full Shakespeare, Chekhov, and Restoration performances in workshops during the second year.

The third year, which is the performance year, gives our actors a chance to try out what we have instilled and what they have discovered. Students go on tour for six weeks and perform an English classic in various professional theaters. For instance, this year they are touring the Netherlands with *A Midsummer Night's Dream*. We have been doing this since 1979. It enables actors to establish themselves away from LAMDA and return with what they have learned about performing in front of an audience.

Do You Offer a Course for Americans?

We occasionally take Americans and other overseas students into our three-year course, but very few. We have a separate one-year overseas course that is very much a part of the tradition at LAMDA. The one-year course was founded in 1956 at the request of the Fulbright Commission in order to assist American actors in getting training in the classics, and Shakespeare in particular. At that time there was very little available in North America. Today there is a great demand for the study of classics and we offer North Americans a very concentrated course in

Shakespeare, Restoration, and the Russians, together with class work in stage combat, singing, period movement, and voice. Within a year they get quite a thrilling look at the classics in a sequence that they find very helpful. Most of these students feel that it is still difficult to get this training in the U.S. except in one or two schools that are very difficult to get into.

What Differences Have You Found Between British and American Students?

Americans generally want to perform *all* the time, to do productions. When they come to LAMDA I try to make it clear to them that this one year is about learning, about exploring what they find difficult to do or have been unable to do before—but without having to perform in public. At first this is strange for some American students, but when they realize that they can relax and explore without the pressure of public performance, they are able to gain a great deal from the course. Of course, there are public performances at the end of the year, which they relish, but if they had to perform every night, their progress would be slower and they wouldn't be able to experiment.

What I have always admired about American actors, and what they give their British classmates, is their tremendous energy and commitment, and a determination to use every hour to its best advantage. And that, of course, is very healthy in any drama school.

What Do You Foresee for the Future of Training at LAMDA?

I would like to extend the training period to four years so that I could include a greater range of plays, like Greek drama, for example. There is no doubt that doing Greek drama is one of the best ways to free up the voice. Also, given the state of general education today we have more to teach incoming students about the theater and the wide range of drama as well as the theater's social history. And we could use another year to do this. I'm not alone in thinking this. Within the profession there is quite a strong feeling that we could extend the training period.

The other thing I would like to see changed (which hasn't strictly to do with training) has to do with the actor's right to work. After they have trained at an accredited school, actors should be able to have their Equity card without more ado. Acting is the only profession in this country where people undertake a very difficult training and are then prevented for as long as possible by their colleagues and their union from entering the work sphere. I think this is unjustified. There is better news on this point lately, and it seems likely this will be reformed.

Caroline Eves

Caroline Eves teaches acting and directs productions at the London Academy of Music and Dramatic Art (LAMDA). She has been an associate director of four major English theaters and has worked on a wide range of productions in repertory theaters, including Cardiff, Lincoln, and Watford. She frequently directs Shakespeare and classical plays in the U.S. and formed two touring theater companies that presented productions throughout Europe.

Ms. Eves received her training at the East 15 Acting School under Joan Littlewood and later co-ran the Theatre Workshop there when Ms. Littlewood retired. Although she works primarily on classical plays, she directed the original productions of Pam Gems's Dusa, Fish, Stas and Vi *and Micheline Wardor's* The Old Wives' Tale. *She was part of the original Women's Theatre season at the Almost Free Theatre.*

Most of my work at LAMDA is teaching acting and that means doing workshop productions as well as classes. I usually teach improvisation classes during the first year because I get annoyed if I do a production with students and they can't improvise properly. During the first year I teach students how to research a play so that when we work on productions in the second and third year, everybody knows how to do that as well.

During the first year we do specific exercises rather than setting students straight into a play. The very first exercise I will have them do is an improvisation. I tell them, "You have all just left home and have come to a park. There are the gates. Relate to each other." That's all I give them. And they all come in acting their socks off because it's the first or second day of class and, of course, they want to impress. Then I say, "Anyone who doesn't know specifically where they came from and how they got here, please go back and arrive again. If anyone doesn't know precisely where in the park they are sitting, leave the class and arrive again and decide where you are going to sit." Basically, I ask the students to go through the five senses and answer the questions who, what, where, why, and how. I always quote Kipling: "I keep six honest serving men who teach me all I know. Their names are what and why and when and how and where and who." I try to make them understand that they have to answer those questions every time they get up to work.

Eventually I ask students to find a reason why they might need to speak to someone in the park. At first they will usually create a dramatic confrontation, but then they will learn simpler things such as, I am late for my appointment and haven't got a watch, and they will ask someone for the time.

Another group improvisation is what I call the "bus incident." I ask them to create reasons for an incident. They are allowed to discuss how, what, and where because they will have done the park exercise by now, but I don't want them to decide what will happen in this improvisation. I use these improvisations so that they will learn how to give and take from each other based on what happens spontaneously. Sometimes they come up with simple things, like losing a contact lens and trying to find it, and sometimes they place these bus stops in the most outlandish places. Once a group of students created a bus stop outside of Auschwitz. They were all leaving the concentration camp and the Führer himself came down and murdered about half of them. It's at these times that I point out that most often a bus stop is a place where people just wait for a bus and get on it when it arrives.

What Kinds of Incidents Are You Looking For?

It could be anything so long as it's logical, coherent, and motivated. That's the major point of this exercise. I will also give improvisations, such as an engaged couple meet both sets of parents and go to a restaurant. There is the waiter, the wine waiter, and the head waitress. All I am interested in is, Do the actors order the meal? Do they perform the proper greetings? Do they eat? Do they do all the normal things? Later on students do improvisations that involve more dramatic events, such as fighting authority. I ask them to give me an example of a severe injustice they might have experienced, perhaps at their school, and we then create an improvisation based on that. Or I might ask them to think of a time when they were very sad, or of something that made them cry. We will talk about these and then put them into improvisations so that the situations are based on real feelings. I don't want students to become self-indulgent, however, so I wouldn't do this kind of work beyond the first year. They have to learn the mechanics of how to do it and the techniques with which they can draw out their emotions. That's important.

I might well use improvisations in working on a play, not for the sake of improvising around a play, but to clarify the content. I trained at the East 15 School and the whole of our first year was improvisation. That was a very good background, but I have developed it in my own way. At East 15 it was about content. Now I am very interested in form, but I am not sure how much students can learn about form in a drama school or whether one should just concentrate on content. You really need more than three years to practice it all.

What Do You Mean by Form?

Form is the technical shape of things, the style that is demanded by a particular period. It involves the ability to use your voice and body in ways that are appropriate to the lives you are playing, to the period and place in which the play is set. Here's where the research comes in. Understanding the different perceptions of people in different periods is taught in the second year. I love working on form and style and I am a great one for never deviating from what the authors have written because they are the lifeblood of the theater. We couldn't do anything without them and our job is to interpret what they have created. Form is about serving the play and how to do that with your voice and body. Content refers to the emotional quality of a scene. A scene about a tea party is not just about having tea, but perhaps about who is the superior one in a battle of wills. Content is the human event that is taking place.

When we work on a play I teach students to divide it into units. Most people do this now, but I am very strict about it. I ask students to divide the play into small sections of action and label what each one is about. It might be that having tea is the action, but the characters are discussing a potential murder victim, let's say. I ask each character to find out what he or she is really doing in each section.

Is a Unit Defined by an Objective?

A unit is coupled into its own objective, but the action of the unit, its beginning and end, define its limits. Say in a scene someone comes in the door with a telegram that announces that my mother has died, and I burst into tears and the person leaves. The scene needs to be divided into small units. My overall objective might be: don't upset me too much with this impending information because I can see that you have bad news. Within the little units the sequence might be: who is this person?; give me the envelope; don't see that I am upset as I am reading it;

leave immediately, please, because I don't want to break down in front of you—or please don't leave, I want you here. Although the units sound very strict, how the actor interprets them is still a very free process. The units make the scene very clear for the actor. But I don't think you can go on doing this forever. One can get too tied up in these sorts of exercises and once actors have left drama school they may have to work in different ways with different directors. With older actors I might not mention the word *unit*. They may not want to stand around and do tableaux to demonstrate the name of the unit, or they might find it great fun. I've just directed a production of *Top Girls* by Caryl Churchill at Cardiff Repertory and we broke down the first scene into units to get it very clear. This group of professional actors enjoyed doing tableaux and wanted to rehearse the rest of the play that way.

What Do You Mean by "Tableaux"?

It's like a frozen Victorian photograph that clearly demonstrates the title of a unit. For instance, we broke down the first scene into seventeen units. We labeled the first unit "the arrival" and I asked the actors to get into any pose that came into their heads that would demonstrate that unit title. The second unit was "Marlene garrulously dominates the table," and so on. My objective is to see if the tableaux they come up with reflect the title. That's merely an exercise, but third-year students also seem to like doing it and I like it because it sets the skeleton or framework of the play in the actors' heads. Then, of course, we have got to flesh it all out. But I always tell actors, if you forget your lines, ask yourself which unit it is—ah, yes, unit five: Marlene garrulously dominates the table—and you will know exactly what to say.

How Do You Help Students Who Have Difficulty Expressing Emotion?

One has got to look at the root cause of why something isn't being expressed. Often a student has an idea of what he or she is experiencing and it stops in his or her head. I always say, "You may have lovely thoughts in your head, but your body and voice have to tell us what they are." If they say, "Oh, I just can't do it," I often say, "Sorry, I've paid twenty-five pounds for this ticket. You've just got to." I do think one needs to hear that occasionally. One can't be overly self-indulgent. However, a student may never have experienced that particular emotion and then it is the teacher's job to find a way to get it out of that person. But we are not psychoanalysts, we don't do therapy. When I think of some of the work one did in the seventies, I wouldn't touch it now with a barge pole. It was most intrusive on people and I don't like that. If an actor really can't let himself be vulnerable, if he hasn't a clue about what that emotional experience is, he can never play it. I don't mean that I want to see students wallow in the feeling or become upset and get traumatized, but we have got to find a lever to help them experience that emotion. It may be that they can use an emotional memory, it may be that you give them ideas.

CAROLINE EVES

If Students Are Working on the Balcony Scene from Romeo and Juliet, *for Example, and You Don't See* Juliet Expressing Love, How Would You Help the Actress?

If I knew that she understood the essential elements— that Juliet has just fallen in love, that it's very dangerous because the nurse is in the room, that she has been up very late at her first party, that the man she fancies is a family enemy and forbidden fruit—if I knew that the actress understood all those things I would say, "Have confidence and go a lot further because it's all too small." I might say, "You are doing it as a miniature artist or in watercolor and I want poster paints." Or, "Give me an oil painting." These things may sound silly outside of the classroom, but they can help. I might even have to help her use her body to express feeling. Gesture is so significant on stage. The English are not very touchy people and we are also very nonverbal. We have to be shown how words and gestures can help. I might also tell the actors to swap roles and say to the actress, "Now you see what Romeo needs to receive." Or I might tell another student, "Go do it like the actress playing Juliet is doing it, and you, Juliet, sit here and watch. Now, what do you think that performance needs?" So if I felt that the performance was real and the actress understood what was going on, that's probably what I would do to make her more expressive.

How Would You Help a Student Make It Real?

Let's say that Juliet was behaving as though Romeo were a wet load of porridge. You have to say quite bluntly, "What's just happened to this girl? She has a sexual feeling for the first time. Can you remember when you had one?" I don't ask the actress to describe it, that's not important. I say, "Just think how you felt, where you felt it, and what you would do. Hasn't anyone ever arrived at your garden gate and because your parents were upstairs, you weren't allowed to speak to him? How did you feel?"

Do You Use Terms Like Objective and Obstacles?

Yes. I often say that an objective is like sailing from *a* to *b*. You want to go in a straight line, but because of winds and tides, you tack and change course. I do a little exercise to help students understand this. I write two different objectives on pieces of paper and ask each student to pick one. Then I ask them to create an improvisation based on two objectives—which can be in conflict. I always ask students to think of their objective in the imperative form because it's more immediate. For example, an objective might be, "Give me some money," not, "I want you to give me some money." Another might be, "Shut up because you talk too much." When they do their improvisation the class has to guess what their objectives are. If the class can't, I tell the actors to repeat the improvisation in its crudest or most basic form. It's amazing how often actors think they are playing an objective and, in fact, nobody can tell what it is they want. Then I will ask them to play their objective in its most subtle form or to play the exact opposite of their objective to see what will happen. And I might ask them to try six or seven different ways. This exercise demonstrates that an objective is not just something to be played like a battering ram. It can be played with subtlety in many different ways.

What Is Your Approach to Text?

Although I am not the only one who teaches Shakespeare at LAMDA, I work on it a lot. My class is geared toward teaching students how to lift the words off the page and how to understand any play they are working on. Learning the implications of the language of any play comes from research, and learning how the language affects your behavior comes from understanding the style of the writing. Often actors think they can paraphrase the dialogue in modern plays, but it doesn't work because contemporary playwrights, for example, Edward Bond and Caryl Churchill, have very strong styles. So it's important that students learn to read dialogue properly and understand how their characters are revealed through the dialogue.

How Do You Work on Shakespeare?

I like students to get a chance to work on meaty scenes from Shakespeare. They might each get the Romeo and Juliet balcony scene or Coriolanus turning away his mother or Richard III and Queen Anne. I also give them another scene where they are a listener so they can learn how to do that. We will spend a lot of time breaking down the text into units and overall objectives, but I also ask students to write down the text in contemporary English and then let them work on their scene using their own words. But they have to translate all the words, including the allegorical references, the allusions, and the word plays that we no longer use today. Often students just leave those out and end up not knowing what they are saying. I make them say exactly what those now obscure references mean so that every phrase is clear and understood. Then they can do it in their own words before going on to the text. I think it's very important to do that.

Do You Teach Students to Scan?

Yes. I make sure they have scanned it all. I will not let students break the rhythm of the meter. I make sure they know what an enjambment or whatever is and understand what it means. Shakespeare tells the actor how to feel through his use of grammar. You might have a speech that contains five question marks and four exclamation marks followed by five lines that are one uninterrupted sentence. If you do it as written, it will produce a specific feeling in you.

I am also very strict on the rhythm of the whole scene. Shakespeare doesn't write pauses at the end of speeches, but actors often put pauses there. I don't agree with that. As in real life, you listen, you hear, you assimilate, you think, and you respond. After all, we usually only need to hear two-thirds of a sentence before we know the rest. I don't normally let actors put in pauses between speeches—which a lot of them tend to do. If you break up the speeches in the wrong place, you lose the rhythm of the scene.

Text research is so important. For instance, once you understand what society was like under Cromwell's Republic you can understand why Restoration plays were filled with adultery and swear words. Under the Republic those were crimes that earned you the death penalty and the Restoration period was a reaction against the repressive policies of the Republic. When theater was restored during the Restoration period, every play was filled with them. Text research is so vital for the practicing actor because it tells the actor how to play the text.

How Would Text Research Help the Actor Develop a Character?

First of all, it's important that all the basic rules about being real and logical still apply when you do Shakespeare or any of the classics. People tend to forget that. The style comes out of how people felt. Juliet, for example, is a Roman Catholic as portrayed by Shakespeare. That would dictate how she should be played. Everything she does is dangerous and illegal by the Church standards of the time. That implies that everything she does is terrifying to her. When Romeo says he wants to kill himself, the Friar asks him, "Are you an animal or a man?" During Elizabethan times it was a big insult to be looked upon as a beast of the field because it implied you had no soul. Also, it is basic to Roman Catholic theology that you

237

never take the life that God gave you. Consequently, the Friar should be very passionate or fervent in his attempt to dissuade Romeo. We forget that today. Later, when Juliet is found dead on her wedding morning and everyone is weeping and wailing, the Friar, who is also filled with guilt, says, look, she has gone to a better place. She has gone to God. Why are you weeping? Today, as parents, we might find that difficult to accept and a minister probably wouldn't put it that way. But we can't play that scene with our contemporary beliefs.

The scene where Richard III coerces Lady Anne into becoming his wife is always a big dilemma for the actress playing the part. You have to point out that Lady Anne has no alternative: her father is dead and her father-in-law and husband have been killed by this man. There is no one left to protect her. If she wants to live she must marry him. It's important to understand these things.

In *Top Girls* a courtesan comes to the dinner party that is in progress and asks Pope Joan why she didn't get rid of her child when she was pregnant. The courtesan explains how her children were all taken away from her right after their birth. A woman today would play that scene with a great deal of anger, but the courtesan understands the social mores of her time and knows that if she is to remain with the Emperor in the imperial court, that is exactly what must happen. Research is indispensable in helping an actor understand what his character is experiencing and why.

At the end of the first year we have a project in which students are given three weeks to create a play through research and improvisations on a given topic. It is a summation of their year's work. For a play on the war in the

Falklands students did the following: they did all the research using primary and secondary sources; they learned how to use Reuter's news service: how to find people who were involved in the conflict; and they interviewed people connected with the event. Everyone picked one area of research. Some researched how one becomes a British private; some interviewed RAF officers. One girl found the Portsmouth wives who had been left behind during the war. Someone else got to know a nurse involved in the conflict. Students also interviewed Ministers of Parliament. We also did a lot of factual research from books about military training. We used as much documentary information about the war as possible.

Then we broke the students into six family groups. They chose who they were and what happened to them. Obviously, different events occurred in each group, such as birthdays being celebrated, soldiers leaving for the Falklands, some coming back, some not. The play they created was structured by family groups so that students understood all the different emotions involved. We also included an Argentinean family. We followed these people throughout the course of the war and explored how they felt about it—then how the actors felt about what had happened.

All that was put together into a play that followed the history of the Falklands and highlighted the ongoing issues and controversies. The play emerged from improvisations that were set down and performed. We saw the historical events through the lives of the six fictitious families, following what happened to them, their fortunes and misfortunes, their joys and sorrows. It's very hard work. It's also the first time that students learn that they must have an attitude toward their work, that they need to have a point of view. They might not agree with something they have to play, but they learn that it is necessary to play it with conviction anyway. And this is very helpful in fringe companies or Theatre in Education companies where they may well have to devise plays based on historical or contemporary events. There are so many different types of theater forms as well as film and television work in which the actor may be employed that the students must be able to deal with it all.

Helena
Kaut-Howson

Helena Kaut-Howson is a staff director and acting teacher at the London Academy of Music and Dramatic Art (LAMDA). In addition to the many plays she has directed at LAMDA, Ms. Kaut-Howson has also presented productions at the Greenwich Theatre, Leeds Playhouse, and Haymarket Theatre. Her productions span a wide range of theater styles and periods, from Tennessee Williams's Vieux Carré, *to her own translation of* The Werewolves *by Lubkiewicz, to an adaptation of Dostoyevsky's* The Possessed.*

Born and educated in Poland, Ms. Kaut-Howson is a graduate of the Polish State Theatre School. She has been a resident of the United Kingdom since 1965 but continues to direct and teach internationally. She is a frequent director for the Habimah National Theatre and the Cameri Theatre in Israel, as well as the Centaur Theatre in Montreal and the National Theatre School of Canada.

Our approach to acting is organically connected to the development of the theater; that is, acting training is inseparable from the state of the theater. You cannot just say that acting affects the shape of the theater, or the shape of the theater affects acting. They mutually affect each other. In the sixties and seventies there was a different type of theater we were working for; therefore, there were different training approaches that entered the bloodstream of teaching. We were experimenting with nonlinear plays and the emphasis was on group work. We did not use Stanislavsky's method, but rather the techniques of Peter Brook, Grotowski, Joe Chaikin, and The Living Theatre. I've abandoned many of the Grotowski exercises I used in the sixties that focused on communing with the other actors, resonating different parts of the body, etc., because our theater no longer calls for that. The sixties were an explosive reaction against the boring bourgeois theater of the time and theater became almost a religious experience. But that kind of theater no longer exists—even in Poland. We have to train students for what we perceive to be the immediate future of theater.

Today the existing theater has become more uniform. Actors have to be trained to be comprehensively employable. There are no longer strong distinguishable trends. The fringe theater is not so vastly different from the commercial West End. You can see Lorca's *The House of Bernarda Alba* in the commercial sector and you can see a commercial play at the National and even on the fringe. So actors have to be accomplished in all styles.

For instance, there is a changing attitude toward Shakespeare. Today the focus is on how to make his plays relevant. This is probably a reaction against the academic interpretation of Shakespeare during the seventies. So theater keeps fluctuating, doesn't it? We also have the Royal Court Theatre, which is committed to developing socially conscious and politically committed actors. Their productions are in the tradition of Brecht and their goal is to make the audience aware of contemporary social realities. The Royal Court playwrights and directors do not want the actor to "spill his guts" for the audience. They believe that all the actor's character choices should have a social foundation because a character's behavior is socially and culturally determined. In fact, Brecht's theory is the complete opposite of Stanislavsky's. It is alienation as opposed to empathy—a social comment as opposed to emotional identification. It's not a school of acting, but an approach committed to the idea that theater has a certain role in society. We in drama schools have got to take this into account and expose our students to Brecht as well as Stanislavsky.

As teachers and directors we are continually developing and looking for new ways of making students aware of the state of the theater. We are not simply being eclectic, nor do we simply reject a doctrine on principle; it simply depends on what we feel may best respond to the demands of the times. I'm sure that every teacher has his own particular method that derives from his individual background, experience, and vision of the theater.

How Do You Approach Shakespeare?

When LAMDA gives a Shakespeare summer workshop the emphasis is on the verse. Teachers try to make the students aware that the verse carries the emotion, that the length of the phrase and the pauses and beats carry exactly the measure of the emotions. We emphasize that if students look carefully, without closing off their feelings, they will find the right emotion because it's a bit like following a music score. A phrase has a certain number of beats or stresses, and if there are some missing, it's for a purpose.

When I work with professionals or third-year students in a production, my emphasis is different because my awareness of language is somewhat different. It's a cultural thing. My background is Eastern European, and I think of Shakespeare as a universal writer. My focus on language is not just on its shape but on what it communicates. Like my compatriot Jan Kott, I believe that Shakespeare continues to be our contemporary.

I recently directed *All's Well That Ends Well* with professional actors, and without losing sight of the fact that it is verse and has to be recognizably verse, and without breaking the poetics of the piece, we arrived at the strands of the play, the relationships, through quite a lot of improvisation. One could have approached the play with a much stronger emphasis on the text, but I was looking at the play as something modern, not a period piece. I looked at the language as an extension of the characters' social and cultural background rather than as an aesthetic entity. What I mean is that in my work on Shakespeare the emphasis is not only on the language. There is a lot of emphasis on action.

For instance, we found that the central theme of *All's Well* could be seen as a piece of manipulation by two of the characters. So I asked the actors playing these two characters to improvise and to act like conductors, to manipulate the other characters in the play, to whisper to them, guide them—like devils whispering into their ears and dictating to them what to do, where to go, and what choices to make. You can view the other characters as being prodded to take action by some force sitting on their shoulder. This play is about making moral choices. The whole play could be looked at in this condensed way and improvised along those lines. And that's what the actors actually did. We found that each time an actor got bogged down by the language, he could go back to the actions he discovered in the improvisations and overcome his block. You find a lot of threads like that in Shakespeare, of characters who are not in control of their own impulses, who act as if they were under a magic spell. *All's Well* is a bit like that.

When You Direct Students, How Do You Advise Them to Work on a Play?

I start by asking students to research the period, to steep themselves in the material of the world that they are about to enter, whether it's a Russian play or an English play, whether it's classical or modern. The first weeks of rehearsal are usually taken up with research work. Everyone chooses a topic and then we collate it by getting together and sharing what we've learned. That's invaluable.

Do You Have Techniques to Help Students Learn to Develop a Character?

In Gorky's *The Lower Depths*, which I'm at present rehearsing with the third-year students at LAMDA for their final production, there are several minor characters who sit on stage and don't do much. One of these is a Tartar who has only five lines. I suggested to the student playing the Tartar that it might help him find a character if he observed Moslems. He did so and it contributed to creating the role: he prayed silently through much of the play.

There is another minor character in the play that we know nothing about. No background is given and the actor couldn't make an imaginative leap and develop a full portrait. One day I brought him a small picture of a peasant boy receiving his first communion. I told the actor to imagine this was a picture of his character at his first communion and had been given to him by his grandmother. And from this picture the actor was able to build a whole biography of his character and a whole scenario that was not written by Gorky. As a result he could engage in activities that gave his character a life. He spent the first act being ill and homesick. Then he unpacked his bags and took out the picture and pinned it above his plank bed. Then he produced an old squeaky harmonica and played it. The character changed during the course of the play; he went from being shy and withdrawn in the first act to trying to emulate the tougher men around him in the last act. This was particularly effective because the character had only one line of text. There are so many ways to feed and stimulate an actor's imagination and our role as teachers is to guide it, not to impose dogma.

When you work with students in this way you hope it won't be strange to them if you say that for such and such a character they have to "inhabit" somebody else, not just use themselves. If they have an artist's imagination, then they don't just copy, they actually inhabit. So a student might find a neighborhood tramp, for instance, and get to know him and study his movement patterns. One of the actors who plays a tramp in *The Lower Depths* did this kind of work when he was developing his character. I find that this approach to training is more useful given the state of contemporary theater.

If an actor has got an inclination to speak and move in a particular way, and if the character he is playing is expected to speak and move in a different way, we try to get the actor to extend himself toward the character, not to adapt the character to himself. I think that's one of the chief differences between English and American acting: the American method often focuses on the actor knowing how to embrace the experiences of the character and find them in himself, whereas the English approach includes that and also focuses on the actor extending himself toward something that is outside his immediate pattern of behavior, temperament, and rhythms of speech.

At LAMDA we do an animal exercise that is helpful for this. It helps the actor discover that his body, his spirit, can live in a body that moves very differently from his own, and has different vocal habits from his own. It's a wonderful sight seeing actors do this. At the end of the first term, students go to a large room that has been divided into cubicles that look like cages. Each student becomes the particular animal they have worked on and eats what that animal would eat. Students spend the entire morning, about four hours, being the animal. We have an audience that just mills about from cubicle to cubicle. Sometimes nobody comes in, but the students still remain in character. We video this "performance" and students get a chance to see it.

What Was Your Own Training?

I trained first as an actress at the Warsaw Theatre School. The main approach was Stanislavsky except we were not encouraged to be too emotional because it was considered an indulgence. A more intellectual approach was encouraged. A bit later, when I trained as a director, Grotowski's work was emerging and we also became aware of Peter Brook's experiments in the Theatre of Cruelty.

As a director I think that it is useful to know what it feels like to act. Very often teachers or directors, and even voice teachers, don't know what it feels like. Some things that seem easy to do are not so simple from the inside. It is a mysterious and complex process and we can only guide actors and inquire how it feels rather than tell them dogmatically what they *should* feel. What I hope for before each production is not to complicate and confuse actors, and not to block their creativity. I just want to step in when I can be useful.

John Waller

John Waller is Combat Master at the London Academy of Music and Dramatic Art (LAMDA), the Guildhall School of Music and Drama, the Arts Educational School, the Drama Studio, and the British and European Studies Group. He is a member of the British Society of Fight Directors. Mr. Waller's stage work includes choreographing sword fights and stage combat at the Royal Court Theatre, Regent's Park Theatre, and the Glyndebourne Festival Opera.

Mr. Waller is also an expert horseman, archer, and falconer and has worked on many films, including Monty Python and the Holy Grail, Anne of the Thousand Days, and The French Lieutenant's Woman. His television work spans a wide range of projects from TV movies and BBC series, such as Dr. Who and Bleak House, to commercials and documentaries on archery and weapons.

Mr. Waller has had a lifelong interest in ancient

weapons and medieval customs and is a frequent consultant on historical film projects.

The course I teach is called Stage Combat, but the same techniques are used in film and television as well as on stage. What I try to do is choreograph a sword fight to look as it would have in the period in which the play takes place. If a play is set in the nineteenth century, for example, I will base the fight scenes on how people fought at that time.

If you were producing *Romeo and Juliet* and you wanted it set in sixteenth-century Italy, you would expect your choreographer to choreograph a pavane or a galliard for the dance scenes; you'd want your lighting designer to create the effect of candlelight instead of oil lamps, and you'd expect the set design and costumes to be of that period as well. Why shouldn't you expect the fight director to create the combat scenes using all the shapes of that period, which are, in my opinion, more beautiful than any contrived modern theatrical shapes. If you changed the setting of the play to nineteenth-century England, then I would choreograph a nineteenth-century fight. Of course, I take certain liberties. It is not always possible to be a purist, but it is something to strive for.

How Has the Approach to Stage Combat Changed?

Most contemporary fight directors choreograph combat scenes using modern fencing techniques, regardless of the period the play is set in. Originally, English actors just learned contemporary fencing with masks. Then Bill

Hobbs, who was instrumental in upgrading the idea of stage fight, turned it into a balletic form of swordplay while using some period shapes. But I believe his emphasis is more on movement than authentic shapes. In drama schools today there are two schools of thought. Some schools teach this form of balletic swordplay, but in the twelve schools where I and my colleagues teach, students are taught through my historic "shapes" approach.

Sword fighting is not what you see in Hollywood movies, which do not use period fighting styles. What we do is teach the actor how to move like a swordsman of a specific period as much as possible. Then I incorporate certain techniques to develop the actor's stage awareness. I don't just teach Elizabethan or Georgian sword fighting. I teach actors certain moves that denote the style of the period in which the play takes place. In addition, students learn how to maintain eye contact, how to develop their peripheral vision, their sense of balance, and sense of center—all of which makes the fight appear motivated and authentic. I teach the student to move in ways that are, according to my research, Elizabethan or Georgian, etc., and these moves lend a certain authentic shape to the fight.

Could You Give Me an Example of the Difference Between the Elizabethan Shape and Some Other Period?

In the Elizabethan period, swords were much longer and heavier than they are in modern fencing, as a visit to any museum will show. Therefore, if I impose a modern fencing stance on an actor using Elizabethan weapons, it changes his sense of center and sense of balance, and alters the intention he will convey to an audience. Modern swords are lighter and enable the actor to stand much more square on and use more arm movements. An eighteenth-century or Georgian swordsman is more like the modern fencer except that he still had vestiges of movement left over from earlier times. People today are preoccupied with Eastern martial arts because they find them so graceful. In my opinion Elizabethan sword fighting is just as graceful because, given the size and shape of the weapons, these movements are the most efficient ways to defend yourself. There are no extraneous movements and its simplicity gives it a pure and elegant form.

How people fought also depended on the clothes they wore, whether it was armor or Georgian cuffs, and particularly the kind of boots worn during the period. For instance, during Louis XIV's reign, people in his court walked with big bucket boots. They either had to walk bow-legged like a cowboy, or pass their legs round each other—which is how they danced; hence one of the ballet steps was developed. If the boots can affect the way you dance, and the way you carry a sword can affect the way you bow, then those things can affect the way you sword fight.

How Is Your Class Structured?

Our basic teaching starts from students learning how to maintain eye contact. There isn't a martial art that doesn't work from the eyes. Then we teach the actor how to hit a mark on the floor while maintaining eye contact with his partner, and this helps to develop his peripheral vision. The better you get at looking at your opponent's eyes, the better your peripheral vision becomes. This, of course, helps the actor become more sensitive to what is surrounding him on stage.

We start off with a basic choreographed cutting sword routine based on a series of attacks and defenses. The routine is designed to start the students moving together and they learn how to stretch their balance—that is, maintain balance while they lunge. Having mastered a sword fight in a basic style that is suitable for any weapon from a Viking sword to a U.S. Cavalry saber—that is, cuts and defenses with a long cutting weapon—we then add a dagger in the other hand. Then students repeat the basic routine but incorporate a dagger. Now they have to use both hands.

After the simple sword and dagger work we teach a different set of moves that incorporates thrusts and cuts.

As we go along we teach stage awareness, how to make the thrusts safe, whether they should be upstage or downstage, and how to move the body, all the while increasing the student's awareness of his center. But it all stems from the very first lesson of looking into each other's eyes and not at the weapons.

Having accomplished a sword routine with Elizabethan sword and dagger, we then teach students how to disarm each other and add this to the fight routine. So they start with a simple sword and dagger fight, then one disarms the other of his dagger and ends up with two weapons against one. Then the other student is disarmed of his dagger and they go back to the basic routine they learned with just swords.

Up till now students have been using large swords, which require what we call "in-distance" fighting. In-distance means that I always thrust *past* your belly, not at you, while you step back or to the side as you naturally would if we were really fighting and the sword were coming at you. The audience doesn't see that the sword actually went *past* you. They see you withdraw and it looks to them as if I would have stabbed or cut you if you hadn't moved. The illusion of reality is created by your *reaction*, not just by my thrust.

The next step is to teach eighteenth-century small sword fighting, which requires a completely different technique. These weapons are smaller and lighter and are more like modern fencing swords. Now we teach "out-of-distance" fighting, which means that instead of thrusting past your body, the swords are thrust toward the body, but never come closer than eighteen inches. In-distance technique also creates the illusion that the sword would go through the body. Out-of-distance technique creates the illusion that the small sword thrust, which is always made toward the torso, is stopped by the opponent's sword. I teach both in- and out-distance techniques, whereas the traditional approach to sword fighting has emphasized the latter.

Next we teach unarmed combat. Students learn how to roll, swing a punch, and take a slap, etc., without contact by the actors. For example, the noises of the slap can be made either by the deliverer or the receiver. We teach students how to safely throw someone over a table, like they do in cowboy movies. Even if an actor is never called upon to do this, being able to fling someone over a table builds confidence and gives a student the physical courage to try other things.

What we are also trying to teach is a philosophical attitude, not just a technique. We teach theatricality based on reality. By that I mean that the actor should give the audience the impression that he is really trying to kill his opponent, and the opponent should respond as if his life were really in danger. One should always react truthfully. In this way the illusion of reality is created. Since the actor is moving realistically, we believe you don't necessarily have to add theatrical flourishes. It's truth first: move like a swordsman or deliver a punch as you would in reality. The tricks are how you hide it from the audience.

I work with two associates, Rodney Cottier and Mike Loades. Together we teach stage combat at twelve drama schools. Of course, the three of us have slightly different styles, but we all believe in the same basic philosophy.

Most of our students study stage combat for the first two years of their three-year course. At the end of the first year's training, students take an exam that is set by the Society of British Fight Directors. If they can perform a fight scene that includes a rapier/dagger fight, a small sword fight, and an unarmed combat sequence all at performance pitch, they receive a certificate. They can then choose to train an additional year to develop their skills with different weapons and learn how to choreograph themselves. LAMDA also has a one-year course for overseas students that includes an intensive course in stage combat, and they take the same exam as well.

At LAMDA we have also started to teach students archery and horseback riding. The training is for theatrical purposes. It helps them overcome any fear they might have and teaches them the different styles of riding. It also helps them learn how to deliver lines on horseback, which they might be asked to do in film.

Although all stage combat is choreographed, there is a certain spontaneity at the end of training when good students can create their own moves, when they know how a sequence should progress logically. It is very exciting when students can do this. They are young and are not yet locked into patterns. My work is then fed and enlarged by watching them create their own moves. I am constantly learning from them.

How Do You Work with Actors in a Production?

How I choreograph a fight will be based on the director's interpretation of the characters. I use my knowledge of the period and weapons and build around what the director wants. My only preconceived ideas are of the shape of the period and how the weapons were used. Then I ask the actor how he sees his character and build around that. The fighting style must reflect the character's behavior and motivation, as well as each particular actor's body. I also try to help the actor understand why one particular thrust or blow is stronger or more appropriate than another. For example, the reason Mercutio challenges Tybalt is that he feels ashamed because Romeo won't respond to Tybalt's provocations; he challenges Tybalt in order to get rid of this shame. So it's probably not an all-out aggressive challenge, but rather more of a defiant one. Therefore, in the fight Mercutio might not move in too closely or aggressively on Tybalt. He might approach it more as a contest than a blood feud.

When I work with actors I first ask them to read the scene for me and from that I can tell how they view their character. Then I ask them to try certain moves and incorporate what they think they should be doing with my understanding of the weapons and the period.

How Do You Incorporate Acting Techniques into Your Stage Combat Course?

It's a question of motivation. When a student is learning a routine for the first time, I ask him to think of why his opponent might make a specific move. Have you overextended? Has your opponent seen an opening? Is he trying to kill you? When he tries to kill you are you expecting it or are you caught unawares? Perhaps you have been caught because your aggression carried you too far or made you back off a bit more than you should have. Those are simple instinctive reactions that are often missing in worked-out routines because the actors have come to believe their fighting is safe. And it's never safe—even when it's choreographed. They must never believe it is safe because then it's not real. You must always jump back as if someone were trying to cut you in half. The audience's belief hinges on your *reaction*.

Recently a student mentioned that he had seen a particular production that had some very elaborate sword fights. I asked him if he believed the actors were trying to kill each other. He thought for a moment and said, "It was very clever, but no, I didn't." That's the complete opposite of what we teach.

The Royal Academy of Dramatic Art

Founded in 1904 by Sir Herbert Beerbohm Tree, the Royal Academy of Dramatic Art (RADA) has provided continuous and comprehensive training for the professional theater ever since. The Academy's curriculum was originally based on a study of the classical repertoire combined with intensive work in voice, movement, and text analysis. In recent years, under the principalship of Dr. Oliver Neville, the school has added contemporary European and American techniques that emphasize an organic approach to actor training.

Shortly after its foundation the Academy was established in its present site in Gower Street. The school has two fully equipped theaters, the VanBrugh and the George Bernard Shaw, and a small studio theater, which enables students to perform in open stage and in-the-round productions.

RADA offers a three-year Acting Course, a two-year Stage Management Course, and a Specialist Diploma Course in Scene Design, Stage Carpentry, Stage Electrics, or Property Making. Intensive Drama Workshops are offered in the summer.

Oliver Neville

Oliver Neville is Principal of the Royal Academy of Dramatic Art (RADA). He studied stage design, singing, and clarinet before taking up a career as an actor in 1951. His first professional performance was in Sir Tyrone Guthrie's Tamburlaine *at the Old Vic with Sir Donald Wolfit. He then worked for ten years as an actor and appeared in productions at the Birmingham Repertory, the Manchester Library Theatre, and the Old Vic, where he played Claudius in* Hamlet *as well as other leading Shakespearean roles.*

Dr. Neville turned to directing and founded his own company at the Manchester Library Theatre. He also became an Associate Director of the Old Vic, where he directed The Tempest *and* Macbeth. *At the age of thirty-nine he decided to accept the offer of a place at Kings College, Cambridge, to read English and was awarded the Le Bas Research Studentship to complete his Ph.D. on Ben Jonson. He taught at London University and was*

The Royal Academy of Dramatic Art

Senior Lecturer at Bristol University Drama Department before taking up his post at RADA in 1984.

During their time at RADA students encounter every possible kind of world drama at all levels, from the Greeks to what's on at the Royal Court Upstairs tonight, and the latest fashion in soaps. Any student here during the last three years will either have worked on or seen the work of other students in Sophocles, Euripides, Shakespeare, Jonson, Farquar, Middleton, Shaw, D. H. Lawrence, Pirandello, Sartre, Chekhov, Gogol, Molière, Ibsen, Strindberg, Orwell, and an equally eclectic list of contemporary writers, all in fully mounted productions. They not only work on established scripts but also create new texts based on literature from all over the world. Recently, we had projects based on Balzac's *Cousin Bette*, Pushkin's poems and stories, the Victorian Gothic novel, and Arthurian legend. Creating these texts is very demanding. They are group projects for students in their fifth term. They require the ability to create a dramatic scenario through the creation of characters that are appropriate to the text and communicated with clarity and theatrical force to an audience. Because the source material is vast, complex, and not written as dramatic literature, these projects require intelligence, a sense of dramatic shape, aesthetic judgment, physical and vocal skills, and the knowledge of how to research into the historical, geographical, and social background of the material. Each group member works toward contributing his individual skills unselfishly and enthusiastically to the piece as a whole. These projects are an important part of our training here.

OLIVER NEVILLE

How Do You Approach Shakespeare?

I am often told by American students who audition for me that what they think we can teach them is "classical technique." There is a great misconception students have, not only Americans, that one can somehow clip on "classical technique" to an actor's natural imaginative process. Instead what we try to do—successfully, I think—is to go back to the students' own cultural roots and approach Shakespeare's texts from there, while giving intensive classes in the study of verse, voice, and movement related to Elizabethan and Jacobean theater.

American students typically fall into one of two traps when they approach Shakespeare. Sometimes they impose superficial contemporary values onto the text, values that reflect popular culture today, but which, it seems to me, often fail to grasp what is universal in human behavior. On the other hand, they often try, as I have already mentioned, to clip on external physical and vocal patterns of sound and movement that make their performances artificial, inhuman, and mannered. They think of this as technique.

One should not strive for technique at the expense of meaning. Technique, as nearly as I can define it, is the ability to combine all of the acting skills into a harmoniously appropriate interpretation of the text (or of the action in nonverbal theater). Technique should be undetectable. As soon as someone tells you, "I admire your technique," you can be certain you've got it wrong. I fear that what people mean by technique is the visible and audible display of an actor's external skills enjoyed for *themselves* by the performer. He is acting "Acting." It is anathema to me!

However, when we are talking about speaking verse, there are guidelines and basic rules that should be known—though some actors have a natural instinct for it. Attention to syntax and the formal values of verse will allow a playwright's intentions to emerge fully. Verse cannot be treated as prose. Naturalism is certainly not enough—not for me anyway. On the other hand, rules can also become a straight-jacket inhibiting the imaginative and emotional flow; then the actor must rebel against them.

Many of our American students have had training in aspects of Stanislavsky's method, sometimes to the neglect of the vocal and physical skills that Stanislavsky took for granted. Although we don't practice a "hard method" approach at RADA, the first year is spent investigating and working on basic principles derived from Stanislavsky. These principles are applied to contemporary and classical work alike. The details of this work I leave to Doreen Cannon, whose foundation work here in the first and second year is central to our program.

What Classes Do Students Take?

They spend an average of six and one half hours per week on voice, ten hours on movement, and nine hours on acting exercises in the first term, plus work in improvisation and physical skills, such as unarmed combat and falls. There are also individual lessons in the Alexander Technique and singing. Later we add armed combat, phonetics, speech, dialect, the rudiments of music, group singing, dance, the study of contemporary texts, technical crafts, and stage management skills. This gives us a very full and expansive timetable.

How Has Actor Training Changed in the Last Decade?

In the past, training at drama schools was pretty basic. Most young actors received their training by working in repertory companies, progressing from assistant stage manager positions with small parts to "juvenile" leads, as they were known then. Only very few made it into the West End or leading classical companies. Many of our most distinguished actors and actresses came through this system, and it was a very good one—many actors never went to drama school at all. The young actors worked alongside older actors. Plays at that time were mostly preoccupied with the problems and exploits of the mature citizen; in most plays the majority of the cast were over thirty years of age. So for young actors it was often quite a long apprenticeship. All that has gone. There are now few theaters to learn in, and the experienced older actor tends to stay in London, where expenses are less and opportunity hopefully greater, with television, film, radio, etc. At the same time, there is more work available in plays, films, and television for young actors. Nowadays, students are often required to play very important roles immediately after they leave drama school. The problems are obvious. With less opportunity for the majority to complete their apprenticeship "on their feet," the training at the schools has to be more complete, which means more performances in full productions. This is expensive, but unless training is completed at drama school, there is a great danger that our young actors will not be able to cover a full range of parts, and will be used once and discarded—like paper tissues.

How Are You Attempting to Compensate for the Lack of Opportunities in the Provinces?

Our course has been extended from seven to nine terms. This gives students more time for rehearsal, working with professional directors under professional conditions. We do many performances, as I've described. We also introduce students to the skills of setting up their own companies, including learning the basics of sponsorship, funding, booking, touring, box-office budgeting, and targeting an audience for the kind of work they want to do. This is proving very popular with our students, who recognize the importance of making their own work.

You know, if you had interviewed me five or six years ago my concerns would have been solely with the art and craft of acting and its teaching. That is still my primary focus, but more and more we must pay attention to the problems of sustaining and remaking an environment where acting can be taught and theater made in today's economic and social climate. We must do this without losing the inheritance of the past, and the circumstances and skills that made it so rich.

Doreen Cannon

Doreen Cannon is Head of Acting at the Royal Academy of Dramatic Art (RADA). She was born and raised in New York City and worked extensively as an actress in theater and television. She trained with Uta Hagen and Herbert Berghof at the HB Studio, where subsequently she was asked to teach classes of her own. In 1960 marriage brought her to England, where she continued her career and started her own studio for professional actors.

In 1963 Ms. Cannon was invited to create and run the acting department at Drama Centre, London, the first Method drama school in Britain. She also founded her own theater company in the West End and directed plays to provide an ensemble theater for actors who had studied with her. In addition she travels extensively throughout Sweden giving master classes and acting seminars to theater companies.

In 1985 she was invited to join the faculty of RADA.

She recently returned to New York to teach at the HB Studio during the summer.

When I was a young actress in New York I studied with Uta Hagen and Herbert Berghof as well as other teachers at HB Studios. Then I came to England and wanted to continue my workshop activities while looking for acting work, but amazingly, there were no acting workshops to be found in London. At that time Irene Dailey, who had been Uta's assistant in New York, was in a West End show and was giving classes for her cast and interested professionals. She invited me to join and to take over the teaching when the show closed and she returned to New York. I did, and since then I have had my own professional workshop.

How Did You First Start Teaching in Drama Schools?

In 1963 I was invited to teach at the Drama Centre, London, a new acting school whose emphasis was an organic approach to acting. Consequently it became the first Method drama school in England. Its success over the years is a tribute to Uta Hagen and Herbert Berghof, whose work and ideals inspired me to care about the acting process. The graduates achieved a very high standard of work as a result of three years of intensive acting training. Until that time and indeed, even now, the drama schools in England did not teach acting. The emphasis has been on voice, speech, and movement. The acting process was something that "happened" during the rehearsal period. I have now joined the faculty at RADA, a school that has a history of being traditional in its approach, but the new principal, Dr. Oliver Neville, is changing the school's orientation. Of course, there is some fear that the training will get too American or too Russian, that RADA will lose its English identity. However, this has not happened yet and it cannot—not with the completeness and unity of the training. RADA is very committed to an organic approach to acting. The students are intent on finding the inner truth of creating a character, and the productions are strengthened by the ensemble playing. We hope this approach will have a beneficial effect on British theater, and that we will see even more organic performances from a wide range of actors.

Do the British Have a Particular Acting Style?

The traditional English approach to acting has been representational—the actor represents the character but doesn't necessarily experience what the character is going through emotionally. English actors have developed an extraordinary external skill so that to an audience their portrayals appear to be a true representation of the character they are playing, and the audience is intellectually stimulated. The text has been analyzed intelligently and played well. The skill is undeniably there, but to me it remains an external performance without real depth or involvement. Of course, there are some actors who, even when they are representational in their approach, do have real feelings and create a strong emotional experience for the audience. But often acting stays external.

The other extreme is the naturalistic actor who trades

on his own personality. He turns every character into himself so that what we see is virtually the same performance in every part he plays. It can be truthful, but it's always the actor's truth. After a while these performances become predictable. I would like to think that what I teach is a way of acting in which the truth of what the actor experiences changes every time he plays a different character. It's trying to find that truth that we slavishly work for. So one could say that I train students to work from the inside out, to find their own truth first, which they then express in a heightened reality. I believe that every time an actor goes out on stage he must use his own truth, and must stretch and extend that truth so that it becomes real to him for the time and place in which the play is set. It may not be the actor's 1980s truth, but it's a truth that he takes from different parts of himself.

What Changes Have You Seen in British Training Since You Came to London?

The present economic problems have traumatized the theater community in Britain. The repertory system used to turn out very experienced actors, but when so many provincial repertory theaters closed down, everything changed. Actors used to attend drama school for three years, then go into repertory, perform for forty weeks, get their Equity card, and stay in the provinces. Even those who didn't train would work and try to learn as they acted. The tradition was to work rather than train. I think one of the reasons there have always been so many workshops in the U.S. is the lack of available work. When I first

came to London I heard actors complain when they had
been out of work for two weeks! They had not thought of
and had no need for workshops. Now, unfortunately, actors in England are unemployed for longer periods of
time. That, in my opinion, has created the need for continuing training. Workshops are springing up all over the
place and the theatrical community is more readily accepting of the idea that an actor needs to remain flexible
to keep his creativity alive.

I still think there is a deep resistance in Britain to the
teachings of Stanislavsky. There seems to be a school of
thought that equates Method with "indulgent emotions"
and the "airing of dirty linen in public," and this goes
against British reserve. Unfortunately, a lot of the resistance stems from being exposed to overindulgent actors
who misuse the work on both sides of the Atlantic. You
still find many directors who will not hire a Method
actor—and in some quarters they certainly frown on professional actors taking classes. The traditional attitude still
prevails that once you've trained and are a professional,
you needn't train again.

What Do You Teach at RADA?

What I teach is called acting technique. What I try to do is
give students a foundation, a methodical approach to acting so that they have a technique to fall back on when a part
isn't readily accessible to them. This approach focuses on
action work. Actors concentrate on what they are *doing*
rather than what they are feeling. The idea is that feelings
emerge as a result of what one does. Sometimes it's diffi-

cult to get students to understand the simplicity of this procedure. They want to show feelings and attitudes immediately. After a while they begin to understand that the acting process is doing things truthfully for a purpose.

Initially, students work on themselves, not a character, through structured improvisations focusing on concentration, inner truth, the use of objects, and relaxation. They also do animal exercises and work with songs as well as sense memory and affective memory exercises. Afterward, when they work on a character, they also do research into the background of the play, the history, and the socioeconomic influences on the character. Later on they also work on text analysis.

The approach is based on Stanislavsky, my training at the HB Studio, and the changes I have made based on problems that are unique to British and European actors.

I begin with a list of eight questions that students must answer fully and personally before they get up to work. They are:

1) Who am I? When students are playing themselves they must make truthful choices about their own likes, dislikes, fears, passions, relationships, etc. Later, when we work on a play, they make choices of the same kind for themselves as the character. They must also decide where their character was born, who their parents are, what schools they went to, who their friends are, etc. This is an actor's research that has nothing to do with intellectual or academic study.

2) Where am I? We explore the fact that we respond differently in places or to objects that are familiar or unfamiliar.

3) When is it? Is it early morning, late afternoon, etc. Is

it spring, summer, winter, or fall? All these factors condition how we behave.

4) What do I want? This I call the action. An action is a want, a desire, an intention. When I teach English and European students I change it to, what do I *need?* because although the word *want* is understood, it is not strong enough.

5) Why do I want it? This is a justification for an action because one can never have an action without a reason.

6) Why do I want it *now?* I stress this question in England because the English have difficulty in responding to immediacy. The immediacy of an action gets the inner motor going. Herbert Berghof used to say that an actor has to have all four burners going at once—it not only gives him energy but it keeps the action alive.

7) How will I get it? By doing what? This can be answered by a transitive verb: you beg, plead, tease, sympathize, etc., in order to push ahead your action.

8) What must I overcome to get it? What is the actor's obstacle or resistance to fulfilling his action? There must always be an obstacle in a dramatic situation.

Have You Had to Adjust the Exercises for British Students?

Yes. Generally speaking, British students have a natural guard against expressing their true feelings. Americans plunge right in. One has to tread carefully with the British and slowly build up their confidence and trust. It's not that they don't want to explore their feelings, but their upbringing and education are an enormous barrier to overcome. They want to answer those questions from an intellectual standpoint rather than explore the organic subtext. They prefer to present everything through the verbal use of the text. Because of the preponderance of the Method in the States over the past forty years, American actors try to relate their character's experience to their own life and feelings in order to find a deeper personal involvement. Much of what is basic and second nature to an American-trained actor is a revelation to an English actor.

When I work with improvisations I change the question "What *would* I do if I were in this situation?" to "What *could* I do?" This opens up enormous possibilities. The word *would* makes actors behave too naturalistically and limits their imagination. Basically, the training consists of exploring all the possibilities of what you *could* do in order to get what you want. It stretches the imagination and can produce exciting, dramatic, compelling work. It can free the actor physically, psychologically, and verbally.

I also try to explain to students that this training does not produce immediate results. Often actors will come back years later and say, "The penny has just dropped" or, "Now I understand. I wish I could start the training all over again." To grow as an actor can take many months. It can even take years to strip away the layers of reserve and inhibition that are a barrier to finding one's creative freedom. The struggle is to bring back the naiveté that one had as a child and find the joy of "make believe" all over again.

I dislike the term *Method*. There is no one way of solving acting problems. All one can do is try to open doors so that each person can find his own way in and his own individual method.

Could You Describe How You Do an Affective Memory Exercise?

First, I ask students to choose an experience that they would like to recall. When we are working on an affective memory it can be any experience that brings them from one state of being to another: receiving good or bad news, having a fight, losing keys, etc. When it's an emotional memory, which I do in the second year, they work with a traumatic event that must be at least five years old. They do both these exercises by visualizing and recalling the event through their five senses—what they saw, heard, smelled, tasted, touched. There is no story line. They lie down with their eyes closed and I take them through relaxation exercises by systematically relaxing all the muscles. Then I ask them to imagine a black screen, something like a movie screen, inside their forehead. On the screen they must visualize a beautiful and relaxing panoramic scene, a place where they are relaxed and happy. They imagine themselves alone basking in the peace and quiet of the scene. Then I ask them to hear whatever they might actually hear in that place, see, smell, taste, touch—everything associated with their surroundings. This takes about fifteen to twenty minutes. After this, they go to the affective memory by concentrating on their sensory recall and allowing a free flow of their memories toward their experience.

The objective of this exercise is to find the trigger that

sparked off the actual emotion. This trigger can then be used to personalize an emotional event in a play when the actor cannot find it in the given circumstances of the text. All these techniques are intended to become part of the actor's homework, something he can do by himself when he gets into the professional theater.

How Often Do You Do These Exercises with Your Students?

At RADA I do them once or twice a week during the first and second year of study. Each term is twelve weeks and there are three terms a year. The acting training is broken down into two areas. The first concentrates on improvisations and technique; the second area is character work based on classic Greek texts, Restoration, Shakespeare, Chekhov, Ibsen, Strindberg, and Molière. They also get the time to work on modern plays as well. By the third year they should be able to use this training to fulfill the lives of the characters they play in their public productions.

How Do You Direct?

I am presently directing *Tartuffe* at RADA and I hope to show that inner substance is not only essential for realistic drama but for all theater styles. At the moment, because of my busy schedule of acting and teaching, I am only directing internal productions that are seen within the school and are an adjunct to the teaching.

Do You Have Any Specific Techniques for Helping Students Become More Expressive?

That is a hard question to answer since all the exercises I do are designed to give the student the freedom to become more expressive. The actor's instrument—his body and voice—must be finely tuned so that he can express whatever impulses come from his emotions, intuition, and imagination. The students at RADA have very good training in movement and voice, and I use a great many animal exercises to create a different physical center. I also use songs as a way to help students learn to express themselves.

How Do They Use the Song Exercise in Their Acting?

For instance, if a student needs an emotional preparation for tears before coming on stage, a song can be used to produce those tears. In class I would ask a student to choose a song that has a powerful melody and strong rhythmic beat. It must not be chosen for its sentimental value or because of its associations with an experience. These associations tend to be unreliable and dry up with time. The song will be effective in arousing feelings through the repetition of the beat and tempo. In class the student sings the song repeatedly, perhaps twenty to thirty times until the beat produces the emotion response. It is important to use these songs specifically— otherwise there is a danger that the student will end up playing the "mood" of a song, and, in Uta Hagen's words, "Mood spelled backwards is DOOM!"

What Do You Hope to Contribute to British Acting?

An enjoyment of the learning process, a commitment to inner truth, and an honest emotional life; a technique that encourages spontaneity and exploration, not only in the rehearsal period but while playing in a long run; and, of course, actors who involve the audience not just intellectually but organically. I think that the English, without admitting to it, admire the American style of acting. They admire the energy and commitment of American actors. On the other hand, Americans could learn from their English counterparts the importance of discipline and of training in movement and voice. For me to get a blend of what is strong in both—the inner and outer technique— is a very exciting challenge.

Andy Hinds

Andy Hinds teaches acting and directs classics at the Royal Academy of Dramatic Art (RADA). He began his career as a trainee director for the Irish Theatre Company in Dublin before forming Playzone, a Belfast-based touring company. He received a grant from the Arts Council of Great Britain to establish and extend his work in England. Since moving to London he has directed for the major repertory theaters as well as the London fringe theaters and touring companies. His productions include All's Well That Ends Well, The Winter's Tale, A Midsummer Night's Dream, Mother Courage, Fidelio, The Beggar's Opera, *and* Le Malade Imaginaire.

Mr. Hinds also directs opera and has worked for the Glyndebourne Touring Company, Scottish Opera, and the Wexford Festival.

Mr. Hinds has been an Associate Director for the Bristol Old Vic, where he is currently working on a production of Macbeth.

I am presently teaching a ten-week course for foreign students at RADA called Acting Shakespeare. I particularly like this course because the actors are professionals and from different cultures. There are Americans, Canadians, and Danes taking the course. The North Americans came, by and large, expecting to be taught a technique specifically for acting Shakespeare, and believed it would be based on how they spoke the lines as opposed to how they expressed themselves artistically through the lines. We are now in the third week of this course and it has only been in the last couple of days that I feel they have begun to understand what we are doing.

What Is It You Believe the Overseas Students Need?

They need training in how to kindle the creative imagination through contact with the text. They thought they would get up to act and I would say, "Stand like this," or, "Intone like that." One student said she had had a wonderful English actress who came to lecture at her school and told the students to use an upward inflection at the end of every line, and to come in on a pitch above the one they ended on in the previous line. All the students started to do that and, she said, they started to get more laughs. If only they could learn more "techniques" like that. The point, of course, is that an inflection is not funny or otherwise in itself. It has a particular effect on an audience because of what it implies about the attitude and energies of the speaker. The more a performer includes such effects in his performance without their having grown out of carefully evolved feeling, the hollower it will ring. I think a lot of students believed they were coming to acquire a large repertoire of such effects. That's not what they need. They need to learn to say the words with sufficient depth of feeling, and I know they can do that because as professionals they have learned to do it with other material. What they wanted was something technical, to learn to work from the outside in, and I wanted to start from the inside out.

For example, a few students said, we have been told that in Shakespeare the emotion is carried on the vowels and that intensity is expressed through the consonants. How do we apply this to what we are doing? Now, they believed this was an accessible and concrete technique that English actors use. Of course, there is truth in this, but it doesn't really say much more than you have to breathe to speak. They were very confused because they couldn't marry what we were doing in class to statements like that, and they wanted techniques they could use immediately in their acting. They wanted simple answers and simplistic techniques. There are some well-known Shakespearean actors who embody what some North Americans think is good Shakespearean acting. They use the rolling vowels sounds and sing the text. The connection between the meaning of the text and the chosen mode of delivery is sometimes merely the performer's determination to impress the audience as to how "well" he has spoken it. It's appalling, and I teach students to avoid those techniques.

How Do You Teach Shakespeare?

I don't think there is any special trick for Shakespeare. It's just more difficult. As a performer you have to condition yourself through the rehearsal period. With Shakespeare students often have preconceptions about him that don't allow them to condition themselves in the same way they would in a role where the language is more accessible. But as far as I am concerned it's exactly the same process. It's the preconceptions that interfere. What I try to do is help people get over the initial shock of the complexity and sometimes the difficulty of his language. I want them to understand that what one is looking for in Shakespeare's characters is an emotion that is fundamental to all humanity so that the audience will recognize something of themselves in that character. That may sound like a cliché, but it's important. The students thought Shakespeare was about something entirely different. The other big shock to students is discovering just how good he is. Once the text explodes in your face in every direction and you think you can't conceivably contain all it is giving you, everyone gets very excited.

Another problem is that Shakespeare isn't done enough in North America and actors don't have much practice performing his plays. Students don't have practice in how to look for the clues in the text that tell them what emotions are called for.

What Do You Mean by "Clues" in the Text?

Every scene, every line seems to contain in essence the whole play; every image too. For instance, we are working on *All's Well That Ends Well*. In the play Bertram says to Diana, don't speak about my marriage vows to my wife every time I try to get into bed with you. I was compelled to marry her, but I love you. "By love's own sweet constraint." It helped the actor playing Bertram to realize that although Bertram was in pain at the time, there was also a sweetness in the agony of not being able to consummate his love. The class then found examples of that all through the play, and we realized that every character was undergoing some form of constraint that on the one hand they enjoyed and on the other they were desperately trying to escape. Suddenly, many connections could be made. In the play Helena gets some form of exhilaration out of sacrificing her entire life for Bertram, but at the same time she is miserable in her frantic pursuit of him. Since texts usually aren't this good, we are not used to digging that closely and seeing how much one phrase can illuminate the entire text.

Another thing that I think is essential is that in order to do a single scene from one of his plays, every character has to have a shared understanding or agreement as to what the center of the play is. There is a tendency for everyone to simply get up and only do his or her own bit.

What Do You Mean by "Shared Understanding"?

It seems to me there is one central impulse that sparks off the whole of any piece, and when I am directing I have to feel that I have touched that. It's usually fundamental, and therefore very simple, and every single character can be interpreted in terms of that single spark. If we can all touch that together every character will make sense and everyone will discover the limits within which they can create and develop the complexity of their character without distorting the piece or interfering with other characters. In one sense it's a restriction, but it provides a form within which you can build and express your character's need.

For instance, the class was working on a four-woman scene from *All's Well* and we couldn't work out who they were or how they ought to be played until we understood the scene as a whole. We agreed that Italy, where the play is set, embodied unhealthy sexuality and relationships between the sexes. Once we understood that, we could see how every character reflected an aspect of the overall theme and was in some way connected with that center. For instance, one woman pretended to be pure, but was in fact always titillating men and using her sexuality as a way of controlling them. We could then go on and say, I think that the widow is extending her own sexuality through her daughter, but because she is a hypocrite, she won't let men near the young woman. And suddenly all the men made sense as well. We understood that Bertram needed to maintain his relationship with Helena because he had to sort out his sexuality; and we understood why Helena was still attracted to him: she could sense it was a sexual problem that prevented him from opening himself to her, and if that could be gotten rid of, he would be sufficiently confident in his own masculinity to enter into congress with her femininity. That's a big problem in the play: how does this woman even consider going after Bertram, who is such a pig? That's one way to solve the problem and one which I believe ties all the other elements in the play together.

The students learned this process of analysis very quickly—really too quickly. They didn't want to digest it all. We got to the stage where we could make grand statements about the play and say, for example, that Bertram has an Oedipal problem. That's all very well, but how do you act that? After scrutinizing the text with the intellect, then you must let it work on you. I believe that when you exercise your brain in this way on a text, you massage your subconscious automatically; areas of yourself become more open and the text penetrates. It's a mysterious process.

How is This Ten-Week Course Structured?

What students are being offered is a full term at RADA with emphasis exclusively on Shakespeare. Students in the overseas course study acting with me every day, and take other classes in voice, tumbling, singing, dance, and stage combat. When they are not in acting classes they are taking the standard courses that other students take.

This semester we have spent four weeks working on scenes from *All's Well*. We started with four groups of four-person scenes and five groups of three-person scenes, and Oliver Neville and I are each taking half the group for two-person scenes. So it's very intensive and detailed. We have been resisting letting students get up on their feet until the last moment because of the tendency to make the jump to performance and bypass the building up of the layers.

As the students go from the bigger scenes to the smaller ones, they learn more about their characters. Then we will go back and redo the bigger scenes with what we have built and learned. After this we will work on *Twelfth Night*, which is a very different kind of play with a more translucent text. It will be like a holiday for them after *All's Well*.

How Do You Help Students Become More Expressive?

I try to invite actors into opening up through the text. For instance, I ask them, "Why did Shakespeare use this word instead of that one?" I try to provoke them through the text. I keep asking them what it is that they are actually saying. The clearer they are, the clearer the emotion they want to express will be. Sometimes I will simply tell a student, "You are posturing instead of feeling." I might say, "Imagine the last time you were in love. What did it feel like?" But lack of imagination is generally not the problem. The problem is more fundamental than that. The reason they are posturing is because they don't sufficiently realize what the text is about. They haven't opened themselves to the text.

I am suspicious of actors who want directors or teachers to force them to have emotional breakdowns in acting classes, who use what I call the "assault technique." When a student has a strong emotional response to some heavy psychological exercise, is it the actor or the character who is crying and screaming? It might help a performer personally, but there is still a vast gulf between how an actress or actor will cry and how their character will cry. I prefer to work within the framework of the text. First of all, you must create an environment where it is possible for actors to be genuinely vulnerable, which I don't think happens very often.

I know actresses who felt very resentful after being treated with the "assault technique" because they realized it was *they* and not the character that was emotional—and that's not what actors want. They want to connect and establish their relationship to the audience via the text so that their emotion is metamorphosed and expresses the character's life. That's how they want to express themselves. It's no one's privilege to psychologically kick actors around.

Do You Teach Scanning?

Part of a line's meaning lies in its rhythms, but with me it is usually in the context of trying to understand a line or an exchange that the rhythm, metrical anomalies, etc., are scrutinized. I know teachers who drill students in the basic iambic pentameter so it might "sink into their bones." This is probably useful. Perhaps more so for North Americans if you believe, as some do, that the pentameter embodies the basic rhythm of English as spoken in England but not as spoken in North America. I don't know where that leaves an Irish person, as I am.

Do You Believe Students Must Always Maintain the Rhythm of the Verse?

Yes, in one way or another. Sometimes actors seem to let the rhythms run away, but it still feels right. They are perhaps still within the pentameter but in a more complex way.

In any play a current of rhythmic tension should run unbroken from the first line to the last. In a verse play this rhythm has a more heightened artificial form. The appropriate shape of the play and its tensions can therefore be achieved only by observing the form in all its details. Observing the rhythms of the verse in itself, however, guarantees neither clarity nor interest, not unless they seem to be necessary and exactly appropriate to the feelings of the speaker at that time.

What Do You Feel American Actors Have to Offer When Working on Shakespeare?

I don't see many differences. If an actor is good, he's good; if he's not, he's not. But a classic beginner's problem that some American students have is that they tend to pull the energy out of themselves rather than out of the scene. That can happen when a person has been trained in an approach that leads him to go into himself and actually works against the scene or the play. It has to be the person, of course, but the person with one hand on the pulse of the entire play, one hand on the pulse of the character, and one hand inside his own heart.

The Royal Scottish Academy of Music and Drama

The Royal Scottish Academy of Music and Drama grew out of the Glasgow Athenaeum, a pioneering body founded in 1847 to provide further education for adults in commerce, science, and the arts. In 1939 the Academy became one of the Central Institutions, a network of colleges throughout Scotland undertaking vocational training. The School of Drama was originally founded by James Bridie in 1951 as the Glasgow College of Drama.

The Academy recently moved to a new building especially built to house the music and drama departments. The School of Drama's premises include a full theater, a laboratory theater, a television studio, and a sound broadcasting studio.

The Academy offers a three-year course in Dramatic Art designed for those intending to act professionally, a B.A. in Dramatic Studies validated by the University of Glasgow, and a two-year course in Stage Management.

Edward Argent

Edward Argent is Director of the School of Drama at the Royal Scottish Academy of Music and Drama. After graduating from the Royal Academy of Dramatic Art he worked as actor, stage manager, and director in various provincial companies, among them the Bristol Old Vic, the Cambridge Theatre Company, and the Royal Court Theatre, Apollo Theatre, and Vaudeville Theatre in London. While acting with the Royal Shakespeare Company in 1962 he was invited to teach at the Guildhall School and launched his career as a teacher.

Mr. Argent went on to become Head of the School of Theatre of Manchester Polytechnic and in 1974 took up the post of Director of Drama at the Royal Scottish Academy. He is a Fellow of the Guildhall School, a Governor ex-officio of the Royal Scottish Academy, and a director of the Citizens Theatre and Garret Mask and Puppet Centre, Glasgow.

What Is Your Background in Theater?

When I first started teaching in 1962 I found that I didn't have very much to draw from in the way of teaching techniques. My own training at the Royal Academy of Dramatic Art (RADA) had been very formal and old-fashioned, and I was one of the last generation of students to be taught under Sir Kenneth Barnes, the original principal at RADA. The style was still almost nineteenth-century. But after graduation I found a London offshoot of The Actors Studio run by an actor called David de Keyser. He had worked with Lee Strasberg and set up classes based on his work. There were some interesting young actors around who came to de Keyser's class and it was a very exciting time. I spent about one year discovering a lot about acting, which together with my formal training gave me a direction in which to go. Later, I joined the Royal Shakespeare Company as an actor at the Aldwych, and I talked Peter Hall into letting me direct a Sunday-night production. I had hoped an invitation to direct would come out of that, but instead I was invited to teach at the Guildhall School of Music and Drama. Eric Capon, who was the new head of drama there, was a brilliant man, and he was trying to introduce new ideas into the school, so he asked me to teach a class. It was all very off the cuff. I kind of made it up as I went along.

At the same time there were some strange but interesting experiments going on at the Royal Court so I went to watch. These were mask and clown sessions being run by Keith Johnstone. I found this absolutely fascinating. Actors were experimenting with various improvisation techniques that were completely different from anything I had been doing. I saw that this would be useful with my students. Since I couldn't afford to purchase masks I had to make my own, and I did. I came up with one and started to use it with my students at Guildhall. The results were very encouraging so I made a few more. As soon as word went out that there was another young professional actor willing to teach (I was appearing then at the Aldwych and on television), I got invitations from all over and quickly found myself teaching at three schools at the same time. So I had to develop techniques quite fast. Teaching made me very aware of what I had been doing as an actor—what I had been doing wrong as well as right— and I began to realize that rather than pursuing directing, I had something useful to offer as a teacher.

What Was It About Mask Work That Appealed to You?

I found that the work with masks got to the root of what I was trying to do in improvisational work. I wanted to get away from teaching acting by way of simply rehearsing scenes or plays and presenting them. It's obviously important to put actors to the acid test of performance so they get feedback, but new actors need a lot more than that. The first class I taught had students as new to acting as I was to teaching, and we all started exploring together, trying to find the core of what acting is. If acting is just learning the words of a play and getting up and doing it, what do we need a school for? So what I developed over the years—and I have taught a new crop of students every year since 1962—has become a basic part of my life. What I hope to help students look for is the roots of acting in themselves, the degree to which everyone role plays. I try to make them aware that they have a vast range of experience that they haven't tapped into but which they can draw on subconsciously. They know and can imagine a great deal more than they give themselves credit for. I agree with Keith Johnstone's basic premise that the process of socialization is not one of addition but subtraction; that is, although education gives us a certain amount of factual information, it also systematically narrows down the young person's potential because it's inconvenient for society to have too many fully imaginative artists around. Thus, people are shriveled down into suitable artifacts for the wheels of our civilization. I think there is an awful lot of truth in this. Most people need to be reminded that they are artists and that artists are not different from other people except that they have retained more of childhood. If people can recreate the world of a five-year-old, if they can loosen up and feel rather than suppress or channel their feelings into socially acceptable forms, then they can find new forms for communicating their feelings to others.

Can You Give Me an Example of an Exercise You Use to Help Students Expand Their Imagination?

One exercise I use in my improvisation class and also for auditioning a student for the Academy is to ask him to imagine that up until this moment he has lived on a far distant planet. I say, "Imagine you have a totally different body, different in whatever way you want to imagine. Maybe you are enormously large or microscopically small; maybe you are heavy and dense, maybe light;

maybe you have no body at all, but are pure intelligence; maybe you are all body and hardly any consciousness at all; maybe your body is very skillful with dozens of senses and appendages; maybe it is very clumsy and has only one essence with which to perceive the world. Invent anything you like. Then imagine that a scientist has invented a machine that can take your consciousness out of your strange body and transfer it into the body you now have. So you go to sleep on your planet and you wake up on earth in this body and you are in a totally alien environment, and in a totally alien body. And part of the environment you have to explore and learn about is composed of sentient beings like you who also move about." I allow that improvisation to run for about an hour. Afterward, some students will be able to look back and analyze their experience clearly, and some will need to be told that what they have done was to recapitulate being born. They had to learn to observe and make comparisons and connections and discover the need to express the things they felt, as well as how to escape from dangers and follow up on gratifications, and so on. Since they need to communicate they soon discover the need for a language. If I let the improvisation run long enough we end up with a primitive society that has a language, engages in tribal battles and alliances, etc.

How Do Students Communicate in This Exercise?

First, they have to find out whether or not they can talk. They start with noises because, remember, their bodies are totally strange to them. They may discover purely by accident that they can communicate by making a noise.

This is a basic exercise that we use to free students from their preconceptions about acting.

I also give students lots of observation exercises. I will ask them to observe someone and re-create that person in class. I ask them to observe someone they are familiar with or someone they can study. It can be someone from their past who they remember clearly, someone they've seen on the street, or a person sitting opposite them on a bus, for example. They must then demonstrate how that person sat, talked, etc., and do everything and anything they can to convey that person physically and mentally. In this way they begin to explore things like how an individual's work can affect his behavior and what he thinks about himself and the world. Before he knows it we are discussing politics, economics, sociology, and poetry—what songs that person might sing, what poems he might know.

Then I put students in pairs and ask them to present their person to each other and then teach their person to each other. They can correct their partner until the partner demonstrates their person as well as they can. So now they have switched characters. Then this pair meets up with another pair who have learned each other's characters, and they have to teach their new character to another person. In this way students get to the essential characteristics of a person, the essence of that person, since they can't convey all the details. This exercise gets them to observe, and perform as well.

I teach these kinds of exercises in the drama course for ten weeks, ten hours a week. After a few weeks I will introduce masks as a way to crystalize everything and bring it all together. The essence of the mask experience is this: I tell them, "Every aspect of you, consciously and unconsciously, communicates something about you: your choice of dress, the way you wear your hair, the way you sit, etc. But the most individual signal of all is your face. Where did that come from? Heredity, of course, but your face has also been sculpted by experience out of the raw material that has been given you by your genes. So if I can wave my magic wand and give you a different face, you will find a different person inside yourself—someone you might become in the future or someone you might have been under different circumstances. With a new face you have the freedom to become any of the millions of people that you might have been. Your mask is your new face."

A student starts mask work by looking into the mirror at his own face and trying to see it as if it were a stranger's face. What does that face tell you about that person? If you were observing that face on the bus, what would it tell you? That's a start.

Then the student turns away from the mirror and I give him a mask, or a new face as I call it. I don't call it a mask at first because that word has certain connotations. I use a version of a *commedia dell'arte* half-mask that covers the eyes, nose, and forehead. The masks have expression, some being stronger than others, but that is quite irrelevant. It's just a trigger. We get the mask comfortable on the face and go back to the mirror. Now the student sees a different face and I say to him, "Don't see your face with a piece of cardboard covering half of it. Don't try to see two separate things, but blend them together and see a whole new face and a whole new person, and allow yourself to be that person. Allow that new person to express himself through the whole of your body and voice. Let that person in." Five people will see five different things through the same mask. The same person will produce five different characters on five different occasions with the same mask. It's a matter of having the courage to allow something to happen.

Once a student experiences the impact of the mask and sees who he has become, he comes away from the mirror and I ask him to sit in a chair in the middle of the room and ignore the other people. Now I start to talk about the mask as the "new person." I start with just one mask at a time and I talk to him, get to know him. What I ask will depend on what I see. I talk to the student very gently trying to find out who he is. Very often he will be a sad person because sadness seems to be nearest the surface, I suppose. So I try to help him deal with his pain by having him express it in very simple terms. Then I begin to put two or three or four masks together and they interact with each other as the mask characters. All kinds of things emerge and people start to experience states of exultation, depression, whatever, *as their mask character.* One of the marvelous things is that the students who are watching can say whether or not the exercise is working, whether someone has actually found a new person or if he is simply performing for the rest of the class. You can't get away with anything in mask work. If you "act" while wearing a mask it's immediately obvious. I have about thirty or forty masks now and they are all different.

It's important that masks be well made. Mass-produced masks don't work because they lack intention. The ones that produce the best results, that are the most helpful to the imagination, take the longest to produce because they are individual and unique.

Mask work is one of the most intense and productive improvisational techniques for developing the actor's imagination, as well as his mental and physical techniques.

When Do You Introduce Text Work?

After the mask work I introduce text by typing up sections of plays and giving them out. I leave out any indication of the play's name, the author, characters, or locale, and there are no stage directions, just the dialogue. The actors then memorize the words and use the text in a variety of ways to find out what is essential in that script, what is demanded in that piece, without making assumptions based on the name of the author, etc. I want them to avoid stereotypes. I use these anonymous texts to pry students loose from presuppositions and to make them aware of acting as a creative art. I never understood the notion that the actor is purely an interpretive artist and that it's the playwright who is creative. Not so. The playwright has produced something that provides raw material for the actor's creativity, and the actor, in recreating it, has to go through the same process as the dramatist. It can be very liberating for actors when they realize that they can be as creative as anyone else, that they don't simply have to do what they are told. I always tell students that their challenge is to be creative within the limits set by the dramatist, the director, the set designer, etc., and to use it all as raw material.

Do You Admit American Students to Your Drama Course?

Yes, but we never admit more than about two or three at a time out of a total intake of twenty students. Although we would prefer to audition in person, we know Scotland is a long way to go, so we consider applications from students who send us a voice or videotape. If accepted they enter our full three-year acting course. We don't as yet have a separate course for foreign students, but we are thinking of starting a summer course to include overseas students when we move to our new and larger facilities. We also have a three-year degree course that we teach jointly with the University of Glasgow's Department of Theater, Film, and Television. About eighty percent of that course consists of practical classes, and students do a lot of the same work as our regular acting students. However, it's not as intensive in terms of performance and includes academic work as well.

Some of the Teachers I Have Interviewed Feel That the Emotional Range of British Actors Could Be Expanded. Do You Agree?

I work a lot on stimulating emotions and bringing them forward, and I don't find that very difficult to do. I think what makes English acting so good is that our actors do what all good actors do, but with a high level of intensity and skill. British people act a lot. They have a high awareness of the nuances of speech. Shaw said that no Englishman can open his mouth without making some other Englishman despise him. Our whole social system is built on that. It goes round in a circle and it can also lead to reverse snobbery as well. A lot of young people who come from backgrounds where their accents might be highly aristocratic and educated have learned to talk a kind of bastard cockney, particularly if they are going into the world of the arts, because they feel they wouldn't be accepted if they spoke in their natural accent. The British are sensitive to speech, so much British comedy, at least as far back as Shakespeare, is about social pretensions, about a lower-class person trying to get above himself— like Malvolio, for instance. And Shakespeare loved comedy based on people using words incorrectly, like Dogberry, for example. We have the most complicated, finely graduated system of social placement in the world. We have a civilization built on the fine nuances of social behavior and speech. Obviously our theater is very rich in these subtleties.

What Is It About British Acting Training That Permits the Actor to Play a Wide Repertory of Theater?

I suppose British acting training is as eclectic and non-doctrinaire as British theater. There is no system, no method, no fixed tradition as there is in the Comédie Française, for instance. There is no one way of doing Shakespeare or anything else; therefore, there is an openness and an assumption that an actor is an actor is an actor, and he should be able to turn his hand to any kind of acting. We in the schools reflect this in the way we teach. There are one or two British drama schools that very conscientiously teach a particular method and these may expand the range of British drama training. But most of us are, as it were, presenting a microcosm of the breadth of versatility that is found in British acting. I feel that I, and my school, need some fresh stimulus from the outside at this moment, and we are very positively looking for that by exposing our staff and students to other methods from Europe and America. We are trying to keep our students' attitudes flexible and open to everything. I do want us to look outward more. It's very easy for us to get complacent and believe that British acting is the best in the world and everybody has to come to us. It's too easy for us to believe that we know it all. That would prevent us from continuing to change and develop.

Do You Feel That Young Actors Have to Contend with the Tradition of Past Great Actors and Their Specific Interpretations or Performances—of Hamlet, for Instance?

You bet. But remember, the tradition is very open. Obviously, the competition with the past or even the present is formidable, but it doesn't inhibit or prevent someone from having a go. I was just reading Olivier's new book, and in it he mentions that one of his greatest feats of acting was when he did *Oedipus* and followed it with *The Critic*. He was brilliant in both. A while ago, Derek Jacobi, whom Olivier had given his start to in the National Theatre, proposed to do the same double bill elsewhere.

Olivier sent him a telegram on opening night that said, "Cheeky bugger."

One of the roles that Olivier stamped his image onto most memorably was, of course, Richard III. Everyone agrees that for the first years of his career Olivier was a fine performer and a truly glamorous star with many impressive movie and theater performances. But he stepped into greatness with Richard, a role in which both Garrick and particularly Kean had also excelled. After his opening night in the role, John Gielgud, who owned the sword Kean had used in the part, sent it to Olivier.

Recently, Anthony Sher played *Richard III* and managed to come up with a new image of Richard that was as strong as Olivier's and quite stunning. He played him on crutches as a man who had developed enormously strong arms and shoulders. With them he was able to move faster than anyone else could actually walk, and scurried his way around the stage like an enormous spider. His performance won him the Society of West End Theatres award for best actor in the year when the awards were first named after Olivier, who was there to see him receive it.

Peter McAllister

Peter McAllister teaches acting at the Royal Scottish Academy of Music and Drama. After graduating from the University of London with a B.A. in drama and English literature he trained in the directors' course at the Drama Studio, London. While at the university he spent six weeks in New York attending classes conducted by a number of leading American acting teachers. These included sessions at the Actors Studio under Lee Strasberg. In 1983 he received a British Council award and spent six months in Poland, where he worked with a number of theaters, including the Teatr Studio under Jerzy Grzegorzewski, the Teatr Polski under Kazimierz Dejmek, and the Stary Teatr under Andrzej Wajda. He began his career as Assistant Director to Lindsay Anderson and since then has worked as a teacher and director before taking up his appointment at the Royal Scottish Academy.

First let me begin by saying that I am not really sure either what the "British technique" is, or whether I am one of those who teaches anything that could be called uniquely British. If I had to describe my work as a teacher I would say that it is not so much a reflection of the British theatrical tradition as a reaction to it. I must say I am surprised that actors from other countries often express envy of our tradition because from what I have seen and experienced abroad, we have much to learn from the traditions of others. I am often surprised, for example, when I hear people say that American actors are in awe of British actors. It seems to me that America has its own tradition, and I believe it is a fine one. In fact, my interest in acting really stems from the tradition that originated with the Group Theatre in the thirties, and which was later developed and expanded upon both at the Actors Studio and privately by people such as Lee Strasberg, Uta Hagen, Robert Lewis, Stella Adler, Sanford Meisner, and Harold Clurman. If there is a foundation from which I work, then I suppose it is Stanislavsky. The reason for this is that—apart from the work of Michel St. Denis—it is the only systematic approach to actor training that exists; as such, it has to be one of the cornerstones of any practical program aimed at the teaching of acting.

How Do Your Teaching Methods Reflect This Influence?

All my work is, in the end, based on the approach Stanislavsky outlined in his three major works as available to us in translation: namely, that actor training ought to be divided into two distinct areas: the actor's work on himself, and the actor's work on the role. Class work, therefore, primarily consists of the actor working on his "instrument," while rehearsal work is concerned with the actor working on the interpretation of a part; some work, however, is also done in class on dealing with the problems of interpretation. From my point of view as a teacher of acting, the first is perhaps the more important as it focuses on the essential creativity of the actor—that is, how the actor both inspires himself and stimulates his imagination. This has its roots in Stanislavsky's famous hypothesis: "Are there any technical means by which the creative mood can be made to appear more often than is its wont?" In other words, how can the actor excite his imagination at will? The work in class centers on this problem, and on ways of bringing the impulse within the actor to expression. This is achieved through a combination of exercises, theater games, and improvisations.

Some of these are derived from British acting teachers, but predominantly they are derived from American teachers such as those cited earlier. Others I have learned from teachers that I myself studied with, and there are those that I invented myself. These exercises, theater games, and improvisations cover areas such as awareness, relaxation, concentration, imagination, sense memory, observation of others, situations, relationships, action, language, character, and emotion. They constitute the basic elements that make up a dramatic character, and as such provide the foundation for the actor's work on the role.

PETER McALLISTER

What Kind of Work Do You Do with New Actors?

Initially, exercises in awareness, relaxation, and concentration. In every class I begin with exercises in these three areas, and later I add exercises in imagination. At the start of training my aim is to try to make the actor aware of himself and the world about him, and how his environment affects him. This develops into work on sensory awareness, since it is through our senses that we experience our environment. This work is often done blindfold, in the dark, or with the eyes shut. The aim is to try and reawaken the faculties the actor had as an infant, and the first major improvisation at this stage centers on the recreation of a childhood experience. Sense memory work develops from this, leading into work with objects; it is at this point that the use of the imagination is first brought into play as the actor tries to recreate the sensation of objects which are not present.

This leads into the next stage, which I call "situations," where the actor is asked to try and re-create the sensation of being in a particular place at a particular time, purely through the use of his five senses. These situations are then developed into scenarios; that is, the actor is then given a concrete purpose for being in that situation. For example, he is on a railway platform, late at night, waiting for a train that has not come. The aim is to begin to introduce the actor to the notion of "action," the idea of having a specific reason or purpose for doing something on stage. These scenarios are then further developed into improvisations, which I refer to as "meetings," where one actor meets another actor, knowing who, where, when, and why he is there. The other actor, however, does not know and has to discover in the course of the improvisation the nature of their relationship and situation. The aim is for the first actor to communicate through a sense of place, time, weather, and attitude to the other what the relationship and situation is so that the second actor can discover who, where, when, and why he is there also.

Following these improvisations, work continues on both action and relationships, leading into exercises on character. About this time exercises involving the observation of others and those such as the animal exercise are employed, as are exercises that help to differentiate between the idea of the actor as himself and the actor as the character. This work then further develops into exercises and improvisations dealing with language and emotion, and finally text. At this point the work begins to cross over from the actor's work on himself into the actor's work on the role.

This stage is necessarily more analytical as the actor begins to try and reconcile his demands for truth with those of the playwright. Using texts from a wide variety of theatrical styles, such as Ibsen, Molière, Pinter, Shakespeare, Chekhov, Beckett, Vanbrugh, or Brecht, the actor is asked to analyze these texts for clues as to situation, character, place, time, weather, and so on, and to try to answer the seven questions Who am I? Where am I? What time is it? What is my relationship? What do I want? What's in the way of what I want? How do I go about getting what I want?

All of these things have, of course, already been dealt with in the preparatory work on the self, but the difference here is that they have already been decided by the playwright. I ought to mention that these texts are somewhat altered from their originals and have been carefully expunged of any reference that might indicate their sources. The reason for this is that it is far too easy to start to play a text in a way that is thought to be "Chekhovian" or "Pinteresque," for example, without ever investigating the impulses behind those famous pauses and silences. As a result, all the textual clues are ruthlessly excised from the scripts; the characters have no names, just A, B, C, D, and E, and the stage directions only indicate if a character is either on or off-stage. The actor then tries to establish what is happening in the scene, and tries to pin down any clues as to the style of the piece. For example, is it classical or modern? What sort of language do the characters use? What sorts of temperaments do the characters possess? What sort of country might they come from? Eventually, this information is extended into exercises and improvisations on and around subtext, language, and period. A larger section of text is then used to analyze the play's theme, its structure, and its use of characterization. Finally, the actor works with other actors on various scenes of their own choosing, which they prepare on their own by working on units, actions, character, subtext, and so on. These scenes are then presented to the class.

Some of the Teachers I Have Spoken with Feel That the Weakest Area of British Acting Is Its Emotional Aspect. Do You Agree?

Yes. I suspect this is partly to do with the fact that working on the emotions has generally been avoided in British actor training, due to what I can only assume to be a fear of opening the flood-gates; that is, a fear that the actor will be unable to cope with the emotion once it is released. This may be because the British are generally more reserved than either their American or European counter-parts, and because emotional restraint just happens to be one of those things that is part of the British tempera-ment. But this means that in plays that require a great deal of emotion, British actors are not nearly so successful as, say, either American or Polish or Russian actors. Brit-ish actors are very famous for doing Shakespeare and Restoration comedy and the like—plays that often put a greater demand on the use of language than anything else—but they are not always so successful with plays from either the nineteenth or the twentieth century. In this respect I would agree that our actors are lacking, and it's something we need to pay attention to in our training of actors if we hope to remedy the problem.

Do You Have Any Exercises to Help Your Actors Become Emotionally Responsive?

As I mentioned earlier, I do work in class on emotion, and this often takes the form of improvisations—similar to the "situations" I described—where the actor is asked not only to recreate the sensation of being in a particular place at a particular time but also in a situation with a strong emotional connotation to it.

Another exercise I use is one where the actor is asked to focus on a particular feeling or emotion that they are then asked to verbalize in a short phrase, such as "No-body loves me." This is developed in a series of stages until the actor is told to let go and express this phrase with as full a commitment as is possible. Usually the emotion is so strong by this point that the actor is almost incapable of *not* expressing it. I have found this exercise particularly valuable because the actor is aware that it is not a personal thing, but the expression of a basic human emotion that everybody has felt at some point. I also use music as a stimulus, and what I call "personal objects," which have an emotional connection for the actor concerned. In addition, I do use emotional memory, although I'm wary of the associations that are connected with it. I use it because I believe it's a very useful tool for the actor, and I know of no other exercise that is as effective in dealing with the problem of making an actor emotionally responsive. Unfortunately, the exercise came into disrepute in this country in the mid-fifties, when people like Noël Coward had a very negative response to the emotional work being done at the Actors Studio. If I can, I prefer to use other means to help make the actor emotionally responsive, but I have no personal objection to using it. The important thing about work involving the emotions is that it does require great care on the part of the teacher in the setting up of any exercise. That said, I don't know of any actor who has not found this kind of work of the utmost importance to his training, and I can think of numerous occasions when an actor has said to me afterward, "I had no idea I had it in me."

Would You Describe Some of the Other Exercises You Use in Class Work?

One of the exercises I use to increase the actor's ability to concentrate I refer to as "puppets." I have no idea when or how it originated, but it happens to be one of my favorites. I ask six actors to volunteer to stand in a line and pick a piece of paper out of a bag on which I have written the title of a subject that they will then give a talk on. These subjects are usually quite diverse and often rather banal; for example, "The History of Rock and Roll," or, "How to Housetrain Your Pet." Each actor is told *not* to refer to his subject by title, and to try to address the class without pulling faces, shuffling his feet, or fidgeting with his hands. Each actor is told to listen to the others, as they are all to talk simultaneously, and to try to make out what it is they are talking about. Above all, the actor is told to try to maintain concentration on his particular subject. The reason this exercise is called "puppets" is because I then stand behind them and operate them like puppets by tapping them on the shoulder. If I tap an actor, he is to begin talking; if I tap him again, he is to stop, even if he is in mid-sentence. He has to start and stop, as directed by me, even though this interrupts his flow. Often I have a number of actors talking at the same time, which interferes with their ability to concentrate. I have found this exercise particularly useful in dealing with concentration difficulties, and also because it involves the use of the actor's imagination in talking about a subject, as well as his awareness of himself and others. In addition, it requires the actor to remain spontaneous and flexible throughout while dealing with the problem of performing in front of an audience. Probably because it encompasses so many of the actor's problems at one time, it is the exercise actors ask me to repeat most frequently.

Another exercise I am fond of is one called "contact," which I learned from one of my teachers. I use this exercise, on the whole, in conjunction with a text, because it deals with the disparity between what the text says on the surface and what it says underneath, that is, the subtext. It involves the use of a soft, lightweight object, such as a cushion, which is used by the actor as a means of physicalizing whatever feelings his character may be feeling but are not directly expressed by the dialogue. The aim of the exercise is to make the subtext clear by physically manifesting what the character is feeling. A character might say, for example, "That's a nice suit you're wearing," and within the context of the scene he wishes to express his approval; in this instance the actor would simply choose to stroke the other actor with the object. But perhaps the character wishes to belittle the other character, in which case the actor might choose instead to put the object on the other actor's head. The essential point is that the actor finds some external means of expressing the character's feelings through the use of the object.

Another exercise I use is called the "point of concentration" and is derived from Viola Spolin. I also use a number of her theater games, such as "exits and entrances," "hidden conflict," and "no motion." Keith Johnstone's work on "status" is of particular value in working on characterization, as is Michael Chekhov's on "psychological gesture," and Laban's work on "effort." I also use exercises to do with energy centers that are based on work by Grotowski. All of these can be found in their books.

Do You Have Any Final Comments You Would Like to Make About Your Teaching Methods?

Only that if there is a philosophy behind what I teach, it is this: to help the actor to find ways to excite his imagination and to give him specific things that he can do when working either on his own or on a part. I suppose what I'm talking about is technique. It seems to me to be of vital importance that the actor should have some kind of framework within which to work. How else is he to utilize his talent positively? Too many actors appear to be without any kind of technical know-how, and it is one of the worst criticisms of the British theater that I can think of that actors and directors can still be heard to repeat that old adage, "Just say the lines and don't bump into the furniture." This is not to imply that actor training should be a rigid, inflexible book of rules—far from it—but unless the actor has got something other than inspiration to fall back on, what has he got? Only inspiration.

The Webber Douglas Academy of Dramatic Art

The Webber Douglas Academy of Dramatic Art originally started as a studio school for singers in Paris in 1906. In 1926 Amherst Webber and Walter Johnstone Douglas established a school for opera singers in the Academy's present premises in South Kensington. The introduction of acting studies by Ellen O'Mally, a leading actress in the twenties, led to its development into a school for training actors, with the study of singing remaining an important aspect of the curriculum. Acting training takes place in classes in improvisation and acting technique. However, beginning in the second term students are directed in scenes and plays by professional directors. The school believes this experience is crucial for acquiring a broad and flexible craft.

The Academy offers a three-year comprehensive Acting Course, and a two-year Acting Course that is particularly suited for overseas and older students. There is also a one-year Post-Graduate Course for experienced actors, and a summer course in Acting and Theater.

Raphael Jago

Raphael Jago is Principal of Webber Douglas Academy of Dramatic Art. After graduating from the Guildhall School of Music and Drama, he went on to direct productions at the Theatre Royal, York; the Opera House, Scarborough; and the Arts Theatre, Ipswich. He was Artistic Director of the Opera House, Harrowgate, and was assistant to Joan Littlewood at Stratford East.

Mr. Jago is Chairman of the Conference of Drama Schools.

What Is Your Own Background in Theater?

I went to the Guildhall School and trained as a drama teacher. It was difficult to get a grant to train only as an actor in those days so I wound up doing both courses at the same time. During the course an ex-student from the Guildhall School started a repertory company, which I joined during my first summer vacation from school. I directed a number of plays there, so by the time I left Guildhall I had not only directed student productions but also quite a number on the outside. So I went straight into directing right after leaving drama school as a free-lance director and worked in the repertory system—an experience shared by most of the principals of the drama schools. After that I worked with Joan Littlewood for about a year and a half at her Stratford East Theatre and we went on tour. I also began to teach at drama schools, and then was asked to be principal of Webber Douglas.

What Was the Tradition in Which You Were Trained?

Training at the Guildhall in those days was varied and open. Most drama schools today have become highly organized institutions with very heavy work loads. But in those days it wasn't like that. You did a lot, but you had to initiate a great deal of your own work.

When I was in drama school there wasn't a specific philosophy of acting. That only really started to happen in the sixties. When I took over Webber Douglas the whole issue of the relevance of the Method was being raised. Up until then the Method was only one approach among many, part of an ongoing tradition of doing plays and being in the theater. Students learned from the people they respected in their school or company, or those they met. It was based on carrying on an oral tradition from actor to actor, from one generation to the next. I don't think that the Method approach ever had an overwhelming effect on the English system of training. It had some effect, a general effect. For example, voice work was less stressed during the sixties. But it never blew everything out the window as it did in the U.S. I think part of the reason for that is because many of the established English actors could not or would not theorize about how they worked. But they were so established, and had achieved so much, that they held the balance between theory and practice.

*Did the Important Actors of That Time, Like
Olivier, Richardson, and Gielgud, Have an Effect
on Young Actors?*

We didn't see a lot of Laurence Oliviers emerging in the drama schools when he was at his height. I never came across anything here that was equivalent to Brando's impact in *On the Waterfront*, where the effect on young American actors was so marked. You would see a lot of actors who were simply repeating Brando's performance. That never happened in England. You can still see the remnants of that when students come to audition and are still doing a kind of imitation of Brando, many times removed. But after twenty-one years I can't see the influence of Olivier or Richardson on students today—not in the same way that you can see the influence of Brando on American actors.

Perhaps That's Because There Is No One "Olivier"
Style While There Was a "Brando" Style?

The Americans were marketing personalities in the end.
Although it was supposed to be new and different, it was
just an "inarticulate," as opposed to an "articulate" personality. This occurs less often in the U.K. than in America.
For instance, today, if you mention Judi Dench, most people would say that she is a great actress and highly to be
admired. But I've yet to see anyone audition or work who
tried to look like Judi Dench. They admire her profes-
sionalism and integrity, her approach and values, but they
won't go to the next stage of trying to absorb her style.

England Has a Whole New Generation of Actors,
Like Jeremy Irons, Tom Conti, Anthony Hopkins,
and Derek Jacobi. Have They Influenced Young
Actors?

They are admired, but I don't see that they have set a
trend. I think that's partially because of our emphasis on
the skills of communication. If you emphasize communication you are moving away from a set style. I think American acting has moved away from communication to style:
actors often don't set out to communicate, but rather to
create an effect. Of course, there are not many actors of,
for example, Derek Jacobi's quality in England. There are
really very, very few whom I would call real classical actors. By that I mean actors who are highly imaginative,
have a wide emotional range, and have consummate vocal
technique. Even in England that's not all that common.

What Is the Course of Study at Webber Douglas?

We have one-, two-, and three-year programs. The one-year program is only for postgraduates who already have a degree. The two-year program has certain educational requirements and these students tend to be more mature. The three-year program is for the eighteen- and nineteen-year-olds. We also have a four-week summer course in August. We have Americans on the one- and two-year courses, but we don't have a separate course for them. I'm not keen on having Americans on our three-year course because they often become so Anglicized that they have problems when they go home. Most Americans at our school take the one-year course, but the majority of the students on this course are English. I've never seen the reason for Americans to travel 3,000 miles to train with other Americans, so we've always kept it mixed and never made it exclusive to them.

The one-year postgraduate course is quite good for Americans because one of the things they can do very well is establish priorities and they are very realistic in many ways. There is only one thing they find very difficult: the weather! They never stop being sick. The American students in England fall like flies. The climate is very damp and that makes it difficult for them.

How Is Acting Taught at Webber Douglas?

We have a course in acting technique that is taught in all courses. I also teach improvisation classes, which are basically acting classes, in the second year. However, a lot of the teaching of acting also comes through the relationship between the experienced directors, who are brought into the school, and the actor. We have always emphasized this a great deal because we don't want to end up with a narrow approach. Throughout the whole course of study we bring in professional people from the theater who pass on their knowledge. Directors are brought in to direct scenes from the students' first term on. By the time students are in the third term of their first year, they are doing ten to twelve hours of this work each week. Their acting-technique tutor is only with them three hours a week, so whoever is directing them is with them much more of the time. It's a situation in which the students are working with a whole series of different professional directors whose approaches vary widely. Of course, the Academy's basic values are being passed on by the choice of directors.

What Do You Look for When You Choose a Director to Work with Students?

First of all, I hope I select directors who are not narrow and dictatorial, but can give the actor some space to work. I nearly always choose a director who has been an actor, since when an actor has a problem, directors can deal with it from their own experience. That's fundamental. The directors we have may be working in repertory theaters, bringing productions into the West End, or working on a television series as an actor. They are people who are actually in the business as actors or directors.

What Do You Feel Is the Weakest Aspect of English Acting?

Lack of emotional commitment. But that's an English trait. That's what our improvisation class tries to remedy. The work I do in improvisation wouldn't surprise an American actor, but the English do tend to find it difficult. The English often maintain an element of detachment, which is very useful for technically communicating their thoughts, but this sometimes can take away a vibrancy from their performance.

Are There Any Specific Exercises You Do to Help Your Students Become Emotionally Expressive?

I attempt to address that in the improvisation class and it can get very personal. When you work on students' emotions the dividing line between the character and the student himself gets very thin. And sometimes one finds resistance. But when you are talking about emotional commitment you are talking about the actor as a person because that's what he has to bring to the role.

I find that you can get results much quicker if you start by using the material that is around you, the actual relationships between students as they exist in the class— their jealousies, fears, and concerns. But the class has to be small and trusting. If you are going to focus on students making an emotional commitment, why avoid the material that is right there, why always invent it? Some students will go along with that while others will have considerable reservations. They say, "You can ask me questions about my technique, but not personal questions."

I think that some English acting is not vibrant for that reason. For three years I was on the panel that gives the Olivier Award each year. One year I saw eighty shows, and during the next two years I saw sixty. It came across quite clearly to me that there is a coolness in British acting, and as I said before, an element of detachment. But there is also a higher level of vocal skills than you find in most North American actors.

Students are often not using themselves to their best advantage, not using that side of their personality that is most expressive. In fact, they usually hide it. It's interesting to try to get through those blocks.

Can You Describe Some Specific Techniques You Use in Improvisation Class?

The improvisations are simple. I ask students to create a situation in which two people have known each other for a long time and are at a point of crisis in their relationship. I break up the students into groups of two and they work out the situation for themselves. They present their improvisation and often do not come to the crisis but show us something that happened before the crisis or after it. They rarely choose the critical moment. Then we talk about the character to try to find out what the crisis in the relationship is really about. You know, it's not necessarily that the husband has a critical illness. The crisis may be that his wife is not fulfilling him, for example. And the question is, why has this started to happen? You see, they thought the crisis was the illness, but underneath what's really wrong is that his wife was not fulfilling him. Perhaps the actress herself has similar worries. So this accusation by the husband might hit home with her. Now, the actress needs to let out her own emotional reaction to being told that. If she wants to act truthfully, she will instinctively *want* to use that. If she is more concerned with keeping herself private or saving face or being impressive, she will find every reason not to use it.

Recently, we had five people from the drama school panel come in to watch an improvisation class that was already in progress. The students became inhibited. I said to a student, "Why don't you tell the panel how furious you are with them because they behaved impolitely by crossing in front of you? Just let them know how that ruined your improvisation, and also how you want them to feel that you are the most wonderful actress they've seen in all the drama schools they've visited." That's one example of using the situation at hand to help students overcome emotional blocks.

Do You Ask Students to Redo Their Improvisations and Incorporate This Work into Scenes?

To me the most important thing is to actually key into the student's feeling at the moment it's happening. They can then take it back into the improvisation or into a scene they are working on. But they actually have to make that transference by themselves. I don't worry myself too much about their ability to make the transference. They usually develop enough confidence from this kind of improvisational work so they can start to use these skills elsewhere.

Another way I approach expressiveness is by giving students extreme, even fantastical images to use in expressing their feelings. For example, if someone in an improvisation has just received very good news, I ask him to express how he feels in an extreme way. Does he feel like he's floating on air or swimming up to the sky or bringing the whole world into his arms? I tell him to take that feeling and fantasize with it, to express it fully and to try not to feel inhibited in any way, but to just go with it. This is the reverse of an actor using his fragility as a way to spark an emotion. I tell him, "You are unstoppable, you're super-successful. You are wonderful. Tell us how wonderful and how attractive you are today." He must tell us how attractive *he* is, not just the person he is playing. This brings it back to the person himself.

Do You Do Sensory Exercises?

Yes. That happens as well in the improvisation class. I will prompt students to remember specific things from their past. I ask them to describe that thing specifically, not to generalize, but to focus on its surface, color, smell, and weight. We work on making the experience very real so they can bring the feeling that the object evokes into their improvisations. We do quite a bit of that.

326

RAPHAEL JAGO

What Is Webber Douglas's Strength as a School?

Because Webber Douglas was an opera school until 1945 it still has a very strong singing department. I would say voice/singing is one of the school's major attributes. We don't have a stage management course, so actors have to do stage management for each other, and that helps to create a realistic attitude toward the business aspect of theater and a responsible attitude toward other students. We are also exploring the art of writing and creating original material.

What Is Your Approach to Shakespeare?

We do more and more Shakespeare. That's something I've noticed in the last decade. Students have a Shakespeare class from the moment they come into the school and every student has to prepare a Shakespeare one-man show in the fourth term. They do that by choosing a Shakespearean play and creating a show based on one character from that play. They can write their own material, but it must all be based on the text. They have to have a point of view about the character. They create events in that character's life that occurred before or after the play takes place.

It's a very challenging exercise because they have to do a lot of their own thinking (although there is a member of the staff who will assist them). At the end of the fourth term students present their one-man show to the staff and we choose three to six students out of that group of twenty-four to develop their pieces further and present them to the whole school. We then choose two students and send them to the Poel Festival at the National Theatre. We also participate in an open-air Shakespeare Festival at Cliveden at Maidenhead.

What Do You Consider to Be the Most Important Aspects of an Actor's Craft?

A sense of realism in acting. Also, the actor has to know what his own strengths and weaknesses are, otherwise he'll try to do things and fail and won't know why. Actors also need to become aware of their mannerisms to avoid being trapped by them.

One problem with English drama training is that it is so intense that English actors often feel they no longer need training once they leave drama school. Most American actors, on the other hand, don't have this kind of intense basic training and feel they always have to keep training and improving. Although this situation is improving in Britain, it is still true that a number of our actors stop studying once they start working professionally. Our one-year postgraduate course has changed that to some degree and many other schools are taking in older people as well. That plus the starting of the Actors Centre for professional actors has improved the situation over recent years.

Hilary Wood

Hilary Wood is Senior Coordinating Lecturer at the Webber Douglas Academy of Dramatic Art. Trained at the Royal Academy of Dramatic Art, where she held the Queen Elizabeth Coronation Scholarship and won the George Arliss award, Ms. Wood later performed in repertory, television, and the West End. In the early seventies she embarked on a directorial career and cofounded Coquelin Co-productions, an experimental theater company dedicated to new playwrights and young actors.

Students are responsible to me for their interpretive and artistic development during their stay here. I direct students in productions and teach them a class throughout their entire training in a very misunderstood subject called Acting Technique. This course is intended to help students develop their abilities in a way that one hopes is individual for each of them.

At the beginning of the course I address those aspects of acting that are particularly cogent to spontaneity, which is something I think is very important for the actor. I believe the actor is only as good as he is spontaneous. So I start working on the mental processes that lead to spontaneity right from the start. It's not a class in acting theory. I think one teaches acting by working with students rather than filling them with theoretical ideas. I suppose what I teach is based on my own practical experience in the theater; and what I have learned, other first-rate actors have found helpful in the course of their training and professional work.

I start by using a great deal of improvisation in conjunction with very basic but very carefully structured sense training. I think spontaneity in acting is based on the actor's ability to keep his senses open and sharp.

Do You Base Your Sensory Work on Stanislavsky?

No, I don't. If I were to talk about Stanislavsky I would say that I think of him as a great personal friend, but I feel that he is greatly misunderstood by young students. I take a lot of time at the beginning of the course to explain that Stanislavsky was the director of a company that included many good, experienced actors, and when students read his work they must bear in mind that what he wrote down was based on observing what very good and experienced actors were already doing. He wasn't theorizing and inventing things just out of his head. A problem today's students have with Stanislavsky is his nineteenth-century habit of putting into three chapters what he reasonably could have put into one paragraph. He was a brilliant observer of what actors do, but everyone who works with young students has to find his own methods of conveying those principles to students. I think someone who has been trained in the Stanislavsky system would recognize a lot of things that I do, but I don't think that they would think of it as strictly adhering to the Stanislavsky system.

What Kinds of Sensory Exercises Do You Do?

First, I talk to students about the necessity of becoming super-communicators, and that the only way to do that is to become super-sensuous. I start with a series of very simple exercises that require them to try to use their senses as they did when they were children. The problem is that as we become more sophisticated, our brain works like a computer and closes off our senses to information that we already have. This is lethal for an actor. An actor has to develop an override switch with regard to the use of the senses so that when the brain tries to switch the senses off, the actor can switch them back on. My early exercises are all about that.

We start with observing and examining material objects, then we do the same thing with a person or perhaps several other people. I ask students to see and observe certain things about objects and to note when they feel bored or childish or embarrassed. That's when the brain tries to switch the senses off. I try to take their sense observations beyond that point so they become extraverted in their explorations and glad to be doing it.

Can You Give Me an Example?

I would start with an object first, any object, one that you are absolutely convinced that you know thoroughly, and I would ask you to examine it by isolating it through each of your senses, one at a time, and to ask yourself what information you get from what sense. You would find that you can continually discover new things about the object. I tell students, "The only way you know that your senses are open is when your brain is receiving new information."

Then I ask each student to examine another student, to touch him, first with eyes open, then with eyes closed. He should be able to work out what that person looks like without the use of sight. I then have him sit quietly without saying anything and listen to that person. Just listen to the sound of his breathing or heartbeat to see how much can be picked up by being in a state of silence with someone else. I then let the student talk to that person, saying some of the things that he has discovered about him. Whether students have worked with objects or people, I ask them to share their discoveries with the other people in the class. What I look for is a very fine, detailed, precise description of something they have experienced, not a generalization.

Actors have to learn how to communicate intimately with each other with perfect freedom. Once they can do this it allows them to feel open and trusting, and they begin to acquire a fair degree of sensuality. I think that sensuality is the most exciting and dangerous quality an actor can have on stage. If you were to ask me what kind of actors I am trying to train, I would say "dangerous" ones.

By That Do You Mean Actors Who Are Unpredictable?

By that I mean an actor who can approach a text, even a classical text, and while using all the splendor of his technically trained instrument, still feel as if he is, through subtext, improvising it on the spot, that he is making the thoughts up as he goes along. It's that sense of spontaneity that keeps an audience on the edge of their seats.

Spontaneity happens automatically in improvisations once the actors are relaxed and their senses are open to what is around them. I then give them a series of exercises to teach them how to transfer that ability to text so that all text becomes a form of improvisation—and that also applies to classical text and verse. An actor's talent lies in his capacity to imagine, not in his capacity to feel.

What Kinds of Improvisations Do You Do?

We start with a series of simple improvisation exercises. The word *simple* is misleading. There are certain things in acting that are easy to grasp intellectually yet amazingly difficult to do. What is simple to describe is not always easy to experience. I ask a student to try to convince his classmates to give him back an object that he has voluntarily surrendered to them. I ask him to try to get it back by simply talking to the group, relating to them in a way that would make them want to give the object back. I instruct the group to respond to the student in whatever way he makes them feel. If he bores them, to express their boredom; if he fascinates them, to express their fascination; if they feel antagonized, to show it. Of course, it's important to take care of the student doing this exercise so that he achieves positive results and is not left feeling like a failure.

I then have the students put this into a setting of some sort. For instance, the student is to imagine that he has left an object in a public place, has come back to look for it, and must enlist the help of strangers who are in that place. I ask him to use the actor's process of *relate, accept,* and *build.* By relate I mean keeping the senses open; by accept I mean accepting all the facts that are laid down in the scene; by build I mean that he must imaginatively build upon what he has been asked to accept in order to achieve his objective within the scene. I do a lot of these exercises in the first term so that by the end of the term students are able to be spontaneous in any improvised situation.

I also do a certain amount of work at the end of the first term on texture; that is, imaginative identification with the factual circumstances of a play. It's important, particularly with students who are training in a classical tradition, to understand that style is not something that is imposed on a text from the outside. Every play has its own particular style. Two plays of Congreve are not the same; they deal with different facts, different people, and will have different stylistic details. I use the word *texture* instead of *style.* I ask students to consider the factual

334

elements of a play, including facts about the historical period in which the play takes place. These should be elements that affect the physical behavior of one's character.

Can You Give Me an Example?

In the first term I have students choose simple textures such as age. Age is a texture whether it's being older or younger than oneself. To help a student be younger you can take him back to a time when he was younger. To help a student become older I would ask him to examine the physical phenomenon of aging by observing older people and investigating the medical facts about the structure of the body as people age. I would ask him to use his imagination to apply these facts to himself so that they affect the way he moves. Or I might ask a student to take a very interesting texture like destitution, a condition that can affect anyone from any walk of life. I would start by asking the student to create the sensations of cold, dirt, and hunger to see where his identification with these physical facts takes him. In time, a student can develop an identity through these sensations—a person who exists in that texture.

What Do You Mean by Identification?

I mean the use of the actor's imagination. We take a fact about someone's life, we sense it, we think about it, we imagine it, and it produces a specific physical reaction in

335

us. The information is no longer intellectual. Later on in the course, when students work on style, such as Restoration style, they won't think of it as a pot of paint that they have to splash over everything from the outside. They learn very early on that style is part of content, and that it emerges quite naturally from the circumstances of the play, provided one has done one's research properly.

How Do You Combine Exercise Work with Text?

In the second term students start to mix text and improvisation within the same scene. I write several general-purpose pieces of text and give them out to two students at a time. One is required to speak the text, the other must remain silent. The speaking student may be showing the other around the room, for example, because that's what the text describes. Then they would repeat the exercise, but this time the silent partner can say whatever he likes and the other student has to respond with the same text as before but still must have it make sense. He must adjust his stress and inflection so the text fits organically and logically with what is being said to him.

So the Student Has to Change the Intention of the Lines to Suit the Information He Is Getting from the Other Person.

Yes. And the student has no way of being able to preplan what a line is going to mean until he receives the stimulus that produces it, that is, until he hears what the other person says. Usually, by the end of the second term students are mentally flexible enough to use a text and still respond organically and sensibly to anything that is said to them. Anyone watching would think that both students were using a written text or both were improvising. This is a very good exercise for mental flexibility.

The next area I deal with addresses a problem that a lot of students have: being emotionally expressive when the text calls for it. Most students tend to internalize emotion rather than allow it to be visible. Because theater requires more communication than everyday life, a student needs to express to a far greater degree on stage than he might in life.

What Exercises Do You Give Students to Help Them Become Emotionally Expressive?

Here, too, I use a piece of text that I have written myself. I don't use published texts because should students subsequently work on the play from which I have chosen material for our exercises, it could be ruined for them because they have already worked on it in a very different context. So I write a simple situation for the students in which they have to describe a painful experience they have had. I ask a student to memorize a speech I have written and I say, "Do that as well as you can, based on the information you got from the text. The person sitting next to you will be silent, but you are talking to him." It's usually emotionally charged material. For example, he has just seen an accident on the street and is telling someone about it. The inexperienced young actor tends to internalize emotion so that what one would see may be emotional and dramatic, but is often general and, therefore, unexciting. I then tell the student that the important aspect of his speech is the effect that it has on the person to whom it is being told, and that now that person will be free to respond verbally, if he wishes to. The student repeats the speech and, one hopes, he will develop more sensitivity to the external stimulus; that how he tells it will depend on how the other person is being affected by what he is saying.

What I am looking for is the student's organic response to his partner. Anything could happen because they are basically improvising. The idea is to use text without changing it in an improvisational capacity so that the student learns that a piece of text, be it a play or a scene, is not something that is set in concrete. It is something that flows and changes subtextually because of its internal life and the external life of the circumstances in which it occurs. I think it is always a bad idea to preplan how you are going to execute a speech. Students should totally submerge themselves in the circumstances and facts of the play, and let their imaginative response to it determine what they do on stage as much as they possibly can. Relating to an external stimulus makes that easier. It's much easier to be thinking and feeling in the present if you are continuously being affected by the external circumstances presented to you. It is the other people in the scene who are most likely to be the greatest source of change, the greatest source of external stimulation. The most boring thing that can happen in acting is when emotions are general, divorced from what is going on in the present moment. I find that by using external stimuli

338

I can stop students from generalizing because their intentions become more specific when they are filtered through their immediate response to someone else.

Next we focus on comedy and its different demands. I spend a whole term talking about comedy, trying to do away with that dreadful neurosis—the need to work toward making people laugh. I talk to students about comedy being *selected truth*, that is, truth selected in ways to keep the audience feeling secure. Audiences tend to laugh at what they recognize, at what they feel secure about. Sometimes, though, playwrights push an audience's security beyond what it was when they walked into the theater. Joe Orton did this, and this is why productions of his plays are often unsuccessful.

How Do You Help Students Learn to Be Funny?

In comedy my work gets much more directorial. It's important to talk to students about the seriousness of the play, what it is saying about people. So their first job is to seek an identifiable characterization. For this I ask them to use a great deal of observation.

The very first exercise I ask students to do when they come to the Academy is to go out and find someone they don't know, observe them for a long time, and bring me three minutes of this person. I think that observation is crucial to an actor's process. When we start to work on comedy I ask them to bring on stage somebody they know who has a comedic quality. When they work on comic plays, I remind them, ask them, have they found the character? Have they been out in the streets looking?

My present students are working on three different plays. One group is working on *Billy Liar*, another on *It's a Mad World, My Masters* (about the Silver Jubilee in Britain), and another on *The Importance of Being Earnest*. I try to encourage all three groups to think about what makes their plays specifically unique. I would ask those working on *The Importance of Being Earnest* to consider the texture and attitudes of the period, of how these people are living by social rules that have to be observed at all times. I would also ask them to consider that this is a period in which people spoke for pleasure and recreation; therefore, they must get rid of their contemporary sloppy speech patterns. I would tell those working on *Billy Liar* that this is a wonderful exploration of a family in the 1950s and ask them to draw on their experience in their own families and think about family relationships. I want them to be true to those relationships and not to think about anything else. To the other group I would say that the texture demands that they behave in extreme ways; the play *It's a Mad World, My Masters* is almost an English version of *commedia dell'arte*, which requires inflated impressions of the characters. They can take these characters very far and be quite extravagant.

How Would You Help Students Find the Comic Elements in The Importance of Being Earnest?

Let's examine the tea-party scene between Gwendolen and Cecily. I would ask the student playing Gwendolen to consider, first of all, the serious implications of her situation. Does she realize that she has literally run away from home and has never been out on her own before? She has gotten up very early in the morning and dressed herself, possibly for the first time in her life. She has taken a hackney carriage, which she has never done before, to a railway station. She has bought her own train ticket and has traveled to her fiancé's home in the country. She expects a very romantic situation, and to be greeted by him with tremendous joy. When she arrives he is out. The butler shows her into the garden, where she finds Cecily, a very beautiful young girl who claims to be her fiancé's ward. The information that Cecily gives about herself is exactly the kind of social cover-up that would be given if she were Jack's mistress—not his ward. In addition, Gwendolen is myopic, although she tries to pretend that she is not. She is dying to use her glasses and has to think up witty excuses for it. So she says that her mother has brought her up to be extremely short-sighted. Would Cecily mind if she used her glasses?

Cecily, although unsophisticated, is a great heiress and has had the education of a proper young lady. But she has not yet been out in London society and is not predisposed to being impressed by the glamorous London lady who has come down. As they talk, each piece of information that Gwendolen manages to worm out of Cecily makes her more and more insecure about her relationship to Jack. Finally, Cecily comes out with the information that she is also engaged to Gwendolen's fiancé. I would ask the students to think about this in their own terms. I would say to the actress playing Gwendolen, "How would you feel if someone just asked you to marry him and you went round to his flat and a gorgeous blonde answered the door and said she lived there? Use your own emotional reaction, but express it within the framework of the exquisitely superficial politeness and correctness of that period." I would ask both actresses to explore the emotional circumstances of the scene as well as the manners and to see if they can bring the two together.

Whether I work on comedy or drama I talk to the students about the notion of mentally energizing three specific spaces that are important to the actor: they want to energize their personal space, which extends from their center to the tips of their fingers and the air right around them; they must energize a space that encompasses themselves and their acting partners; and they must energize a space that encompasses the entire auditory area, that is, a space that embraces the audience and draws them in. Stanislavsky was very clever to discover that the energy spaces were circular. A lot of lesser actors project in a linear way, which is inefficient. Circularity embraces, linear pushes away. If my mental energy force travels in a line toward an object or person, I push it away from me. If my mental energy force travels toward that person or object in a circle, I surround it and pull it toward me.

What Exercises Do You Use to Teach the Notion of Mental Energy?

I simply ask them to draw the first circle of concentration on the floor by holding a piece of chalk and swiveling. Everyone's first circle of concentration is a different size, depending on that person's size and shape. I then ask them to sit in it and just focus on themselves in their own personal space. They practice until they can do that easily. I would then ask them to energize their space simply by feeling very happy in it, breathing in it, and seeing if they could make their space feel bright. Then I have to apply the same process to progressively larger spaces.

When Do You Direct Students in Productions?

The fifth and sixth terms are where I pick students up as a director. What I try to do is have nice long rehearsal periods—five, six, even seven weeks for about twenty hours a week, and use plays in which students can stretch their imagination. Ideally, I like to do one play with no double casting. Then we present the play, which is often a Chekhov or Gorky play, to the school.

My working methods vary depending on the play. With Restoration comedy I spend a lot of time working specifically on the text, while with a Chekhov or Gorky play I do a lot of improvisation. I might ask the students to improvise the first time their characters met and encourage them to explore as much of their individual character's past as they can in this way. By doing these kinds of improvisations they become so filled with their characters' motivation and relationships that the text often plays itself.

Webber Douglas Has a Finals Company. Would You Describe It?

During the last two terms of the diploma course students are invited to join a finals company. That means that they will do six plays during their final two terms of training. They have to demonstrate that they are capable of playing

343

six totally different characters. Students are invited to join; it isn't automatic. A student has to have reached a certain sophistication in his interpretive ability and a certain standard of technical excellence; and he should be able to demonstrate his employability as an actor, and, one hopes, as a classical actor. Final productions are performed for an invited audience that includes agents, casting directors, and the general public.

Occasionally, we work on classical plays in finals. I just directed *The Roman Actor* by Massinger. During rehearsals I said to the students that I wondered if agents and casting directors would come to see a classical play as readily as they would a contemporary play. One of my students who was playing Caesar said to me, "I don't care if no one comes to see me in this part. The opportunity to play it, and what it is going to teach me, strikes me as being the most important experience I could have at this stage of my career." It is very rewarding when students feel their work to be this valuable. And it gives them so much confidence to be able to work on these kinds of plays because they won't get the chance again for a while—unless they are extremely lucky.

Addresses

The Bristol Old Vic Theatre School
$\frac{1}{2}$ Downside Road
Clifton,
Bristol BS8 2XF
0272-733535

The Central School of Speech and Drama
Embassy Theatre
Eton Avenue
London NW3 3HY
01-722-8183

The Drama Centre, London
176 Prince of Wales Road
London NW5
01-267-1177

The Drama Studio
1 Grange Road
Ealing
London W5 5QN
01-579-3897

The Guildford School of Acting and Dance
20 Buryfields
Guildford
Surrey GU2 5AZ
0483-60701

ADDRESSES

The Guildhall School of Music and Drama
Barbican
London EC2Y 8DT
01-628-2571

The London Academy of Music and Dramatic Art
Tower House
226 Cromwell Road
London SW5 0SR
01-373-9883

The Royal Academy of Dramatic Art
62–64 Gower Street
London WC1E 6ED
01-636-7076

The Royal Scottish Academy of Music and Drama
St. George's Place
Glasgow G2 1BS
041-332-5294

The Webber Douglas Academy of Dramatic Art
30–36 Clareville Street
London SW7 5AP
01-370-4154

About the Author

Eva Mekler is the author of books and articles in both theater and psychology. Her theater books include *Contemporary Scenes for Student Actors, The Actor's Scenebook* and *The Actor's Scenebook, Vol. II,* and *The New Generation of Acting Teachers.* She has also been an actress, appearing in Broadway and off-Broadway productions. Her adaptation of Anton Chekhov's novella "The Duel" was produced off-off-Broadway. In 1985 she taught acting and directed productions at the Usdan Center for the Creative and Performing Arts. She herself has studied acting in New York and at the London Academy of Music and Dramatic Art.

Ms. Mekler has a master's degree in psychology from New York University. She co-authored *Bringing Up a Moral Child,* and has published numerous magazine articles on that subject.